The Politics of Genocide

Genocide, Political Violence, Human Rights Series

EDITED BY ALEXANDER LABAN HINTON, NELA NAVARRO, AND NATASHA ZARETSKY

For a list of titles in the series, see the last page of the book.

The Politics of Genocide

From the Genocide Convention to the Responsibility to Protect

Jeffrey S. Bachman

Rutgers University Press
New Brunswick, Camden, and Newark, New Jersey and London

978-1-9788-2146-0 (cloth)
978-1-9788-2150-7 (paper)
978-1-9788-2147-7 (epub)

Cataloging-in-publication data is available from the Library of Congress.
LCCN 2021055667

A British Cataloging-in-Publication record for this book is available from the British Library.

⊗ The paper used in this publication meets the requirements of the American National Standard for Information Sciences—Permanence of Paper for Printed Library Materials, ANSI Z39.48-1992.

www.rutgersuniversitypress.org

Manufactured in the United States of America

For my wife, Jeannie, and my family,
for their never-ending support.

Contents

The Politics of Genocide

Introduction

GENOCIDE AND STATE IMPUNITY

> Memory—of what has been, of acts of commission or omission, of a responsibility abdicated—affects the future conduct of power in any form. Failure to adopt some imaginative recognition of such a principle merely results in the enthronement of a political culture that appears to know no boundaries—the culture of impunity.

At its inception, the United Nations was designed in a way that belies the organizational principle of the "sovereign equality" of all of its members.[1] Evidence of this can be found not only in the fact that there is a Security Council that is akin to an "elite club"[2] but also in the fact that the power vested in its permanent members, as insisted upon by them, makes them "the ruling oligarchy of the United Nations."[3] The Security Council institutionalizes a difference in status between its members and nonmembers. It also institutionalizes differences in status between its permanent members and the rotating nonpermanent members by the very fact that five members (known as the P-5)—the United States, Russia, France, the United Kingdom, and China—are permanent fixtures on the Security Council, whereas the nonpermanent members hold seats for only two years at a time. Moreover, the P-5 hold the veto power, which they can use to veto any Security Council resolution that might threaten their various interests.[4] Thus, though the United Nations was supposedly established in part to create "conditions under which justice and respect for the obligations arising from treaties and other sources of international law can be maintained,"[5] the organization's structural inequality all but ensured that justice and respect for international law would be uneven at best.

Examples of injustices perpetrated by P-5 members and their client states and of their lack of respect for international law are far too many to recount here.[6] It is sufficient to say that such injustices and violations of international law occur in all areas of the international legal landscape: severe violations of human rights and crimes against humanity, systematic and widespread violations of international humanitarian law, wars of aggression, and genocide. Importantly, the lack of meaningful accountability for the actions of the P-5 has contributed to a culture of impunity that becomes more deeply embedded with each new injustice and violation of international law committed—or, as Wole Soyinka put it, the exercise of the P-5 prerogative has resulted in "the enthronement of a political culture that appears to know no boundaries—the culture of impunity."[7]

This book aims to show how the P-5 have been able to establish a culture of impunity for themselves (as well as other states when their interests align), specifically in relation to the crime of genocide. Having powerful states that are permanent members of the Security Council and can exercise their veto at will does not alone explain the emergence and maintenance of a culture of impunity. This fact has been lost in the considerable debate over whether the Convention on the Prevention and Punishment of the Crime of Genocide (hereafter, the Genocide Convention) or politics among the P-5 is most responsible for the failure to take timely and effective action to prevent genocide.

In the expansive literature on the historical failure to prevent genocide, blame for the failure to give practical meaning to the promise of "never again" has been levied against both the deficiencies in the Genocide Convention and the indifference and lack of political will among the P-5. Beginning with the former and the idea that the Genocide Convention was designed to be primarily a symbolic text, Lassa Oppenheim wrote, "It is apparent that, to a considerable extent, the Convention amounts to a registration of protest against past misdeeds of individual or collective savagery rather than to an effective instrument of their prevention or repression."[8] Similarly, Barry Schiller stated, "Ironically, one of the most palpable examples of man's inhumanity to man has given birth to an international Convention which presently may be conceptualized as existing primarily in a symbolic universe."[9] What Oppenheim and Schiller essentially argue is that the United Nations felt obligated to register some form of protest against the policies that led to the attempted exterminations of the Armenians and the European Jewish people. However, the form that protest took was a treaty that was missing the teeth needed to prevent the very crime it rhetorically prohibits.

Payam Akhavan and René Provost view the Genocide Convention as an instrument constructed to create the facade that the international community was making progress in its fight against genocide. They argue: "The Genocide Convention was hailed as a triumph for international law. . . . But the vow to 'never again' allow such horrors to happen soon became an empty mantra as millions more became the targets of genocide. . . . These immeasurable tragedies speak to our repeated failure to give effect to righteous declarations and lofty utterances that create the illusion of progress."[10] Peter Ronayne refers to the numerous cases of genocide that followed the Genocide Convention's entry into force as evidence of its failure: "Despite the good intentions of the UNGC [United Nations Genocide Convention], post–World War II history has proven with disturbing clarity that the Holocaust was not the twentieth century's last genocide."[11]

Gareth Evans criticizes the international community's failure to invoke the Genocide Convention when it would have been appropriate to do so. Expressing an argument similar to that made by Schiller, Evans argues: "But it was almost as if, with the signing of the Genocide Convention, the task of addressing man-made atrocities was seen as complete. It took the major powers years (in the case of the United States, forty years) to ratify it, it was rarely invoked, and has never been effectively applied in practice either to prevent or punish actual atrocities."[12] The failure to invoke the Genocide Convention while a case of genocide is ongoing is an important point. Without recognition of ongoing cases of genocide, the void in international law that existed prior to the adoption and entry into force of the Genocide Convention remains, for all intents and purposes. Before preventive measures can be taken to remedy the violation of the prohibition against genocide, it must first be recognized that the prohibition is being violated.

Samuel Totten has placed the failure to prevent genocide squarely at the feet of the P-5: "It's not the UNCG [United Nations Genocide Convention] that has failed but the way it has been applied and the way nations and the international community have maneuvered their way out of complying with it. Yes, the UNCG has various components that are ambiguous . . . but ultimately individual nations and those comprising the Permanent Five in the UN Security Council have resorted to realpolitik to undergird their actions/inactions."[13] Mary Robinson, Ramesh Thakur, and Leo Kuper echo Totten's sentiment that the blame for the failure to prevent genocide resides more with the P-5 than with the Genocide Convention. Robinson implores us to "count up the results of fifty years of human rights mechanisms . . . and endless high-level rhetoric," because we will find "the general impact is quite underwhelming" and that the "failure of implementation" is of a "scale that shames us all."[14] Thakur notes that the continued use of the slogan "never again" "requires chutzpah."[15] Kuper provides a more aggressive critique: "I have been driven to this study by the realization that genocide is all too common in our own day, and that the organization charged with its prevention and punishment, the United Nations, responds with indifference, if not with condonation."[16]

At the risk of being perceived as deeply cynical so early in this book, I argue that debates such as this one, on some level, wrongly accept the views that the Genocide Convention was negotiated in good faith and that at least some of the P-5 might be willing to place humanitarian interests above their own interests when the two conflict, although so far they have often failed to do so. Just as important, there is an underlying belief that the same states do not commit or contribute to the commission of genocide. Therefore, their failure is not in their own actions but in their acts of omission. The idea that the Genocide Convention was negotiated in good faith is evident in the sentiment that the convention is representative of the "promise of the United Nations and international law."[17] This view seems to ascribe good intentions to the states that negotiated the terms of the Genocide Convention, even though there has been acknowledgment that the negotiations were influenced by national interests. As should become clear throughout this book, good intentions were not a dominant motivator. Beth Van Schaack more accurately describes the intentions when she writes that the drafting of the Genocide Convention "reveals the way in which political bodies may attempt to limit their obligations under international law when they reduce customary law norms to positivistic expression in multilateral treaties. In this case, the Convention had to respond to the tragedy of the Nazi Holocaust. At the same time, however, the Convention could not implicate member nations on the drafting committee."[18]

Each P-5 member has contributed in some way to the creation and maintenance of an international system that allows the P-5 to act with impunity when it comes to the crime of genocide. The contributions have been uneven, with the United States and the Soviet Union or its successor, Russia, having been the most active in this regard. Nonetheless, all five states have contributed either to their collective impunity or to their individual impunity. These contributions have been both legal and political. The P-5 were able to negotiate the terms of the Genocide Convention in ways that would limit its potential application to their practices, while also ensuring a form of territorial jurisdiction for the prevention of genocide—specifically, intrastate cases of genocide. Thus, their approach could be described as two pronged, with goals being to limit the scope of the Genocide Convention on the one hand and to prohibit interference in their internal affairs on the other, even when their actions fall within the Genocide Convention's limited scope. The other parts of this story are the maneuverings among the P-5 to ensure that post–Genocide Convention developments do not challenge their impunity for genocide by revising the international framework they devised.

An Ideal Lemkinian Genocide Convention

Because a significant portion of this book focuses on the changes made to the Genocide Convention at the behest of P-5 members during the drafting and negotiating processes, it is instructive to identify what an ideal Genocide Convention would have encompassed, based on what was envisioned by Raphael Lemkin, the individual who coined the term "genocide" by combining the Greek word *genos* (race or tribe) and the Latin word *cide* (killing). It is with this ideal type that differences in what was originally hoped for and what resulted from years of politically motivated negotiations can be seen. Because of Lemkin's significant participation in creating the Draft Convention on the Crime of Genocide (hereafter, the Secretariat Draft), it would be easy to look to this text as representative of his ideal.[19] However, as numerous scholars have pointed out, even the Secretariat Draft, as close as it was to Lemkin's intentions, "was a highly political text"[20] informed by "political compromise."[21] It is more fruitful, instead, to turn to Lemkin's writings that predated the onset of realpolitik in addressing genocide.

The ideal Genocide Convention can be constructed by identifying Lemkin's perspective on five basic components: groups protected; acts prohibited (*actus reus*, meaning "guilty act"); mental element (mens rea, meaning "guilty mind"); preventive elements; and punitive elements. In 1933, Lemkin presented his "Acts Constituting a General (Transnational) Danger Considered as Offences against the Law of Nations" at the Fifth Conference for the Unification of Penal Law in Madrid.[22] As Donna-Lee Frieze points out, it was at this conference that Lemkin described genocide "in its incipient forms: 'barbarism' and 'vandalism.'"[23] Lemkin's barbarism and vandalism encapsulate the acts he identified as genocidal in nature. Acts of barbarism consist of "attacks carried out against an individual as a member of a collectivity," with the purpose of the acts' author being "not only to harm an individual, but, also to cause damage to the collectivity to which the later [*sic*] belongs."[24] More specifically, barbarism includes "acts of extermination," such as "massacres" and "pogroms," as well as "actions undertaken to ruin the economic existence of the members of a collectivity" and "all sorts of brutalities which attack the dignity of the individual in cases where these acts of humiliation have their source in a campaign of extermination directed against the collectivity in which the victim is a member." Lemkin writes that when taken as a whole and committed against "ethnic, religious or social collectivities whatever the motive (political, religious, etc.)," these acts "constitute an offense against the law of nations" and represent "a general (transnational) danger." He similarly describes acts of vandalism as a general danger to humanity. According to Lemkin,

> An attack targeting a collectivity can also take the form of systematic and organized destruction of the art and cultural heritage in which the unique genius and achievement of a collectivity are revealed in fields of

> science, arts and literature. The contribution of any particular collectivity to world culture as a whole, forms the wealth of all of humanity, even while exhibiting unique characteristics.
>
> Thus, the destruction of a work of art of any nation must be regarded as acts of vandalism directed against world culture. The author [*of the crime*] causes not only the immediate irrevocable losses of the destroyed work as property and as the culture of the collectivity directly concerned (whose unique genius contributed to the creation of this work); it is also all humanity which experiences a loss by this act of vandalism.

So far, three of the five elements have been addressed. Groups protected, though imprecisely defined, include ethnic, religious, and social collectivities. Prohibited acts include those that constitute Lemkin's acts of barbarism and vandalism. The mental element includes the intent to cause damage to or destroy the collectivity to which the targeted individuals or cultural heritage belongs. The motive is indeterminate. The remaining two elements—preventive and punitive—are implicit in Lemkin's categorization of barbarism and vandalism as offenses against the law of nations. According to Lemkin, as such offenses, they should fall under a form of universal jurisdiction for their prevention and punishment. As he notes, the concept of such offenses "comes from the interdependent struggle of the civilized world community against criminality." These offenses require enforcement of a "principle of universal repression" that is based on the idea that an "offender can be brought to justice in the place of where he is apprehended (*forum loci deprehensionis*), independently of where the crime was committed and the nationality of the author." This is because violators of the law of nations are regarded as "the enemy of the whole international community and in all States he will be pursued for crimes universally harmful to all the international community." Finally, Lemkin states that offenses against the law of nations in one state should cause spontaneous reactions in other states, including critical media coverage, mass public protests, and "even in diplomatic actions on behalf of the victims of such violations (humanitarian interventions)."

What Lemkin presented at the Fifth Conference for the Unification of Penal Law could be considered as having contained the elements of his ideal Genocide Convention. As Lemkin writes, he finally had a forum for action and believed that it was the right time "to put before the conference my idea, which had been maturing for so many years."[25] Nonetheless, it is instructive to include in Lemkin's ideal Genocide Convention his deliberations on genocide in *Axis Rule in Occupied Europe: Laws of Occupation, Analysis of Government, Proposals for Redress.* In that book, he first uses the term "genocide" in print and expands on ideas expressed at the conference. Furthermore, *Axis*

Rule in Occupied Europe also preceded Lemkin's foray into the politics of negotiating binding international law on the crime of genocide.

In *Axis Rule in Occupied Europe*, Lemkin defined genocide as "the destruction of a nation or of an ethnic group."[26] More specifically, and consistent with his presentation at the conference, Lemkin wrote: "Generally speaking, genocide does not necessarily mean the immediate destruction of a nation, except when accomplished by mass killings of all members of a nation. It is intended rather to signify a coordinated plan of different actions aiming at the destruction of essential foundations of the life of the national groups, with the aim of annihilating the groups themselves."[27] The objectives of genocide are to disintegrate "the political and social institutions, of culture, language, national feelings, religion, and the economic existence of national groups, and the destruction of the personal security, liberty, health, dignity, and the lives of the individuals belonging to such groups."[28]

As Lemkin's ideas about what constitutes the crime genocide progressed, he added to the acts that contribute to the crime's commission. He did so while also offering a unifying concept: the destruction of the essential foundations of the life of a group. Out of acts of barbarism and vandalism grew Lemkin's eight techniques of genocide by which the foundations of life can be destroyed. The techniques are political, social, cultural, economic, biological, physical, religious, and moral.[29] Without going into great detail here, it is important to note that each of Lemkin's techniques has some relationship with one or more of the other techniques. For example, as I have argued elsewhere, the political technique merges with the social technique, as together, they seek to destroy local institutions necessary for self-government, impose a new system of institutions and administration, and abolish local laws and courts.[30] The political and social techniques then intersect with the cultural technique in its prohibition of the use of the local language in schools and in print. As the ability to resist politically and socially is altered, so too is the physical ability. The economic technique not only destroys the "foundation of the economic existence of a national group," but it also lowers the standard of living, creating "a daily fight literally for bread and for physical survival."[31] The weakening of the ability to physically resist makes the members of a targeted group more susceptible to forced removal or forced assimilation, as well as the biological and physical techniques of genocide.

In summary, an ideal Genocide Convention for Lemkin would contain protection for social collectivities in all their forms, prohibition of acts that undermine the foundations of life, and universal repression of genocide by preventing and punishing the crime. Similarly, Anton Weiss-Wendt notes, Lemkin "was particularly concerned about (1) universal jurisdiction; (2) a future ICC; and (3) cultural aspects of genocide."[32] What an ideal Genocide Convention would not be is one that contributes to a culture of impunity for the P-5—or any other state, for that matter. However, for the P-5 to be able to act with impunity concerning the crime of genocide, they could not permit there to be an ideal Genocide Convention. Moreover, legal and normative developments that followed also required P-5 intervention to maintain the culture of impunity that has its origins in the Genocide Convention negotiations.

Chapter Overview and Theoretical Framework

The first two chapters of this book show how the political processes of drafting, negotiating, and adopting the Genocide Convention eliminated many of the key elements of Lemkin's ideal convention. The third chapter shows how similar arguments made during Genocide Convention negotiations were employed to limit the applicability of a key element of the text of the convention that remained intact. Chapter 1 focuses on the evolution of the preventive language found in the convention. It argues that the original formal draft of the Genocide Convention (the Secretariat Draft) incorporated a form of universal preventive jurisdiction. However, during negotiations, at the behest primarily of the United States but also of the Soviet Union and France, this was replaced with territorial preventive jurisdiction. Chapter 2 focuses on the omission of political groups and the exclusion of the prohibition of acts constituting cultural genocide. Along with universal preventive jurisdiction, the Secretariat Draft included protection for political groups and the prohibition of cultural genocide.[33] Both were also included in the second formal draft of the Genocide Convention, the draft Convention prepared by the Ad Hoc Committee on Genocide (hereafter, the Ad Hoc Committee Draft).[34] Once again, however, specific P-5 members worked to ensure that political groups (Soviet Union) and cultural genocide (the United States, the United Kingdom, and France) were excluded from the final adopted text of the Genocide Convention.

Less than three years after the Genocide Convention was unanimously adopted by the General Assembly, on December 9, 1948, the International Court of Justice (ICJ) delivered its Advisory Opinion on Reservations to the Convention on the Prevention and Punishment of the Crime of Genocide.[35] At the conclusion of the Genocide Convention negotiations, culminating with its adoption, the process of "emasculating" the convention was incomplete.[36] Though some problematic elements were revised or excluded during negotiations, Article IX of the final adopted text of the Genocide Convention gives the ICJ the authority to hear disputes between states concerning state responsibility for genocide.[37] Therefore, as written in the Genocide Convention, all states that become party to the convention accept the jurisdiction of the ICJ to hear cases involving alleged violations of convention obligations. Chapter 3 shows how arguments similar to those made by P-5 members for the omission of protection for political groups and exclusion of acts constituting cultural genocide were made once again when the ICJ considered the question of what impact reservations to the Genocide Convention have on the reserving state and states that object to the reservations. Together, chapters 1, 2, and 3 demonstrate how P-5 members effectively wrote the law of genocide and limited the applicability of a crucial element of the Genocide Convention that remained intact.

Though it does not necessarily contribute to the creation or maintenance of a legal hierarchy (which results in inequality before the law), the greater ability of some states to determine the content of legal rules is key to the first three chapters.[38] Malcolm Shaw notes: "The notion of equality before the law is accepted by states in the sense of equality of legal personality and capacity. However, it would not be strictly accurate to talk in terms of the equality of states in creating law. The major states will always have an influence commensurate with their status, if only because their concerns are much wider, their interests much deeper and their power more effective."[39] Of course, this can have practical implications concerning the various inequalities that exist outside of legal personality. Put differently, the haves hold a greater capacity than the have-nots to make rules that then apply to all states.[40] Indeed, the ability to influence the content of legal rules means that some states can use their power to mold such rules in ways that protect their interests. Thus, even if it is accepted that all states are equal before the law (sovereign equality), which entails a "responsibility of all states" to "comply with them [legal obligations] when they have been created,"[41] what is legally obligated can still be understood—at least in part—as an imposition created, disseminated, and applied (or not) by powerful states.

The significance of the capacity of some states to determine the content of legal rules is especially evident in the positivistic nature of international law. Positivist doctrines of lawmaking require the consent of states to incurring legal obligations. In other words, when it comes to treaty law, of which the Genocide Convention is a part, states "are bound only by those treaties they ratify or those to which they accede."[42] Therefore, when it comes to the crime of genocide, states are not bound to accept Lemkin's concept of genocide or the definitions of genocide included in the early drafts of the convention (the Secretariat and Ad Hoc Committee drafts) that preceded the final adopted text that entered into legally binding force. Of course, genocide is prohibited in customary international law. Hence, states that do not ratify or accede to the Genocide Convention, a surprisingly large group,[43] are nonetheless bound by the prohibition.

It is worth noting that the influence of power on determining the content of legal rules extends also to the capacity to influence the development of customary international law. In *Custom, Power and the Power of Rules*, Michael Byers writes that different forms of power, such as military, economic, and diplomatic, "would seem to be important within the customary process because they determine, either separately or cumulatively, whether and to what degree different States are able to contribute to the development, maintenance or change of customary rules."[44] Similarly, Charles de Visscher wrote in 1957, "among the users are always some who mark the soil more deeply with their footprints than others, either because of their weight, which is to say their power in this world, or because their interests bring them more frequently this way."[45] However, it is the Genocide Convention that defines the specifics of the crime and the related obligations and prohibitions. In other words, genocide is prohibited both by customary international law and the Genocide Convention, but it is the convention that makes the prohibition concrete.

Because of the role power plays in the development of international law, including the Genocide Convention and developments after its implementation, rules may easily become little more than acceptance of the doctrine that might is right. When it comes to the most powerful states, realism is still the dominant paradigm for their relations with other states. Hans Morgenthau and Georg Schwarzenberger are two notable realist thinkers who nevertheless expressed their concerns about an international legal system that is dominated by the mighty. Concerning international law's enforcement system, Morgenthau wrote: "There can be no more primitive and no weaker system of law enforcement than this; for it delivers the enforcement of the law to the vicissitudes of the distribution of power between the violator of the law and the victim of the violations. It makes it easy for the strong both to violate the law and to enforce it, and consequently puts the rights of the weak in jeopardy."[46] Schwarzenberger makes a further connection between what Morgenthau wrote and the use of power in situations where humanity is the least of concerns, taking a back seat to national interest. Schwarzenberger asserted that "in a society in which power is the overriding consideration, the primary function of law is to assist in maintaining the supremacy of force and the hierarchies established on the basis of power, and to give this overriding system the respectability and sanctity law confers."[47]

The culture of impunity for genocide in which the P-5 tend to operate requires more than the power and privilege of influencing the development of new legal regimes. It requires what Gerry Simpson has called "legalized hegemony."[48] Simpson defines the phenomenon of legalized hegemony as "the existence within an international society of a powerful elite of states whose superior status is recognized by minor powers as a political fact giving rise to the existence of certain constitutional privileges, rights and duties and whose relations with each other are defined by adherence to a rough principle of sovereign equality."[49]

In more detail, legalized hegemony is composed of four principles. First, there needs to exist a legal basis for the dominance of some states.[50] For the P-5, the legal basis includes their permanent positions on the Security Council and their veto power. Second, regardless of material differences, there remains a level of sovereign equality among the dominating states.[51] Clearly, there are material differences among the P-5. This was true at the inception of the United Nations, and it remains true today. Nonetheless, even beyond the shared veto power, the P-5 members have a similar hierarchical position in relation to other states within the international system. Third, powerful or dominating states will act together to achieve certain goals within the international order. As Simpson writes, "these powers have an interest in and prerogatives over, not only their own narrowly defined interests, but over the whole international system."[52] Of course, for the P-5, protecting their individually defined interests may require working in concert to place restraints on elements of the international system. For example, the omission of political groups and the exclusion of cultural genocide were achieved by a compromise between the Soviet Union and the United States. Similarly, there was a form of implicit cooperation between the Soviet Union and the United States during ICJ proceedings regarding treaty reservations in the countries' shared opposition to the orthodox approach to reservations.[53] Fourth, legalized hegemony is imposed by the powerful and accepted by those below.[54] As Simpson explains, "the powers and privileges afforded the Great Powers in the Security Council . . . in the creation of new legal regimes are examples of . . . special law-making powers and tend to suggest that strong legislative equality does not exist in international law despite a general commitment to sovereign equality."[55]

In response to Samuel Moyn's tweet about how it is the use of law, rather than its abuse, that "leads to domination and hierarchy,"[56] Adil Haque noted, "Discretionary non-application of laws is an exercise of domination and hierarchy."[57] Chapter 4 shifts from the processes by which P-5 members created a culture of impunity to the ways in which the P-5 have exploited the legal deficiencies they negotiated into the text of the Genocide Convention to politically and discretionarily avoid applying the convention, pursuant to their own interests, in three historical cases: Pakistan, Rwanda, and Bosnia. By analyzing the official and verbatim records of Security Council meetings held throughout each of these three cases, chapter 4 demonstrates the importance of narrative, framing, and naming at the Security Council because of their impact on what, if anything, will be done in response to a suspected case of genocide. Hence, the changes made to the Genocide Convention must be seen not only as harmful but also as determinant.

There is an element of narration that comes into play as the P-5 choose the words they use to describe events. Security Council narratives inevitably frame events in ways that will promote or reject particular outcomes. The restrictive legal definition of genocide negotiated into the text of the Genocide Convention acts as a facilitator of this narrative process by providing space within which the P-5 can select and highlight some facets of the events "to promote a particular interpretation, evaluation, and/or solution."[58] Simply put, the legal definition offers opportunities for the P-5 to exploit its limitations by situating events either within or outside the scope of the Genocide Convention. However, when situating events outside the scope of the Genocide Convention, alternative narratives, labels, names, and descriptions are required.

In *Silencing the Past: Power and the Production of History*, Michel-Rolph Trouillot highlights the significance of naming events. For example, he writes that the "Castilian invasion of the Bahamas" is a more accurate representation of what has been commonly described as the "discovery of America."[59] The former description portrays a group that arrives at a destination and attacks its inhabitants, whereas the latter portrays the arrival of a group to a land on which no human has previously set foot. Thus, Trouillot writes: "The naming of the 'fact' is itself a narrative power disguised as innocence. . . . Naming the fact thus already imposes a reading and many historical controversies boil down to who has the power to name what."[60] At the Security Council, comparable to Trouillot's "innocence" is the idea that the P-5 operate in good faith. That is why, as this book shows, they have gone to great lengths to not only avoid naming events genocide but also to use and defend alternative names, frames, and narratives. Importantly, the "discovery" narrative is evidence that there is no rule that precludes false depictions from having real world consequences. As David Carr aptly puts it, "some histories may be inaccurate and some stories *invraisemblable*, but nothing in principle prevents such narratives from succeeding at their aim."[61]

Chapter 5 draws connections between the first two chapters and the political and discretionary nonapplication of the Genocide Convention. Through a comparative analysis of the changes made to the convention and the responsibility to protect doctrine (hereafter, R2P), chapter 5 shows that R2P addresses many of the legal deficiencies negotiated into the convention. Nevertheless, the chapter also shows how the P-5 maintain the culture of impunity within which they act concerning the crime of genocide by controlling when R2P is applied. Because Russia and China refuse to invoke R2P, the remaining P-5 members largely determine when it is invoked. The idea that liberal democracies are in a position not only to judge but to also take action against illiberal states is central to what Simpson refers to as "liberal anti-pluralism," a form of liberalism "endowed with a sort of moralistic fervor, a conviction and, at times, an intolerance of the illiberal."[62]

Because R2P is invoked in some cases and not others, chapter 5 also demonstrates how R2P is representative of a discretionarily applied international doctrine, as well as how discretionary nonapplication of R2P further contributes to P-5 impunity concerning the crime of genocide. Discretionary noninvocation of R2P is connected to the criticism that R2P is selectively applied based on the interests of P-5 members—meaning the United States, United Kingdom, and France, as they are the P-5 members that have invoked and are likely to invoke R2P. There exists an abundance of literature that grapples with selective intervention. For example, Jennifer Welsh writes: "One could never completely erase the possibility of abuse or the selective application of the practice [of humanitarian intervention]. But these objections in and of themselves are not strong enough, and should not prevent action where 'right' motive joins together with the capacity to make a difference."[63]

Even when acknowledging R2P's selective application, some scholars are reluctant to do so explicitly, seemingly out of concern that it would undermine R2P's normative value. For example, Thomas Weiss dismisses criticism of R2P while also criticizing the Security Council for "dithering since 2003 [in relation to Darfur]" and for failing to "address the even longer-running woes and the millions dead in the DRC [Democratic Republic of the Congo]."[64] Weiss laments the lack of international political will to stop atrocities, thus acknowledging—without using the term "selective"—the selective mustering of that will for the use of military force for alleged humanitarian purposes. He then fails to address why intervention occurs in some cases and not others and criticizes those who would offer considerations of national interest as the source of the selectivity he implicitly acknowledges. Aidan Hehir also invokes Darfur and the DRC, along with Sri Lanka, but offers a more biting critique of the failure to protect: "If R2P meant something and had real influence, why was this? Supporters argue that R2P constitutes more than military intervention and such action is not always prudent. A more accurate explanation, however, is that the response of the 'international community' remains dependent on the interests of the P-5."[65]

What is missing from the selectivity debate, which is also addressed in chapter 5, is an analysis of how the P-5, by working in concert even if their actions are not meant to be a sign of cooperation, ensure that R2P will not be invoked against them or their interests, thus maintaining their impunity. For all intents and purposes, the P-5 are immune from the application of R2P based on their permanent veto-wielding positions on the Security Council. The ideological positions of the P-5 also facilitate a narrative in which the United States, the United Kingdom, and France are moral supporters of the prevention of genocide that would do more if Russia and China would stop impeding them.

The book concludes by arguing for a new conception of the outlaw state. Currently, there is a direct relationship between antipluralism and outlaw states. Outlaw states are defined by their lack of compliance with or adherence to individual human rights regimes and international norms. More specifically, outlaws are illiberal states that violate the rights of their populations and/or commit acts of aggression against their neighbors. In the conclusion, I argue that true outlaw states are those that have fully situated themselves outside the reach of laws and norms—in this case, those related to genocide—thus giving themselves the ability to act with impunity. Though this describes all P-5 members to a certain degree, the United States and China are likely the only two true outlaw states.

Chapter 1

Territorializing Prevention of Genocide

A little more than twenty-five years ago, the United States Office of the Secretary of Defense circulated a discussion paper on Rwanda. Dated May 1, 1994—approximately three weeks into the genocide of Tutsi in Rwanda—the now-infamous discussion paper stressed, "Be Careful. Legal at State was worried about this yesterday—Genocide finding could commit USG [United States Government] to actually 'do something.'"[1] Perhaps more than any other event since the Genocide Convention was adopted in 1948 and entered into force in 1951, the genocide in Rwanda, together with the political response that unfolded at the United Nations Security Council, sparked a debate regarding whether state parties to the convention are legally obligated to take extraterritorially applied coercive preventive action when genocide is recognized as such and is ongoing.

There have been a number of coercive external interventions in active genocides subsequent to the adoption of the Genocide Convention and its entry into force. India intervened to stop Pakistan's attacks on its own Bengali and Hindu populations, including supporters of the Awami League, in East Pakistan (present-day Bangladesh) in 1971—a move that was condemned, most notably by the United States and China. In 1978, Vietnam intervened in Cambodia. This, too, was condemned by the United States and China, as well as others.[2] Importantly, in both cases, the Genocide Convention was invoked primarily by the intervening state, rather than by the Security Council's five permanent members. Additionally, the justifications for the use of force were not connected to any legal obligation under the terms of the Genocide Convention. Instead, India and Vietnam referred to the firmly established inherent right to self-defense to justify their actions.[3]

The above cases of genocide occurred during the Cold War, a period when "the salience of human rights and humanitarian issues rose in international politics, but no government . . . was prepared to contemplate a general right of humanitarian intervention."[4] However, the end of the Cold War brought with it optimism that members of the international community would put past differences behind them and work together to promote and protect human rights, including preventing genocide. As Luke Glanville notes, "with the increased activism of the Security Council after the Cold War, there did emerge a belief in some quarters of international society that the Genocide Convention imposed a duty to intervene beyond borders in response to genocide."[5] Similarly, Samantha Power claims: "Interfering in a genocidal state's internal affairs . . . was not only authorized but required by the convention. If a government committed or permitted genocide, signatories would have to take steps to prevent, suppress, and punish the crime, which no instrument had ever required before."[6]

Article I of the adopted text of the Genocide Convention is the obvious source of this belief. It states, "The Contracting Parties confirm that genocide, whether committed in time of peace or in time of war, is a crime under international law which they undertake to prevent and to punish."[7] Furthermore, the convention's formal title places prevention alongside punishment as central to its purpose. However, Eyal Mayroz argues, "Unfortunately, those who drafted the Convention did very little to clarify what specific measures states had to take to comply with the duty."[8] Similarly, William Schabas states: "Perhaps the most intriguing phrase in Article I is the obligation upon states to prevent and punish genocide. . . . Yet, while the final Convention has much to say about punishment of genocide, there is little to suggest what prevention of genocide really means."[9]

As this chapter demonstrates, the Genocide Convention is actually less ambiguous regarding prevention than some scholars believe. Indeed, a comprehensive analysis of the convention's text and the preparatory work for it reveals that prevention of genocide was firmly rooted in a system of territorial jurisdiction, meaning that there is very little states are obligated, let alone legally permitted, to do when genocide is committed within the sovereign territorial borders of another state. This should hardly be surprising. As Hirad Abtahi and Philippa Webb note, "the Genocide Convention is the product of its time: a document reflecting the sociology of immediate post-WWII inter-state relations."[10]

Yet, as the introduction to this book suggested, this was not always the case. Raphael Lemkin's ideal law against genocide would have incorporated a form of universal jurisdiction for the prevention of genocide. Moreover, as this chapter discusses, the first official draft of the Genocide Convention (the Secretariat Draft) included language that universalized genocide prevention. However, consistent with the overall argument of this book, P-5 members—in particular the United States, the United Kingdom, and China—used the Genocide Convention's drafting process to eliminate universalizing language, thus situating the convention in the existing international system of territorial jurisdiction. In doing so, these members succeeded in protecting their interests by constructing limitations on the enforcement of the prohibition of genocide. Evidence of this can be found in a comparative analysis of the three formal drafts of the Genocide Convention and an analysis of the preparatory work for the treaty. Other scholars have tracked the evolution of the convention using the preparatory work to gain a better understanding of the positions of the negotiating parties and to better interpret the terms of the treaty, but these efforts have largely focused on the punitive element. Thus, the scholarly literature contains gaps regarding the convention's preventive language and what that means for the prevention of genocide.

The United Nations: A System of Territorial Jurisdiction

The United Nations was formally brought into existence by its original fifty-one members on October 24, 1945. The international organization was based on a charter that institutionalized a Westphalian nation-state system in which individual states maintain exclusive control over their boundaries and everything therein. What this means is that states have both prima facie exclusive jurisdiction over a defined and recognized territory and its residents and an obligation not to intervene in territory that is in the area of exclusive jurisdiction of another state.[11]

The United Nations Charter emphasizes the need for "international cooperation" and the use of "collective measures" to maintain international peace and security.[12] In Article 2(4), it also explicitly requires that states "refrain in their international relations from the threat or use of force against the territorial integrity or political independence of any state." In case the prohibition on the use of force or the threat thereof in violation of another state's sovereignty was not clear enough in Article 2(4), Article 2(7) reaffirms the point: "Nothing contained in the present Charter shall authorize the United Nations to intervene in matters which are essentially within the domestic jurisdiction of any state or shall require the Members to submit such matters to settlement under the present Charter." Article 2(7) does clarify that the nonintervention principle based on the sovereign equality of all states does not "prejudice the application of enforcement measures under Chapter VII" of the charter. In this regard, Article 2(7) refers to one of only two conditions in which the sovereignty of a state may be violated—with Security Council authorization. The other condition is in self-defense against an armed attack.

It is within this context that the drafting of the Genocide Convention began less than two years later. Therefore, it is also within a strict system of state sovereignty that the terms of the convention were negotiated. What this means is that the prevention of genocide would be confined to the same limitations as established by the United Nations Charter unless the terms of the Genocide Convention very clearly stated otherwise.

As noted above, there is a belief among some scholars that the Genocide Convention is essentially a self-executing treaty in that recognition of genocide requires and, therefore, makes legally permissible a coercive response that involves the violation of another state's sovereignty for the purpose of preventing genocide. However, a comparative analysis of the three formal drafts of the convention (the Secretariat Draft, Ad Hoc Committee Draft, and adopted text) and a review of the convention's preparatory work reveal that a majority of the negotiating parties prioritized state sovereignty over all else when debating the terms of the treaty. Key among these negotiating parties were P-5 members—especially the United States and Soviet Union, along with France and the United Kingdom. Though the United States and Soviet Union approached the question of how genocide would be defined in terms of its status under international law and what form of preventive jurisdiction the Genocide Convention would establish, both used their power and influence (with the support of various other actors) to ensure that the crime of genocide would have special status in name only, and that preventive jurisdiction would rest with the state on whose territory genocide is committed.

Genocide: Just Another Crime under International Law?

How the Genocide Convention defines genocide within the confines of international law (of which the convention is a subset) is central to the jurisdictional framework. Article 2(1) of the United Nations Charter establishes the sovereign equality of all states. And as noted above, Article 2(4) prohibits the use of force or the threat thereof against the territorial integrity of another state—a prohibition that can be overridden only by the inherent right of states to act in self-defense under Article 51 or by the Security Council acting under its Chapter VII authority.[13] Thus, defining genocide as a crime under international law alone does not give genocide a special status that would require, or even permit, states to take preventive action outside of those allowed under the existing parameters of the international system.

Article I of the Genocide Convention defines genocide as "a crime under international law."[14] Article I also takes the logical next step, requiring that the treaty's parties undertake to prevent and punish genocide. Without such a commitment, defining genocide as a violation of international law would have little practical meaning.[15] Yet, though the commitment added a specific and egregious form of a crime against humanity to the body of international law, defining genocide as a violation of international law did not add much else to that body. The systematic murder of innocent people was already a violation of international law. In the Nuremberg trials, crimes against humanity were defined as "murder, extermination, enslavement, deportation, and other inhumane acts committed against any civilian population, before or during the war; or persecutions on political, racial or religious grounds in the execution of or in connection with any crime within the jurisdiction of the Tribunal."[16] Also, during the so-called Doctors Trial, the indictment against Nazi physicians stated, "The said crimes against humanity constitute violations of international conventions, including Article 46 of the Hague Regulations, 1907, the laws and customs of war, the general principles of criminal law as derived from the criminal laws of all civilized nations, the internal penal laws of the countries in which such crimes were committed, and of Article II of Control Council Law No. 10."[17]

Significantly, while the Nuremberg trials officially recognized crimes against humanity as violations of international law, they also maintained that crimes against humanity "fell within the province of international law if they were committed in preparation for or in connection with international war such as aggressive war and War Crimes."[18] Thus, the commission of *interstate* genocide, as a crime against humanity, was a violation of international law prior to the adoption of the Genocide Convention. Meanwhile, *intrastate* genocide fell outside the province of international law "so as to not infringe in the domestic affairs of a sovereign state merely on the grounds that it was offending against humanitarian principles."[19] The motivation for the creation of a convention that prohibits the crime of genocide was the eradication of the crime through its universal prevention and its punishment. The definition of genocide does not prohibit the application of the term to acts of genocide committed within one set of territorial borders. Yet by failing to define genocide as an inherent threat to international peace and security, which would have brought all cases of genocide within the purview of the Security Council, the Genocide Convention privileges territorial sovereignty.

To illustrate this point, the commission of genocide can take on a number of different forms. Genocide can be committed: (1) across territorial borders against the will of the authority that maintains jurisdiction over the territory in which the crime is being committed; (2) across territorial borders with the acquiescence of the authority that maintains jurisdiction over the territory in which the crime is being committed; (3) within a single territory by the authority that maintains jurisdiction over the territory; and (4) within a single territory by nonstate actors with the acquiescence of the authority that maintains jurisdiction over the territory. In the cases of genocide that cross territorial borders, the failure to define genocide as a threat to international peace and security is less significant. The primary purpose of the United Nations, as established by its charter, is the maintenance of international peace and security. The United Nations organ charged with fulfilling this primary responsibility is the Security Council. By definition, cases of interstate genocide committed without the acquiescence of the authority on whose territory the crime is being committed amount to threats to international peace and security and constitute violations of Article 2(4) of the United Nations Charter. This is so because force is used against the territorial integrity and political independence of the state being victimized. Therefore, such cases clearly fall within the mandate of the United Nations and the Security Council's responsibilities.

The corollary of this is that cases of intrastate genocide, including those committed by foreign agents at the behest of the territorial authority, fall outside the mandate of the United Nations and the Security Council's responsibilities. Because intrastate genocide is confined to a single territory, such genocide does not, under the letter of the law, constitute a threat to international peace and security. In other words, cases of intrastate genocide, without being defined as inherent threats to international peace and security, fall within the exclusive jurisdiction of the territory's authority. Thus, if the territorial authority develops and implements a plan of genocide, the same authority is responsible for the crime's prevention. The international system is predicated on the principle of noninterference. It is only when violations of international law amount to a threat to international peace and security that they cease to be an internal matter of state. Therefore, given the conditions required for the legal use of coercive measures as established by the United Nations Charter, the use of force in response to intrastate genocide is actually forbidden.

Rather than permit or obligate states to prevent genocide, the Genocide Convention requires international cooperation. The treaty's preamble, like Article I, contributes to the formulation of the convention's territorial preventive jurisdiction because it does not create any new legal prescriptions that revise those that exist in the United Nations Charter. The Genocide Convention's preamble states, "Being convinced that, in order to liberate mankind from such an odious scourge, international co-operation is required."[20] The reference in the preamble to international cooperation mirrors the language used in the United Nations Charter. Article 1(3) of the charter states that one of the main purposes of the United Nations is "to achieve international cooperation in solving problems of an economic, social, cultural, or humanitarian character."[21] As noted above, the charter bans the use of force unless authorized by the Security Council or in cases of self-defense. Thus, "international cooperation" must be interpreted to mean that states are encouraged to assist one another when such assistance is sought and required to assist the Security Council when it authorizes preventive measures.

A comparative analysis of the three formal drafts of the Genocide Convention and a review of the treaty's preparatory work show that the primacy of state sovereignty and associated territorial jurisdiction for the prevention of genocide were written into the treaty and explicitly advocated for during the drafting process. During that process, negotiating parties had numerous opportunities to include language in the convention that would have established subsidiary preventive jurisdiction. The idea of subsidiary jurisdiction is similar to the concept of a court of complementarity, as exemplified by the International Criminal Court. While the state on whose territory genocide is being committed would retain primary jurisdiction for its prevention, subsidiary jurisdiction would provide the Security Council with complementary jurisdiction regardless of whether genocide is committed within or across state borders. The rejection of universal and subsidiary preventive jurisdictions is indicative of a commitment not to the universal prevention of genocide, but rather to maintaining complete and immutable control over one's own territory even and especially when in the process of committing genocide.

Evidence of opposition to universal and subsidiary jurisdictions is found in the evolution of the Genocide Convention from the Secretariat Draft to the adopted text. Clause number 2 of the Secretariat Draft's preamble states, "They [the contracting parties] proclaim that the acts of genocide defined by the present Convention are crimes against the Law of Nations, and that the fundamental exigencies of civilization, *international order and peace* [emphasis added] require their prevention and punishment."[22] The analogous text is located in Article I of the Ad Hoc Committee Draft and adopted text. Article I of the Ad Hoc Committee Draft states, "Genocide is a crime under international law whether committed in time of peace or in time of war."[23] Article I of the adopted text states, "The Contracting Parties confirm that genocide, whether committed in time of peace or in time of war, is a crime under international law which they undertake to prevent and to punish."

All three formal drafts of the Genocide Convention recognize genocide to be a violation of international law.[24] Yet while the Ad Hoc Committee Draft and the adopted text left genocide on a par with other violations of international law, the Secretariat Draft elevated genocide to a threat to international peace and security.[25] This is significant because, as noted above, it is only when a violation of international law amounts to a threat to international peace and security that it falls within the mandate of the United

Nations and the Security Council's responsibilities. Therefore, because genocide was not defined as a threat to international peace and security in the adopted text and because, by definition, cases of intrastate genocide do not constitute a threat to international peace and security, such cases remain within the exclusive jurisdiction of the territorial authority.

By defining genocide as a threat to "international order and peace," the Secretariat Draft uniquely elevated its legal status.[26] It distinguished genocide from any other human rights violation by declaring genocide to be an inherent threat to international peace and security, thus awarding the Security Council with subsidiary preventive jurisdiction. Why was this classification omitted from the Ad Hoc Committee Draft and the adopted text? A review of the preparatory work for the convention provides no clear answer to this question. The preparatory work includes only six mentions of "international order and peace."[27] All six mentions came in the form of reproductions of the Secretariat Draft. The negotiating parties that provided comments on the Secretariat Draft did not offer any insight into whether they believed that classifying genocide as a threat to international peace and security ought to be retained.

Though there was no debate over whether the term "international order and peace" ought to be retained, lively debate over the status of genocide in international law ensued in a different context. Article XII of the Secretariat Draft states, "Irrespective of any provision in the foregoing articles, should the crimes as defined in this Convention be committed in any part of the world, or should there be serious reasons for suspecting that such crimes have been committed, the High Contracting Parties may call upon the competent organs of the United Nation to take measures for the suppression or prevention of such crimes."[28] During debates on Article XII of the Secretariat Draft, the Soviet Union argued that all cases of genocide, as threats to international peace and security, should be referred to the Security Council, rather than the more general competent organs of the United Nations.[29]

During negotiations of the Ad Hoc Committee, the Soviet Union proposed the following text for Article VIII, which is where the substance of Article XII of the Secretariat Draft was moved in the Ad Hoc Committee Draft: "The High Contracting Parties undertake to report to the Security Council all cases of genocide and all cases of a breach of the obligations imposed by the Convention so that the necessary measures may be taken in accordance with Chapter VI of the United Nations Charter."[30] Chapter VI of the United Nations Charter details the ways in which the Security Council can promote the pacific settlements of disputes, giving the council the authority to "recommend appropriate procedures or methods" for this purpose.[31] Chapter VII outlines the council's primary authority to determine what coercive action, including the use of military force, ought to be taken in response to threats to international peace and security.[32]

Poland supported the Soviet position, adding that the prevention of genocide was of significant importance and that linking genocide to threats to international peace and security would act as a useful deterrent. Because genocide involves the attempt to destroy a protected group in whole or in part, time is of the essence. To prevent irreparable harm, debates over how to respond must be expedited. Because only the Security Council can authorize coercive measures, it is the only pertinent United Nations organ for such discussions. In other words, if coercive preventive action is to be taken, it must be authorized by the Security Council. Therefore, it would be illogical to call upon any other United Nations organ, because doing so would serve only to delay the case reaching the Security Council This point was not lost on the framers of the Secretariat Draft. According to the framers, "It is essential to exercise constant vigilance, and preventive action must be taken, either before the harm is done or before it has assumed wide proportions, for then it takes on the nature of a catastrophe, the effects of which are to a great extent irreparable."[33]

There was significant opposition to classifying genocide as a threat to international peace and security. Greece and Belgium challenged the Soviet and Polish positions. Greece argued that it was doubtful whether action could always be taken under Chapters VI and VII of the charter in response to all cases of genocide.[34] Had Greece argued that it was doubtful that action *would* be taken in all cases, I would be in agreement. Calling upon the Security Council to take preventive action does not guarantee that preventive action will be taken, nor should it. There ought to be some room for Security Council discretion. Because Greece claimed that it was doubtful that action *could* be taken under Chapters VI and VII in response to all cases of genocide, it is clear Greece did not believe that all cases of genocide constitute a threat to international peace and security.

Belgium similarly argued that it was possible that some cases of genocide might not threaten international peace and security.[35] This position is not without merit. By definition, genocide committed internally without an aggravating factor that would regionalize or internationalize the conflict fails to constitute a threat to international peace and security. Yet the purpose of the treaty that was being negotiated was the eradication of genocide through its prevention and punishment. The negotiating parties were not limited to the literal meaning of a threat to international peace and security. The drafting process allowed the negotiating parties to determine whether genocide ought to be defined as such a threat. With the Soviet proposal, negotiating parties had the opportunity to elevate genocide's legal status to what such a crime deserves.

The Soviet proposal that genocide be defined as a threat to international peace and security and that all cases be referred to the Security Council as the only United Nations organ with the competency to deal with suspected cases of genocide was rejected by the Ad Hoc Committee, five votes to two.[36] With defeat of the Soviet proposal, the Ad Hoc Committee voted on China's proposal: "Any signatory to this Convention may call upon any competent organ of the United Nations to take such action as may be appropriate under the Charter for the prevention and suppression of genocide."[37]

China's proposal was approved by five votes to one, with one abstention.[38] Having been approved, China's proposed amendment became Article VIII of the Ad Hoc Committee Draft, with minor adjustments.[39] Not to be deterred by China's successful proposal at the Ad Hoc Committee, the Soviet Union continued its efforts to include in the convention the obligation that state parties refer all suspected cases of genocide as threats to international peace and security to the Security Council during subsequent negotiations at the United Nations General Assembly's Sixth Committee.[40] According to the Soviet Union, "The basic thought underlying the convention was that every violation was of the greatest importance. Any act of genocide was always a threat to international peace and security and as such should be dealt with under Chapters VI and VII of the Charter. . . . Chapters VI and VII of the Charter provided means for the prevention and punishment of genocide, means far more concrete and effective than anything possible in the sphere of international jurisdiction."[41]

France offered to jointly submit the Soviet proposed amendment if the Soviet Union accepted minor revisions. France's revisions removed obligatory notification and reference to any specific articles of the United Nations Charter because the relevant articles could change from case to case. The Soviet proposal with France's revisions reads: "The High Contracting Parties may call the attention of the Security Council to the cases of genocide and of violations of the present Convention likely to constitute a threat to international peace and security in order that the Security Council may take such measures as it deems necessary to stop the threat."[42]

France noted that the intention behind the proposed amendment was not to replace the current standards of international jurisdiction, but rather to "fulfill a useful function in the prevention of genocide, since that jurisdiction did not exist."[43] This is a significant point. France explicitly recognized the absence of any provisions that established the draft convention's preventive jurisdiction. Had the Security Council been named as a U.N. organ that parties to the convention could call upon, genocide would have been defined as a threat to international peace and security, albeit in a less direct way than found in the Secretariat Draft or the Soviet Union's initial proposal. In other words, because the Security Council's power to authorize collective measures is limited to threats to international peace and security, the mere fact that the joint Soviet-French proposal would have allowed parties to call upon the council implicitly defined genocide as a threat to international peace and security. Thus, the council would have been awarded subsidiary jurisdiction for the prevention of genocide.

The Soviet Union endorsed France's remarks, stating, "It was not simply a question of repeating the provisions of the Charter. The underlying purpose of the joint amendment was to state in the convention that acts of genocide necessitated the intervention of the most important organ of the United Nations. It was essential to state clearly that acts of genocide were likely to bring about threats to international peace and security."[44] Neither the Soviet Union nor France was arguing for universal preventive jurisdiction. Because the purpose of a convention prohibiting genocide was, first and foremost, the prevention of the prohibited crime, the Soviet Union and France essentially argued that the convention ought to say something regarding preventive jurisdiction. The Soviet Union argued that the Security Council should have sole jurisdiction for the prevention of genocide when the territorial authority is unable to prevent genocide or is taking part in it.[45] France's amendment to the Soviet proposal alleviated disagreement over whether notification ought to be compulsory. However, disagreement remained over the requirement that all suspected cases of genocide that are referred be referred to the Security Council.

Iran offered an amendment to the Soviet-French proposal that would have included the General Assembly as well as the Security Council as organs to which genocide referrals could be made. The Soviet Union and France accepted Iran's amendment. The Soviet, French, and Iranian delegations agreed on the following text: "The High Contracting Parties may call the attention of the Security Council or, if necessary, of the General Assembly to the cases of genocide and of violations of the present Convention likely to constitute a threat to international peace and security, in order that the Security Council may take such measures as it may deem necessary to stop that threat."[46] The Soviet Union called for a roll-call vote on the triple amendment, and it was rejected by twenty-seven votes to thirteen, with five abstentions. Notably, the Soviet Union and France voted in favor of the amendment, while China, the United States, and the United Kingdom voted against it.

Because the triple amendment placed the General Assembly (albeit in a secondary role) with the Security Council as the competent organs for dealing with suspected cases of genocide, it is difficult to come up with an explanation for why the amendment was rejected. Coercive prevention of genocide requires that all cases of genocide fall within the mandate of the United

Nations and the responsibilities of the Security Council. Allowing cases of intrastate genocide to escape the U.N. mandate and the Security Council's responsibilities acts as a clear impediment to the fulfillment of the Genocide Convention's purpose. The framers of the Secretariat Draft recognized this, choosing to define genocide as a threat to international peace and security. While the language that defined genocide in that way was excluded from the Ad Hoc Committee Draft and the adopted text, some negotiating parties made efforts to reinsert it. These efforts were rebuked—notably by the United States, the United Kingdom, and China—even though defining genocide as a threat to international peace and security would have strengthened the Genocide Convention's preventive efficacy. Thus, any ambiguity in the convention regarding preventive jurisdiction was not an oversight but was purposeful, which is itself indicative of what is required under the treaty (prevention of genocide within one's own territory) and what is forbidden (intervention in the affairs of another state, even for the purpose of preventing genocide).[47]

Reinforcing Territorial Jurisdiction, One Article at a Time

The previous section showed that the Genocide Convention was negotiated within a Westphalian nation-state system that is based on a foundation of strict state sovereignty. Rather than exempt the crime of genocide from this system, the Genocide Convention's negotiating parties reaffirmed it. Though the Secretariat Draft of the convention would have placed the crime of genocide at the boundaries of this system by conferring on the Security Council subsidiary jurisdiction for the prevention of genocide, the decision not to define genocide as a threat to international peace and security situated the treaty well within the confines of the Westphalian system.

Defining genocide as a threat to international peace and security was only one way that preventive jurisdiction could have been extended beyond a state's own territory. However, Articles I, V, and XII further establish territorial jurisdiction for the prevention of genocide. To reiterate, under the United Nations Charter, there are only two circumstances that allow for the legal use of force in international relations: Security Council authorization under Chapter VII, Article 42, and in self-defense under Article 51. Outside of those two scenarios, the United Nations Charter prohibits the use of force under Article 2(4).[48]

Article I of the Genocide Convention states that genocide "is a crime under international law which they [contracting parties] undertake to prevent and to punish."[49] Article I also commits state parties to undertake the prevention and punishment of genocide without specifying when or where states are to fulfill this duty. The United Nations Charter provides the answer to the questions of when and where: a state may use force if necessary against perpetrators of genocide within its own territory, whether perpetrators be actors internal to the state or external actors who have crossed into the state. States cannot legally prevent genocide through the use of force in any other territory unless authorized first by the Security Council under its enforcement powers granted by Chapter VII of the United Nations Charter. However, even the Security Council's subsidiary jurisdiction is limited to cases of interstate genocide because, as noted above, genocide was not defined as a threat to international peace and security. This places intrastate genocide within the jurisdiction of the territorial authority. Therefore, Article I must be interpreted to mean that states are obligated to prevent genocide only within their territories and are permitted to do so in another state within whose territory genocide is being committed only with the consent of that state.[50]

Article V of the Genocide Convention provides more evidence that jurisdiction is territorially limited. It states: "The Contracting Parties undertake to enact, in accordance with their respective Constitutions, the necessary legislation to give effect to the provisions of the present Convention."[51] Article V also requires that states incorporate the Genocide Convention's provisions into their domestic legislation. Once incorporated, the provisions of the convention become part of each state's domestic law. Each state's domestic law regulates only what happens within each state's territory. States cannot cite their own domestic legislation to justify interfering in the internal affairs of another state. Therefore, states can prohibit genocide only within their own territories through domestic legislation and cannot enact enforcement measures outside of their own territory without Security Council authorization. The combination of an international system grounded in territorial jurisdiction and the limitation on the application of domestic legislation to a state's own territory firmly establishes territorial jurisdiction for the prevention of genocide.

Article XII of the Genocide Convention further emphasizes territorial jurisdiction by its inclusion of an opt-in clause.[52] The article provides that states with foreign territories under their control may "extend the application of the present Convention to all or any of the territories for the conduct of whose foreign relations that Contracting Party is responsible."[53] I refer to Article XII as an opt-in clause because, rather than making application of the Genocide Convention to all foreign territories compulsory, it allows states to decide for their territories whether the convention applies. In other words, states have the option of whether their own responsibility for the prevention of genocide extends to their colonies, territories, and trusteeships. This strengthens the argument that the Genocide Convention relies on territorial jurisdiction for the prevention of genocide because territories under the control of foreign state actors, themselves lacking statehood, cannot become parties to the convention. If a state party to the Genocide Convention can opt out of being responsible for preventing genocide within a territory under its control, clearly no foreign state actor can claim to have preventive jurisdiction over a territory under the direct and proper control of a state party. Furthermore, by making jurisdiction over foreign territories voluntary, the Genocide Convention contradicts established international law concerning the occupation of foreign land. Occupying forces are extraterritorially responsible for human rights violations committed in areas under their control.[54] Yet the Genocide Convention includes an opt-in clause.[55]

The combination of the Genocide Convention's preamble and Articles I, V, and XII clearly establishes territorial jurisdiction for prevention of genocide. Under territorial preventive jurisdiction, the territorial authority—the same authority that could perpetrate genocide—has exclusive jurisdiction over the prevention of genocide within its territorial borders. There was a reasonable alternative to this arrangement. The negotiating parties could have defined genocide as a threat to international peace and security, which would have awarded subsidiary preventive jurisdiction to the Security Council. This would have been consistent with the existing rules established by the United Nations Charter. The Security Council already had subsidiary jurisdiction over threats to international peace and security. Therefore, had genocide been elevated to the level of such a threat, the Security Council would have had subsidiary preventive jurisdiction over genocide. Instead, the negotiating parties chose to limit preventive jurisdiction to each of the individual territorial authorities.

This was not always the case. A number of significant changes were made concerning the Genocide Convention's system of preventive jurisdiction as the convention evolved from the Secretariat Draft to the adopted text.[56] While all three formal drafts of the convention require that domestic legislation be passed to give full effect to the convention's provisions, the Secretariat Draft included a jurisdictional phrase not found in the subsequent drafts.[57] Clause number 3 of the Secretariat Draft's preamble states, "They [the contracting parties] pledge themselves to prevent and to repress such acts *wherever they may occur* [emphasis added]."[58] Because the Secretariat Draft does not contain language calling for international cooperation for the prevention of genocide and because the Ad Hoc Committee Draft does not contain the jurisdictional phrase "wherever they may occur," it can be concluded that the jurisdictional phrase found in the Secretariat Draft was replaced in the Ad Hoc Committee Draft's preamble by the following language: "being convinced that the prevention and punishment of genocide requires international co-operation."[59] Similarly, the adopted text states,

"Being convinced that, in order to liberate mankind from such an odious scourge, international co-operation is required." There is a clear difference between requiring international cooperation for the prevention of genocide and requiring that states undertake the prevention of genocide wherever it may occur. "Wherever they may occur" is an explicit statement regarding preventive jurisdiction. Had this phrase been retained in the Ad Hoc Committee Draft and the adopted text, it would have created a commitment of states to the universal prevention of genocide.

The jurisdictional phrase included in the Secretariat Draft was excluded from the Ad Hoc Committee Draft and the adopted text without any debate over its substance. The only direct reference to this provision came from the United States. The United States criticized the inclusion of questions of jurisdiction in the Secretariat Draft's preamble, arguing that such questions should be addressed in the body of the convention.[60] Retention of this jurisdictional phrase would have designated responsibility for the prevention of all cases of genocide to all parties to the treaty. In other words, had "wherever they may occur" been included in the adopted text, jurisdiction for the prevention of genocide would have been universal, even if filtered through the existing system that awards the Security Council the power to authorize preventive measures. Because the negotiating parties ultimately adopted territorial jurisdiction for the prevention of genocide, cases of intrastate genocide leave the authority most likely to perpetrate genocide responsible for its prevention.

The significance of the inclusion of a jurisdictional phrase in the Secretariat Draft, and its absence in the subsequent Ad Committee Draft and adopted text, cannot be found in the scholarly literature. Similarly, there is surprisingly little mention of Article XII of the Genocide Convention in the literature. Where it or related language is discussed in the literature, the debate during negotiations is typically absent. Article XII of the Genocide Convention—the final brick in the territorial wall—was not added to the text of the treaty until it reached the Sixth Committee. There is no language in either the Secretariat Draft or the Ad Hoc Committee Draft that even suggests such an option for states.

The United Kingdom, which was not a member of the Ad Hoc Committee, proposed the addition of the opt-in clause at the Sixth Committee, with one of its representatives arguing: "It had been the custom during the last twenty or thirty years to include an article similar to the one proposed by this delegation in all multilateral treaties. It was only in recent years that any objections had been raised to the practice and those objections were based on purely political motives and designed to create difficulties for the colonial Powers."[61] Without recognizing the irony of such a claim by a colonial power, the United Kingdom argued further in defense of its proposal by stating that it would be constitutionally impossible for it to decide for its territories—especially those that were completely self-governing—whether they would accept and be bound by the provisions of the convention without first consulting them. The United States supported the United Kingdom's position, stating that it was "extremely reasonable."[62] Essentially, the United Kingdom argued that because colonial territories were not present to represent themselves at the negotiations, those territories could not be obligated by the colonial powers to abide by the terms of the Genocide Convention without first obtaining the territories' consent.

Ukraine challenged the United Kingdom's position, arguing that it was of the utmost importance that the convention apply to all peoples, especially in non-self-governing territories. According to Ukraine, "the peoples of non-self-governing territories were most likely to become the victims of acts of genocide because they did not possess the highly developed organs of information necessary to inform the whole world immediately of the commission of the crime."[63] The Soviet Union also challenged the United Kingdom, referring to the proposal as the "colonial clause."[64] The Soviet Union asked the United Kingdom how many of its territories were self-governing and how many were not, and would the United Kingdom accept compulsory responsibility for its non-self-governing territories? The representative from the United Kingdom responded that he was not a colonial expert and, therefore, could not provide the Soviet Union with precise numbers of the two types of territories. He did claim that at least three-quarters of the United Kingdom's territories were self-governing. And he said that it was technically possible for the United Kingdom to extend the application of the Genocide Convention to non-self-governing territories, but the United Kingdom "did not choose to adopt this course."[65] The United Kingdom essentially argued that almost all of the territories under its control maintained some form of local administration, and therefore it was not up to the United Kingdom to commit those territories to meeting the Genocide Convention's obligations—even though, technically, only it could do so because its colonies lacked the statehood required to be a party to the treaty.

The Soviet Union continued to press the issue, referring to colonial policy as "a dark page in history."[66] It stated that the convention was atypical and that to avoid seeing those "dark pages prolonged by a failure to extend the provisions of the convention on genocide to colonial territories," the "Committee should bear in mind that millions must not be allowed to remain outside the scope of the convention and left to the arbitrary action of the colonial Powers."[67] The Soviet Union questioned the sincerity of the United Kingdom, arguing that it must be concluded from the United Kingdom's position that it believes "that there might be peoples who wished to become victims of genocide."[68] The United Kingdom retorted that the Soviet Union and Ukraine were asking the United Kingdom to impose its decision on its territories (and other colonial powers to do the same on their territories). The Ukrainian and United Kingdom proposals were voted on in that order, and neither vote involved calling the roll. The Ukrainian proposal of extending the application of the convention to all territories under the control of a colonial power was defeated by nineteen votes to ten, with fourteen abstentions. The United Kingdom's proposal was adopted by eighteen votes to nine, again with fourteen abstentions.[69]

Ukraine and the Soviet Union attempted to ensure that all territories under the control of a colonial power were protected against genocide. The United Kingdom opposed the compulsory application of the convention to self-governing and non-self-governing territories. While technically valid, the United Kingdom's arguments against compulsory application of the convention lacked legitimacy. Each of the United Kingdom's arguments, in the words of the Soviet Union, lacked sincerity. First, the United Kingdom noted that an opt-in clause was typical of international conventions, and that it was only in the years leading up to the negotiations concerning the draft convention prohibiting genocide that objections to this type of clause began to be raised. Following World War II and the creation of the United Nations, there was growing opposition to the continued maintenance of colonies by the colonial powers. Therefore, the United Kingdom's reference to what had been acceptable for the two or three previous decades lacked clear relevance to the Genocide Convention's negotiations. The United Kingdom added that the newly founded objections to such a clause were politically motivated. Presumably, that was at least partially the case. However, whether the Soviet Union and Ukraine were motivated by politics based on an effort to "create difficulties for the colonial Powers" does not invalidate the substance of Ukraine's proposal and the positions stated in support of it by Ukraine and the Soviet Union.

During the debate, other negotiating parties made it seem as if Ukraine's proposal would have affected only the United Kingdom.[70] It is difficult to believe, especially when considering the tally of the vote, that other negotiating parties did not think that the proposal would apply to them. Because the United Kingdom was far from the only negotiating party maintaining control over foreign territories, the vote reflected an unwillingness of colonial powers to accept the application of the prohibition of genocide to the territories under their control. It also implies an opposition to a form of universal preventive jurisdiction for the crime of genocide. Whether this was due to a fear that their own policies could have constituted acts of genocide or a fear that their policies were creating schisms between different groups residing in their territories—which could constitute one of the relatively lesser crimes under the convention, such as incitement to genocide, complicity in genocide, or conspiracy to commit genocide—is unclear.[71] Regardless, chapter 2 shows that the colonial powers had a vested interest in removing territories under their control from the scope of the Genocide Convention.

A Nexus between Preventive and Punitive Jurisdiction

During meetings of the Sixth Committee, Iran submitted an amendment that would have established a form of subsidiary punitive jurisdiction for the crime of genocide. While not directly related to preventive jurisdiction, the arguments made for and against subsidiary punitive jurisdiction are instructive. Iran argued that its amendment "was intended to remedy a deficiency in the system of punishment of genocide."[72] Iran argued that primary jurisdiction for trying those suspected of planning and perpetrating genocide rested with the state on whose territory the alleged crimes were committed. However, according to Iran, "if it [the territorial authority] expressed no such desire, it thereby tacitly renounced its right to try him [the suspected perpetrator]."[73] Essentially, Iran was arguing that if the authority with jurisdiction over the territory on which genocide was committed was unable or unwilling to try genocide suspects, or was an alleged participant in the perpetration of genocide, a form of subsidiary punitive jurisdiction was needed. Iran explained that its position was the right balance between state sovereignty rights and the need to ensure that those who plan and perpetrate genocide are punished.

Opposing states argued that subsidiary punitive jurisdiction for punishment of genocide would stand in contrast with the accepted traditional principles of international law by allowing a state to punish a foreigner for crimes committed outside of the punishing state. Furthermore, the opposition argued, because states are often implicated in the commission of genocide, accepting the Iranian position would allow the courts of one state to punish the leaders of another state for crimes committed outside of the punishing state. This, the opposition argued, could result in dangerous international tension.[74] The United States concluded that subsidiary punitive jurisdiction was "one of the most dangerous and unacceptable of principles."[75] The Iranian amendment was overwhelmingly rejected, with twenty-nine votes against, six votes for, and ten abstentions.[76]

Iran's proposed amendment and the debate that followed highlight the fact that a similarly direct and necessary discussion over preventive jurisdiction was never held. Consider Iran's argument in support of subsidiary punitive jurisdiction. Iran argued that such jurisdiction was not a threat to existing international law because it worked in cooperation with, rather than against, state sovereignty. The territorial authority maintained primary responsibility for and jurisdiction over punishing the planners and perpetrators of genocide within the territory it governs. However, if the territorial authority demonstrated itself to be unable or unwilling to enforce the punishment prong of the convention, other members of the international community would be awarded subsidiary punitive jurisdiction, thus making it more likely that the punishment prong would be enforced. In further support of this position, Iran stated: "The source of the jurisdiction vested in national courts was the need for maintaining order in their respective territories. Genocide, however, involved not only the law and order of the State on whose territory the crime was committed, but also the law and order of all States constituting the family of nations."[77]

Clearly, the same arguments made by Iran in support of subsidiary punitive jurisdiction could have been made in support of a system of subsidiary preventive jurisdiction. To allow planners and perpetrators of genocide to get away with their crimes because the authority over the territory on which genocide was committed lacks the desire or ability to prosecute the individuals, as Iran argued, must be avoided. It is arguably even more important that prevention of genocide not rely on the willingness of the territorial authority alone for the crime's prevention, because the territorial authority might also be responsible for the commission of the crime. If the territorial authority is actively engaged in intrastate genocide or complicit in its commission, some form of subsidiary preventive jurisdiction is necessary to increase the likelihood that the prevention prong of the convention will be enforced. Primary preventive jurisdiction would remain with the territorial authority. The explicit establishment of a form of subsidiary preventive jurisdiction would have remedied a deficiency in the system of prevention of genocide.

The problem, therefore, is not that the Genocide Convention does not include universal preventive jurisdiction. Correcting the limitations of territorial jurisdiction with a form of universal preventive jurisdiction would create other liabilities: most significantly, universal preventive jurisdiction would undermine the international system's ability to regulate the legitimate use of force in international affairs. While universal preventive jurisdiction was not the answer, ensuring that prevention of intrastate genocide did not rest exclusively within the jurisdiction of the territorial authority was essential. Yet the negotiating parties failed to complement territorial jurisdiction with some form of subsidiary preventive jurisdiction. This emphasizes why the failure to define genocide as an inherent threat to international peace and security is so significant. Had all cases of genocide been classified as threats to international peace and security, the Security Council would hold subsidiary preventive jurisdiction.

AVAILABLE RECOURSE: STATES ONLY—ALL OTHERS NEED NOT APPLY

As a human rights treaty, the Genocide Convention considers state parties to the convention, rather than the people affected by policies of genocide, as the subjects of the law. As has been emphasized throughout this chapter, this places the victims of intrastate genocide in harm's way by giving jurisdiction for their protection exclusively to those who would commit genocide against them. Unfortunately, there were opportunities to provide victims of genocide standing before international law in relation to the crime of genocide that were rejected.

Articles VIII and IX of the Genocide Convention outline the forms of recourse available to states being victimized by genocide. Article VIII gives states the right to call upon the competent organs of the United Nations to take appropriate measures under the United Nations Charter for the prevention of genocide. Article IX designates the ICJ as the arbiter of disputes between states concerning the interpretation and application of the convention, as well as the fulfillment of obligations maintained by the parties to it.

Because only state parties to the Genocide Convention may call upon U.N. organs for preventive action under Article VIII, recourse is limited to victims of interstate genocide, assuming that the state authority over the territory within which genocide is being committed has not acquiesced to the crime and is willing and able to act at the United Nations on behalf of its citizens. However, for victims of intrastate genocide, the perpetrator and the relevant state authority are one and the same. Therefore, recourse for victims of intrastate genocide under Article VIII would require that the state authority committing genocide call upon the United Nations to stop it from continuing to commit genocide. Furthermore, even in a case of interstate genocide committed with the acquiescence of the territorial authority, interstate genocide still constitutes a threat to international peace and security, bringing it within the Security Council's mandate of maintaining international peace and security. However, members of a protected group being targeted for genocide by their own state or with its acquiescence have no legal standing to petition the competent organs of the United Nations to take action for the purpose of their protection. Therefore, genocide committed within a state's territorial borders excludes the victims from this avenue of recourse unless another state formally seeks its inclusion on the Security Council agenda.

Article IX of the Genocide Convention offers an additional means of recourse to that offered under Article VIII. Article IX recognizes the ICJ as the court to which "disputes between the Contracting Parties relating to the interpretation, application or fulfillment of the present Convention, including those relating to the responsibility of a State for genocide or for any of the other acts enumerated in Article III, shall be submitted."[78] The means of recourse provided by Article IX, like those provided under Article VIII, are limited to states. This is consistent with the ICJ's rules: Article 34(1) of the Statute of the ICJ establishes that "only states may be parties in cases before the Court."[79] Thus, the means of recourse included in the Genocide Convention are available only to victims of interstate genocide through their representation by the state. Individuals targeted by their own government are once again excluded, making it more difficult to prevent cases of intrastate genocide.

All three formal drafts of the Genocide Convention limit available recourse to state actors. This limitation is consistent with the international system: Article 4(1) of the United Nations Charter states, "Membership in the United Nations is open to all other peace-loving states which accept the obligations contained in the present Charter and, in the judgment of the Organization, are able and willing to carry out these obligations."[80] And, as noted above, Article 34 of the Statute of the ICJ states, "Only states may be parties in cases before the Court."

There was only one challenge to this limitation on available recourse. At the Sixth Committee, Haiti proposed giving the affected human groups legal standing to call upon the United Nations for their protection, arguing that if only states were to report genocide, the possibility existed that a state could be the perpetrator of genocide or complicit in its commission.[81] Haiti's proposal failed to elicit debate during negotiations over the Ad Hoc Committee Draft at the Sixth Committee. The chairman of the Sixth Committee noted that Haiti's amendment had been read at the committee's 101st meeting. Unfortunately, the chairman noted, no member of the Haitian delegation was present at the time. None of the negotiating parties at the meeting spoke in favor of the Haitian amendment, so it was presumed that minds were made up on the subject.[82] This raises some questions: Why wasn't a member of the Haitian delegation present? Was the delegation aware that its amendment would be read at the 101st meeting? Why didn't any other negotiating parties speak in favor of the amendment?

Because Haiti's proposed amendment was never debated, it is difficult to comment on the positions of the negotiating parties. However, it is possible that Haiti's proposal, like the subsidiary punitive jurisdiction proposal, was considered by negotiating parties to be a dangerous affront to established international norms. Allowing nonstate actors to challenge the policies of their governments would undermine states' ability to freely govern according to their sovereign rights. Awarding nonstate actors standing to call upon the competent organs of the United Nations would ultimately erode a system based in state sovereignty. Nonstate actors could make unwarranted claims of genocide for political purposes. Because the United Nations as a whole, as well as the Security Council in particular, is essentially a political entity, evaluation of allegations by nonstate actor would be based not on objectivity but rather on considerations of national interest. Of course, the flip side of the drawbacks is that providing nonstate actors with standing before the United Nations would give voice to those who might otherwise be powerless to stop genocide being committed against them by the very state actors that are supposed to protect them.

The impediments to preventing intrastate genocide have once again been highlighted. As noted above, the Genocide Convention offers two avenues of recourse: the right to call upon the United Nations to take appropriate measures under the charter for the prevention of genocide and the right to submit disputes over the interpretation, application, and fulfillment of the Genocide Convention to the ICJ. Both avenues require that the entity calling upon the United Nations or submitting a dispute to the ICJ be a state actor. This leaves victims of intrastate genocide in a perilous position. Regarding the second avenue of recourse, whether victims of intrastate genocide should have access was out of the hands of the negotiating parties. The ICJ's rules, established in 1945, require that parties to disputes before the court be state actors. A similar though less definitive argument can be made regarding access to the United Nations. The U.N. system is based on states being the primary actors in international affairs. However, the negotiating parties had some flexibility here. While only states can be members of the United Nations, its charter does not explicitly ban the participation of nonstate actors in its proceedings.[83] Therefore, the Genocide Convention could have opened the first avenue of recourse to victims of intrastate genocide.

Haiti attempted to include access to the United Nations for victims of intrastate genocide. While the circumstances around the lack of debate on Haiti's proposal are somewhat mysterious, Haiti's proposal would likely have been rejected had it come to a vote. Considering the privileging of sovereignty throughout the negotiations, it is not a stretch to conclude that the majority of the negotiating parties would have voted against an amendment to the convention that would have allowed their citizens to circumvent their authority through direct access to the United Nations. Lack of access to the avenues of recourse for victims of intrastate genocide is not a weakness that could have been easily corrected without creating other liabilities. Because it would have at least provided the Security Council with subsidiary preventive jurisdiction over cases of intrastate genocide, the failure to define genocide as a threat to international security is once again highlighted as a glaring weakness in the text of the Genocide Convention.

Affirming Territorial Jurisdiction for the Coercive Prevention of Genocide at the ICJ

The previous sections of this chapter demonstrated that states have an obligation under the Genocide Convention and associated international law to refrain from intervening in cases of intrastate genocide unless authorized to do so by the Security Council. This is a negative obligation, because it requires that states abstain from interfering in the affairs of other states. The ICJ's 2007 ruling in the Case Concerning the Application of the Convention on the Prevention and Punishment of the Crime of Genocide (Bosnia and Herzegovina v. Serbia and Montenegro) (hereinafter *Bosnia v. Serbia*) has been used by some to claim that a positive obligation to intervene to prevent genocide has been (re)affirmed.[84] According to this position, with a positive obligation comes a legal right to employ coercive measures against other states for the purpose of preventing genocide.[85]

Because the *Bosnia v. Serbia* case was the first time the ICJ fulfilled its role under Article IX of the Genocide Convention as the arbiter of disputes between states concerning the interpretation, application, or fulfillment of the treaty, the court began its review with the most basic question (one that would seemingly have an obvious answer): are states prohibited from committing genocide? The court answered in the affirmative, stating:

> In the view of the Court, taking into account the established purpose of the Convention, the effe[c]ts of Article I is [*sic*] to prohibit States from themselves commiting genocide. Such a prohibition follows, first, from the fact that Article I categorizes genocide as "a crime under international law": by agreeing to such a categorization, the States parties must logically be undertaking not to commit the act so described. Secondly, it follows from the expressly stated obligation to prevent the commission of acts of genocide. It would be paradoxical, if States were thus under an obligation to prevent, but were not forbidden to commit such acts through their own organs, or persons over whom they have such firm control that their conduct is attributable to the State concerned under international law. In short, the obligation to prevent genocide necessarily implies the prohibition of commission of genocide.[86]

It is clear from the ICJ's interpretation that the prohibition against committing genocide is intertwined with what is meant by the Genocide Convention's obligation to prevent genocide. The ICJ essentially ruled that parties to the convention are obligated to prevent genocide within their own territories and are also obligated to refrain from committing genocide in the territories of other states, both directly and through "persons over whom they have such firm control that their conduct is attributable to the State concerned under international law." The ICJ also found that states may incur a positive obligation to prevent genocide based on "the strength of the political, military and financial links" they maintain with the perpetrator.[87] As the ICJ asserted, "the FRY [Federal Republic of Yugoslavia] was in a position of influence, over the Bosnian Serbs who devised and implemented the genocide in Srebrenica, unlike that of any of the other States parties to the Genocide Convention owing to the strength of the political, military and financial links between the FRY on the one hand and the Republika Srpska and the VRS [Army of the Republika Srpska] on the other, which, though somewhat weaker than in the preceding period, nonetheless remained very close."[88]

Further addressing the extent to which the obligations of parties to the convention extend, the ICJ found: "The Court observes that the substantive obligations arising from Articles I and III are not on their face limited by territory. They apply to a State wherever it may be acting or may be able to act in ways *appropriate* [emphasis added] to meeting the obligations in question."[89] While finding that state parties to the Genocide Convention have an obligation to prevent genocide, the ICJ did not do so in a way that can be interpreted to mean that states are permitted or legally required to employ coercive measures against the offending state. Indeed, it limited the obligation of states for the prevention of genocide to "appropriate" means. Such means include those permitted under international law within the existing international system that is based on the sovereign equality of all states. In other words, these means include only those that one state can implement consistent with its obligation not to violate the sovereignty of another state. Hence, the ICJ found that Serbia failed to prevent genocide in Bosnia not because of any failure to employ coercive preventive measures, but rather because it failed to revise its political, financial, and military relations with the Bosnian Serbs when doing so could have had some influence over their decisions. Put differently, Serbia was required to withdraw material and nonmaterial forms of support that might have facilitated the commission of genocide by the Bosnian Serbs. This is a significantly different requirement from one involving supposed obligatory coercive measures directed against the Bosnian Serbs by Serbia. For example, the ICJ referred to its previous orders that required that Serbia "ensure 'that any military, paramilitary or irregular armed units which may be directed or supported by it, as well as any organizations and persons which may be subject to its control, direction or influence, do not commit any acts of genocide, of conspiracy to commit genocide, of direct and public incitement to commit genocide, or of complicity in genocide.'"[90] Offering further clarification, the ICJ stated, "The Court's use, in the above passage, of the term 'influence' is particularly revealing of the fact that the Order concerned not only the persons or entities whose conduct was attributable to the FRY, but also all those with whom the Respondent maintained close links and on which it could exert a certain influence."[91]

The ICJ's findings in the case of *Bosnia v. Serbia* are largely consistent with the International Law Commission's (ILC's) Responsibility of States for Internationally Wrongful Acts, adopted in 2001.[92] The ILC concluded that the commission of an "internationally wrongful act" by a state "entails the international responsibility"[93] of that state. The ILC also included a section on the responsibility of a state in connection with the act of another state. According to Article 16, "a State which aids or assists another State in the commission of an internationally wrongful act by the latter is internationally responsible for doing so if: (a) that State does so with knowledge of the circumstances of the internationally wrongful act; and (b) the act would be internationally wrongful if committed by that State."[94]

In the case of *Bosnia v. Serbia*, the ICJ found that Serbia incurred a responsibility to prevent the genocide committed at Srebrenica by Bosnian Serbs because of Serbia's close political, financial, and military ties to the planners and perpetrators. Based on this relationship, Serbia should have identified the possibility that Bosnian Serbs could or would commit genocide (if not foreseen such genocide) and, therefore, withdrawn its political, financial, and military support and used its political and diplomatic influence in an effort to deter the Bosnian Serbs from committing genocide. Yet Serbia had failed to show that it had taken "any initiative to prevent what happened, or any action on its part to avert the atrocities which were committed."[95] Thus, the ICJ determined that Serbia "did nothing to prevent the Srebrenica massacres, claiming that they were powerless to do so, which hardly tallies with their known influence over the VRS."[96]

Based on the ICJ's ruling in *Bosnia v. Serbia*, it can be said that state parties to the Genocide Convention have an obligation to prevent genocide insofar as can be done through avoiding directly and indirectly facilitating conditions in which another state or nonstate actor can commit genocide—as well as, of course, aiding and abetting genocide or conspiring in its commission. What cannot be said is that state parties have an obligation or legal right to initiate coercive acts against another state when the other state is committing genocide confined to its own territory and against its population.

Readers might view this as a highly pessimistic reading of the ICJ's ruling, but it is not. In fact, I believe that the ICJ's ruling on state responsibility for the prevention of genocide offers promise for the future of genocide prevention. Similarly, Anja Seibert-Fohr notes: "The Genocide Convention, though criticized as excessively focused on criminal measures, offers potentials which have not been fully exhausted so far. Among them is the concept of state responsibility."[97] It clarifies legal responsibility for the prevention of genocide, while also establishing a precedent that can be used to hold external state actors responsible for their role in facilitating the conditions that make it possible for a state to commit genocide. For the ICJ to play a significant role in the future of genocide prevention, its ruling in *Bosnia v. Serbia* needed to offer a warning to third-party actors against aiding in the commission of genocide and from shirking their obligation to prevent genocide. The ICJ's determination that states have an obligation to prevent genocide by using their influence based on their political, military, and financial relationships is consistent with human rights law. States' human rights obligations are extraterritorial. As Seibert-Fohr notes, human rights law "also obliges states to refrain from any conduct contributing even remotely to a human rights abuse. Therefore human rights law does not only become relevant if state officials are the immediate perpetrators or if the abuser can be attributed to the state. The obligations under the human rights conventions are broader than the actual crimes."[98] Nonetheless, for reasons that are discussed in chapter 3, cautious optimism about the role the ICJ can play in the prevention of genocide is warranted.

CONCLUSION

In 1928, Judge Max Huber asserted in his ruling on the *Island of Palmas* case, "Sovereignty in the relation between States signifies independence. Independence in regard to a portion of the globe is the right to exercise therein, to the exclusion of any other State, the function of a State. The development of the national organization of states during the last few centuries and, as a corollary, the development of International Law, have established this principle of the exclusive competence of the State in regard to its own territory in such a way as to make it the point of departure in settling most questions that concern International Relations."[99] Huber did not attempt to include in his ruling a value judgment concerning the principle of sovereignty. Instead, as the sole arbiter in the case, Huber simply applied the conventional legal understanding of sovereignty to the case before him.

According to Matthew Lippman, when the Genocide Convention was adopted by the General Assembly twenty years later, it "broke the barrier of sovereignty."[100] Notably, Lippman also recognizes the "contradiction between asserting that genocide is of international concern while relying on a system of territorial jurisdiction."[101] These appear to be contradictory positions, and analysis of the adopted text of the convention and its preparatory work support the latter—revealing that a majority of the negotiating parties privileged state sovereignty over universal preventive jurisdiction or even a system of subsidiary preventive jurisdiction.

The failure to define genocide as a threat to international peace and security is significant because the United Nations' principal mandate is to maintain international peace and security. The Security Council was given the power to authorize collective measures to fulfill this mandate. However, the council's power to authorize measures that encroach on state sovereignty is checked by the United Nations Charter's protection of that sovereignty. Therefore, the council's power to authorize collective action is limited to cases that pose a threat to international peace and security. Those cases that do not pose such a threat are internal matters of the individual states. By failing to define genocide as a threat to international peace and security, cases of intrastate genocide fall within the exclusive responsibilities of the individual states. Therefore, given the conditions required for the legal use of coercive measures as established by the United Nations Charter, the use of force in response to intrastate genocide is actually forbidden.

The Genocide Convention is firmly planted in the international system of relations between states established by the United Nations Charter. In fact, the negotiating parties that opposed subsidiary and universal forms of preventive jurisdiction were successful in ensuring that the convention did not incorporate such jurisdictions. Key among the opponents were the United States, the United Kingdom, and China—both because of their individual votes against these types of jurisdiction and because of their influence over the votes of other states within their spheres of influence. There were numerous opportunities during the drafting of the Genocide Convention to include either universal jurisdiction or a form of subsidiary jurisdiction for the prevention of genocide. Had the jurisdictional phrase "wherever they may occur" been retained from the Secretariat Draft to the adopted text, the convention would contain universalizing language. However, the phrase was removed from the Secretariat Draft's preamble and was never reinserted elsewhere in the convention, let alone debated.

Had genocide been defined as an inherent threat to international peace and security, the Security Council would have been awarded subsidiary jurisdiction for the prevention of genocide. Primary responsibility would have rested with the territorial authority, but when this authority was committing genocide, acquiescing to its commission, or unable to prevent it, the Security Council would have had the jurisdiction to determine appropriate measures in response.

Additional evidence of territorial preventive jurisdiction can be found in the domestic legislation requirement, the opt-in clause, and the substantial opposition to Iran's arguments in support of subsidiary punitive jurisdiction. As noted at the outset, the Genocide Convention is far less ambiguous on some matters related to prevention than previously believed.

When taken together, the combination of the provisions included in the adopted text of the Genocide Convention and the evolution of the language included in the text from the Secretariat Draft and the Ad Hoc Committee Draft to the adopted text firmly establish territorial jurisdiction for the prevention of genocide. Furthermore, it is clear from the treaty's preparatory work that this was the outcome deliberately sought by most of the negotiating parties. Thus, despite claims to the contrary, the Genocide Convention reaffirmed a strict reading of state sovereignty, most clearly in the fact that the convention does not alter in any way the existing legal and normative structures built into the international system as established by the United Nations Charter regarding the use of force.

Significantly, just as Judge Huber ruled on the *Island of Palmas* case as was required based on international law at the time, the ICJ ruled in the case of *Bosnia v. Serbia* in a manner that was dictated sixty years earlier. State sovereignty ruled the day in the mid- to late 1940s, and it did so again in 2007. In this regard, the ICJ's decision can be seen as an extension of the law as rooted in the Genocide Convention and international system. Lemkin's ideal of universal repression of genocide through universal preventive jurisdiction could not survive the convention's negotiating process, which was dominated by P-5 members. Further evidence of this is presented in chapter 2. Sixty years later, the ICJ chose not to act progressively by establishing a new precedent, deciding instead to adopt a conception of prevention constrained to means within a state's own sovereign control. However, affirming and reaffirming the inviolability of state sovereignty was just one part of the pursuit of P-5 impunity as it concerns the crime of genocide.

Chapter 2

Redefining the Crime of Genocide for Reasons of State

Chapter 1 showed that the adopted text of the Genocide Convention is firmly rooted in a system of territorial preventive jurisdiction. Indeed, any language that would have contributed to even a minimal erosion of state sovereignty rights by the Genocide Convention was removed from the text of the treaty and prevented from being reinserted during the negotiating process. P-5 members held conflicting positions on whether genocide ought to be understood in all cases as a threat to international peace and security, which would have situated both interstate and intrastate cases within the Security Council's purview. Because the Cold War was beginning at the time, it is interesting to note that the United States and the Soviet Union were on opposite sides of the debate over the language even though they were pursuing the same goal: strict control over their borders against external interference in their affairs. Whereas the United States was adamantly opposed to the inclusion of language that could be interpreted to allow such interference, the Soviet Union advocated for the inclusion of language that would have given the Security Council subsidiary jurisdiction for the purpose of preventing genocide. However, there was a bit of smoke and mirrors in the Soviet position: the exercise of Security Council jurisdiction could be restrained by a Soviet veto. Thus, though the Genocide Convention's purpose is the universal prevention of the crime it prohibits, the primacy of state sovereignty and territorial jurisdiction were reaffirmed during the convention's drafting process despite the different positions held among the P-5.

Nonetheless, ensuring that alleged cases of intrastate genocide were considered internal matters of state under the Genocide Convention was not quite the same as ensuring that states negotiating the terms of the treaty would not be implicated in the commission of genocide. Thus, the work of the P-5 was not yet complete. More of Raphael Lemkin's ideal was still to be sent to the chopping block. As Beth Van Schaack puts it, a review of the

Genocide Convention's preparatory work "reveals the way in which political bodies may attempt to limit their obligations under international law when they reduce customary law norms to positivistic expression in multilateral treaties. In this case, the Convention had to respond to the tragedy of the Nazi Holocaust. At the same time, however, the Convention could not implicate member nations on the drafting committee."[1] As this chapter demonstrates, what this meant was different for individual negotiating parties, including P-5 members. The priorities differed among the P-5 members depending in part on the historical position from which they were negotiating. In other words, it was not merely a coincidence that those provisions included in the early drafts of the Genocide Convention that might implicate the members at the time of the negotiations were also the ones typically targeted for exclusion by those members. While using plausible arguments to substantiate their positions, which were framed as principled opposition, the P-5 also maintained a vested interest in the inclusion of some provisions and the exclusion of others.

The two most controversial omissions from the adopted text of the Genocide Convention are protection for political groups and the prohibition of acts constituting cultural genocide.[2] Though Lemkin proved more flexible when it came to protection for political groups, protection for such groups and the prohibition against acts of cultural destruction were important elements of the Lemkinian ideal.[3] Both were also included in the Secretariat and Ad Hoc Committee drafts of the Genocide Convention but were removed during negotiations at the Sixth Committee. For the Soviet Union, the exclusion of protection for political groups was nonnegotiable. Meanwhile, the United States, with the support of the United Kingdom and France, aggressively pursued the exclusion of acts constituting cultural genocide. As Hirad Abtahi and Philippa Webb note, "Two main groups emerged: Western democracies generally favored including political genocide and opposed including cultural genocide while the USSR, along with the emerging Soviet camp, took the opposite positions. The rest of the UN member states followed one or the other of the above groups depending, generally, on their affiliation to them."[4] Importantly, Abtahi and Webb highlight not only the ability of P-5 members to stake out their positions, but also the influence they wielded over other states involved in the drafting process.

This chapter discusses the processes by which political groups and cultural genocide were omitted from the text of the Genocide Convention, thus contributing further to a culture of impunity by exempting "a range of . . . dirty linen from scrutiny."[5] Then it discusses the political factors that drove states to take the positions they did. As will become clear, and as I alluded to above, the positions P-5 members took on political groups and cultural genocide were not mere coincidence but were based on their ongoing quest for impunity.

The Omission of Political Groups

Article II of the adopted text of the Genocide Convention defines genocide as an act perpetrated against national, ethnic, racial, or religious groups. Through the inclusion of some groups and the omission of others, the convention is limited in its application to only those guilty acts committed with genocidal intent against the groups it specifies. Hence, the commission of physical acts enumerated in the convention against a political group, even with the intent to destroy the group in whole or in part, does not constitute genocide because political groups are not protected by the treaty.

Van Schaack identifies the omission of political groups as an oversight that "no legal principle can justify."[6] She argues that the exclusion of political groups from the Genocide Convention equates to the removal from the scope of the convention the "very crime they [political leaders] may be most likely to commit: the extermination of politically threatening groups."[7] Matthew Lippman agrees with Van Schaack.[8] In defense of protection for political groups, Lippman states, "Political groups, in particular, historically have been victimized and, like religious groups, are united by a common ideal and vision."[9]

Lawrence LeBlanc disagrees with those critical of the omission of political groups. He believes that an argument can be made in support of their exclusion: it may have been wise and practical to omit political groups from the scope of the Genocide Convention because "violence against political groups may, in some circumstances, be legitimate."[10] This position coincides with that offered by some Latin American countries during the negotiations at the Sixth Committee. For example, as Lemkin wrote in his autobiography, Brazil's ambassador said: "We in Latin America make revolutions from time to time, which involves the destruction of political opponents. Then we reconcile and live in peace. Later the group in power is thrown out in another revolution. Why should this be classified as the crime of genocide?"[11]

LeBlanc also makes the case that political groups present a problem that the groups protected under the adopted text of the Genocide Convention do not. He does not believe that it is possible to develop a definition of what constitutes a political group for the purposes of the Genocide Convention.[12] He argues that "exceptions to any proposed definition come readily to mind."[13] For example, he notes that to tie political groups to political parties "would result in an unduly narrow and vague definition."[14] He then offers the possibility of groups being identified through their attachment to political movements.

"Examples include," according to LeBlanc, "groups of protesters and others who are attacked by their governments for their political views."[15] He concludes, though, that it would be "absurd to consider such cases as falling within the meaning of genocide as defined by the convention."[16]

Yet even if violence against political groups is legally justifiable in certain contexts, the manner in which the violence is carried out may not be. Political groups peacefully protesting government policies can be dispersed without the use of lethal violence. Take, for example, a significant number of people (say, 100,000) who have gathered in a central location to protest against their government. If the government's response is to surround the protesters and open fire on them, one could argue that such a response would have constituted genocide had political groups been included in the Genocide Convention. While acknowledging that the following point makes malleable the line that separates war crimes committed in civil war and the crime of genocide,[17] it is important to note that even in the appropriate use of force against an armed insurrection, governments can implement measures aimed at avoiding the intentional targeting of unarmed members of the political opposition. Furthermore, LeBlanc's argument that tying political groups to political parties "would result in an unduly narrow and vague definition" is problematic. It is not necessary for the definition of political groups to be as specific as LeBlanc seems to want it to be. The Genocide Convention does not provide a formal definition for each of the groups under its protection. Though it might appear to do so, the definition of each of the groups protected by the convention is not self-evident. What is a religious group? Does a religious group include only those who are true believers in the religion? What about racial and ethnic groups? Into which group do children of intermarriage belong, and by whose determination?

The Genocide Convention's Blind Spot

Importantly, the problems associated with the omission of political groups from the Genocide Convention extend beyond the lack of protection for members of such groups. Not only are political groups unprotected by the convention, but their omission from the treaty also creates a blind spot in its coverage into which those groups that are protected can be pushed. The omission of political groups can serve this purpose by allowing the perpetrators of genocide to create and propagate a narrative of civil conflict, thus removing actual cases of genocide from the Genocide Convention's coverage through defining victims as members of a political group. Members of the international community can lend legitimacy to this framing of events by propagating the same narrative of civil conflict in an effort to avoid recognizing genocide out of considerations of national interest or lack of political will.

Genocide often accompanies some larger conflict, such as civil war. Intrastate cases of genocide could be framed as justifiable responses to political turmoil. When acts of genocide are committed across territorial borders, the resulting deaths could be framed as unintentional collateral damage. Larger conflicts inevitably result in the killing of a significant number of civilians. Therefore, the removal of political groups from the Genocide Convention's protection provides the opportunity for the planners and perpetrators of genocide to claim that the civilian deaths are nothing more than the tragic loss of life that accompanies any war. If members of the international community want to avoid labeling a conflict as genocide, they, too, can continue to focus on the larger conflict at the expense of those being killed through acts of genocide. The members can refer to peace agreements and cease-fires, invoke international humanitarian law, and call upon belligerents on all sides to stop killing each other and respect the rights of civilians. False narratives get their strength from the partial truth they likely contain.

Perhaps the most glaring example of the use of this blind spot can be found in Pakistan's genocide in East Pakistan (present-day Bangladesh).[18] Though India successfully ended the genocide in East Pakistan, it did so only eight months after it began and after as many as a million people had been killed, hundreds of thousands of women and girls had been raped, and ten million people had been forced to seek refuge in India.[19] Archer Blood, U.S. consul general in Dacca, described the violence as "a reign of terror" by the Pakistani military that involved the systematic elimination of supporters of the Awami League, a political group, "by seeking them out in their homes and shooting them down."[20] In its attacks on the people of East Pakistan, Pakistan's military murdered members of the Awami League, Bengali ethnolinguistic group, and Hindu cultural-religious group.[21] The inclusion of political groups in the Genocide Convention would have protected the members of groups such as the Awami League and made it more difficult to hide genocide of groups protected under the Genocide Convention, such as Hindus and Bengalis, behind a narrative of civil conflict. As chapter 4 shows in more detail, the facts that a portion of the targeted individuals were members of a political group and that all the killings took place in the context of a territorially bound civil conflict created the space that Pakistan and its American and Chinese allies needed to frame genocide in Pakistan as a civil conflict that remained strictly in the realm of Pakistan's internal affairs. When combined with the Genocide Convention's reinforcement of state sovereignty and territorial jurisdiction, the task of pushing Pakistan's genocide into the treaty's blind spot was an easy one.

That political groups were not always absent from the text of the Genocide Convention has been widely discussed.[22] Indeed, General Assembly

Resolution 96(I), dated December 11, 1946—which was the seed for the convention—states that "many instances of such crimes of genocide have occurred when racial, religious, political and other groups have been destroyed, entirely or in part."[23] Both the Secretariat Draft and Ad Hoc Committee Draft of the convention also included political groups among those protected. Article I of the Secretariat Draft states, "The purpose of this Convention is to prevent destruction of racial, national, linguistic, religious or political groups [of] human beings."[24] The Ad Hoc Committee Draft defines which groups it protects in Article II: "In this Convention genocide means any of the following deliberate acts committed with the intent to destroy a national, racial, religious or political group, on grounds of the national or racial origin, religious belief, or political opinion of its members."[25] However, the adopted text limits protection to members of national, ethnic, racial, and religious groups. Since political groups were included in the first two formal drafts of the Genocide Convention, why were they omitted from the adopted text?

Sacrifice and Politics: Political Groups and the Life of the Genocide Convention

Before turning to the process by which political groups were omitted from the Genocide Convention's protection, it is important to present Lemkin's complicated and evolving commitment to protection for such groups. In 1933, when Lemkin presented to the Fifth International Conference for the Unification of Criminal Law his proposal regarding "acts of persecution amounting to what is now called genocide,"[26] he repeatedly referred to the targets of persecution as "the collectivity" and "members of a collectivity."[27] In his seminal work, *Axis Rule in Occupied Europe: Laws of Occupation, Analysis of Government, Proposals for Redress*, originally published in 1944, Lemkin first used the term "genocide" in print. He also provided greater, though still limited, insight into what constitutes a collectivity in relation to the crime of genocide. He wrote that genocide involves "the destruction of a nation or of an ethnic group."[28] Lemkin continued, "Genocide is directed against the national group as an entity, and the actions involved are directed against individuals, not in their individual capacity, but as members of the national group." Furthermore, the objectives of a genocidal plan "would be the disintegration of the political and social institutions, of culture, language, national feelings, religion, and the economic existence of national groups."[29] Though Lemkin did not elaborate on what forms a national group might take, he did provide specific characteristics that unify such groups—including their political, social, and religious institutions.

In 1945, Lemkin presented his crime of genocide in abridged form in "Genocide: A Modern Crime." In this work, he continued to describe targets of genocide as national groups.[30] Though Lemkin rarely referred explicitly to political groups as targets of genocide, there are at least two reasons to conclude that he believed political groups were at risk. First, in an undated item, Lemkin wrote that "religious, racial, national and ethnical" and "political" groups have historically been frequently targeted.[31] Second, the first two drafts of the Genocide Convention contained protection for political groups, and according to Lemkin, the Secretariat Draft was prepared with his participation "as an official expert," while the Ad Hoc Committee Draft was prepared with his participation "behind the scenes."[32] Lemkin describes an occasion when the United Kingdom's delegate, Sir Hartley Shawcross, questioned the viability of retaining protection for political groups in the treaty. According to Shawcross, "A Genocide Convention cannot be adopted because of the problem of political groups. To include political groups in the definition would mean to enter the controversial issue of civil war."[33] In response to "the first open attack" against the inclusion of political groups, Lemkin recalls sitting "with a sunken head at a luncheon table on the terrace of a small café near the Palais de Chaillot."[34]

Though Lemkin and the other framers of the Secretariat Draft, Henri Donnedieu de Vabres and Vespasian V. Pella, seemed to have been in agreement initially about the need for the Genocide Convention to protect political groups, Lemkin adopted what might be described as a pragmatic approach when it came to the conflict between protecting political groups and getting the General Assembly to adopt the convention. Lemkin's position regarding protection for political groups would change as the politics of the convention's negotiating process demanded. As Douglas Irvin-Erickson describes it, Lemkin's effort to get the General Assembly to vote on adopting the convention involved "a great number of concessions—not just emotions."[35] His closest associates were surprised by his willingness "to throw anything and everything overboard in order to save a ship."[36] However, it can be seen in the Brazilian delegate's comments above that Lemkin had lost the unconditional support of many Latin American delegations, as they joined the Soviet bloc in opposing the inclusion of political groups. Thus, in the interest of giving the Genocide Convention a chance at life, Lemkin "prepared his first sacrifice."[37]

In 1946, Lemkin was already working to convince the Soviets that General Assembly Resolution 96(I), which defined genocide as a violation of international law, was not part of a conspiracy against them.[38] Such efforts would continue to be necessary to ensure that the Soviet Union would not stand in the way of codifying genocide as a violation of international law that must be prevented and punished. Later, Lemkin's newfound opposition to the inclusion of political groups put him at odds with de Vabres and Pella. For example, when deciding which groups would be protected in the Secretariat Draft, it was determined that human groups are made up of "a certain part of the population whose members have common characteristics distinguishing them from other members of society. From a very general point of view, there are many and diverse human groups." However, "if the problem of genocide is considered from the practical point of view and in the light of past experience, it is obvious that protection is not meant to cover a professional or athletic group."[39] Thus, it was decided that the Secretariat Draft would include protection for five specific types of groups: racial, national, linguistic, religious, and political.

In his formal comments on the Secretariat Draft, Lemkin expressed concern about the inclusion of political groups. According to Lemkin, political groups lack "the permanency and specific characteristics of the other groups referred to," and the Genocide Convention, being of general interest to all, "should not run the risk of failure by introducing ideas on which the world is deeply divided."[40] Meanwhile, de Vabres argued that "genocide was an odious crime, regardless of the group which fell victim to it and that the exclusion of political groups might be regarded as justifying genocide in the case of such groups."[41] Disagreement among the framers of the Secretariat Draft did not result in the omission of political groups from that draft. In the end, the framers of the draft chose to respect the General Assembly's original intentions, as expressed in Resolution 96(I), that political groups be protected.

As noted above, protection for political groups was also included in the Ad Hoc Committee Draft—by a narrow vote of four to three. Lemkin continued to work against the inclusion of political groups as the Ad Hoc Committee Draft was debated at the Sixth Committee, due to his ongoing fear that the Genocide Convention would be nipped in the bud. He worried that the push to protect political groups "might divide the committee almost evenly and would be an obstacle to the adoption of the convention."[42] Lemkin also employed some of the same arguments some delegates used to explain their opposition to the inclusion of political groups. He wrote: "I thought the destruction of political opponents should be treated as the crime of political homicide, not genocide. Every revolutionary regime comes to power by destroying some of its opponents. Later this regime is recognized by other nations, sometimes the whole world. Should political groups be included in the definition of genocide, recognition of a revolutionary regime would imply acceptance of genocide as legal. This would kill the Genocide Convention before it took root in world society."[43]

The Soviet Union argued that including political groups was incompatible with a "scientific" understanding of genocide.[44] Other states claimed that it would be difficult to identify political groups and that such groups lacked internal stability.[45] Still others, as Lemkin had done before, questioned the practicality of including political groups if doing so would undermine the life of the treaty.[46] On the other side of the debate, Cuba expressed concern that the omission of political groups could create a blind spot into which racial and religious groups could be pushed, arguing that the political opinions of such groups could be used as a reason to destroy them.[47] In response to the argument previously made by the Soviet Union that the inclusion of political groups could dissuade some states from ratifying the convention, out of fear that efforts to combat domestic subversion would be labeled genocide, Ecuador noted that police powers necessary to respond to domestic insurrection were distinct from acts of genocide. Thus, according to Ecuador, the inclusion of political groups would not interfere with a state's right to protect itself against internal subversion and that it was up to courts to ascertain the difference between legitimate responses to insurrection and genocide.[48] France added that political groups could be identified, as the Nazis had identified—and attempted to destroy—Communists.[49] Similarly, the Netherlands pointed out that the Nazis had sought to exterminate members of political opposition parties.[50]

The Sixth Committee held two separate votes on whether political groups would be included in the final draft of the convention to be submitted to the General Assembly for adoption. The first vote approved the retention of political groups by twenty-nine to thirteen, with nine abstentions. In a later Sixth Committee meeting, disagreement over whether political groups ought to be included in the final draft was revisited—despite, as noted by William Schabas, "an apparently convincing majority" support for their inclusion.[51] In the end, the principal and most convincing argument for the omission of political groups was not that such groups did not deserve protection, though some negotiating parties certainly made that case. Rather, opposition to the inclusion of political groups was, as Egypt put it, "primarily for practical reasons."[52] In other words, opposition to the inclusion of political groups was a matter of political calculation. With the possibility that the final text could be rejected, the United States and others bowed under pressure, but also with their own interests in mind—specifically, the interest in the reciprocal exclusion of cultural genocide. The renewed movement for the omission of political groups succeeded by a vote of twenty-two to six, with twelve abstentions.

Political groups were omitted from the adopted text despite being included in both the General Assembly resolution that authorized the Genocide Convention's creation and the Secretariat and Ad Hoc Committee Drafts. Furthermore, the arguments made against including political groups were largely unconvincing. The omission of political groups is arguably the Genocide Convention's most criticized weakness.[53] Their omission from the adopted text left political groups unprotected and created a blind spot into which protected groups could be pushed through the creation of narratives of civil conflict. As chapter 4 shows, this is especially evident in Security Council deliberations on genocide in Pakistan in 1971 and Rwanda in 1994. Significantly, the most effective argument made by opponents of including political groups was not that such groups did not belong in a convention prohibiting genocide. Rather, the most effective argument against their inclusion was that opponents would reject the adopted text if political groups were included.

The Soviet Union and the Omission of Political Groups for Reasons of State

Despite being included in General Assembly Resolution 96(I), which authorized the creation of the Genocide Convention, and the first two formal drafts of the treaty, political groups were ultimately omitted from the adopted text. Both the arguments in support of and in opposition to the inclusion of political groups were plausible. Proponents argued that the Genocide Convention should retain the spirit of Resolution 96(I) and that, due to growing ideological divides, political groups were likely to be at risk of genocide in the future. Therefore, such groups ought to be protected under the Genocide Convention. Opponents argued that political groups were not the primary targets in historical cases of genocide and that they lacked the permanency necessary to be protected by the Genocide Convention. The opponents also argued that the inclusion of political groups would interfere with a state's ability and right to respond to domestic insurrection, because appropriate action taken against internal uprisings could be inappropriately labeled genocide.

Concerning the omission of political groups and the implications of doing so, Van Schaack writes: "The exclusion of political groups . . . resulted in a legal regime that insulates political leaders from being charged with the very crime that they may be most likely to commit: the extermination of politically threatening groups. As such, the Genocide Convention is more pertinent as a retrospective condemnation of the Nazi enterprise than as a forward-looking guide for the application of the full international prohibition of genocide."[54] David Nersessian notes that a case could be made on pragmatic grounds that "there simply was a greater *need* to protect certain groups as historically-victimized collectives."[55] Racial and religious groups were the victims of "the most extreme examples of genocide in the 20th century—chief among them the Nazi Holocaust against Jews and the Ottoman genocide against Armenians."[56] However, Nersessian finds this argument insufficient, because members of political groups were slaughtered in Germany and the Soviet Union before the Genocide Convention had evolved into its final form and was adopted by the General Assembly. According to Nersessian, "Historic vulnerability and future needs certainly are sensible factors in *choosing* among groups to cover. But they are not sufficient in and of themselves to explain the groups ultimately selected for inclusion in the Convention."[57]

Nersessian's point is a significant one, especially when it is inverted. If negotiating parties were limited in their commitment to the creation of a treaty prohibiting genocide that would not implicate them, as Van Schaack argues, then it would make perfect sense for some of the negotiating parties to seek to exclude from protection groups within their territories that have been historically vulnerable and/or could be vulnerable in the future. In the case of political groups, at the time of the Genocide Convention's negotiations, there was a recent history of vulnerability in the Soviet Union in particular and a strong potential for such vulnerability to carry into the future.

Though the Soviet Union was not alone in its opposition to the inclusion of political groups in the Genocide Convention, it was the most influential of opponents.[58] It used its influence to garner support among its satellite states, which—in conjunction with support from other states that opposed the inclusion of political groups, such as many Latin American countries—allowed the Soviet Union to force a compromise that resulted in the omission of political groups.

According to Samantha Power, Joseph Stalin feared "that the convention would invite outside powers to punish" him.[59] Soviet history preceding the Genocide Convention's negotiations provides evidence that the Soviet Union's position on the question of protection for political groups was motivated at least in part by considerations of national interest such as that highlighted by Power. Stephen Feinstein argues that it is easy to understand why the Soviet Union was opposed to the inclusion of political groups, "since Soviet ideology and practice had destroyed both opposition political groups as well as having maintained a concerted attack on religion from 1917."[60]

Leo Kuper refers to the massive number of deaths in the Soviet Union stemming from state repression:

> As to the loss in human life, Solzhenitsyn quotes a figure of 66,000,000 . . . from the beginning of the October Revolution to 1959. For the decade 1929–39 alone, Gouldner gives an estimate of 20,000,000 shot, or dying of famine or disease or exposure, as the direct result of punitive action by the Soviet government, to which must be added the slaughter in the decade immediately following the October Revolution, and in the decade of the war years. However unreliable the estimates, it is clear that we are in the presence of the major holocaust of our time.[61]

Nersessian adds crimes committed by the Soviet Union in Poland:

> This position is not surprising when seen in context. In the late 1940s, it is impossible to think that the Soviet Union could sanction a treaty that covered political groups without putting its own *recent* crimes directly into issue. Upon the eve of its entry into World War II, Russian soldiers massacred 4,000 Polish political prisoners. Another 15,000 Polish officers and intellectuals were shot *en masse* in the Katyn Forest because the Soviets believed that they would oppose efforts to 'Communize' Poland. Earlier examples included 10 million deaths during the liquidation of Kukak peasant classes and the deliberate organization of wide-spread famine in Ukraine 1932–33.[62]

While the Genocide Convention could not have been applied to the Soviet Union's treatment of political groups prior to the convention's entry into force—due to the legal principle *nullum crimen sine lege* (literally, "no crime without law")—the same cannot be said for future acts. Because, as Nersessian noted, it was sensible for negotiating parties to consider the "historic vulnerability and future needs . . . in choosing among groups to cover," it was also sensible for negotiating parties to consider their historic treatment of specific groups under consideration for protection under the Genocide Convention. In the case of the Soviet Union, it must have been aware of its record on the treatment of political groups and must have had some idea that such treatment was likely to persist.

Though the Soviet Union offered plausible arguments for excluding political groups from the Genocide Convention, the above evidence suggests that considerations of national interest were a significant factor in the Soviet position. More directly, the omission of political groups was essential to the Soviet Union's ability to act with impunity as related to the crime of genocide. This conclusion is supported by the fact that crimes committed by the Soviet Union both before and after the entry into force of the Genocide Convention would have, with the establishment of genocidal intent, constituted genocide had political groups been included.

The Western powers all supported protection for political groups. Most of them were consolidated democracies, and the motivation for their support for protection of political groups could have included (1) a belief in the importance of political participation and the protection of that right, (2) a belief that political groups were most likely to be targeted for elimination, and (3) confidence that they would not be implicated in the commission of genocide against political groups. Yet the prospect remains that, especially for the United States, support for protection for political groups was also based on the likelihood that the Soviet Union and other nonaligned states would be implicated in the commission of genocide against political groups if they were protected under the convention.[63]

With tension between the Soviet Union and the United States growing since the end of World War II, the two countries often held conflicting positions over provisions "which each anticipated might be used to criticize or condemn their conduct."[64] There was a concern on the part of both the Soviet Union and the United States that if certain provisions were included in the Genocide Convention while others were excluded, one of the countries would be more likely to be implicated than the other. Generally, for the Soviet Union this was the inclusion of political groups. The American Bar Association (ABA) was apprehensive about the possibility that the Soviet Union could evade charges of genocide.[65] According to LeBlanc, "Although they couched their arguments in legal terms, the preoccupation of the ABA representatives with Soviet policies suggests that their objections to the Genocide Convention were as much political as they were legal, and perhaps more so."[66] Thus, there are reasons to suppose that the United States supported the inclusion of political groups not only for the protection of their members, but also because their inclusion would have increased the likelihood of the Soviet Union's being implicated in genocide.

Though the United States initially opposed the omission of political groups from the Genocide Convention and seemingly relented only as part of a compromise, what is generally overlooked is how the United States has also benefited from their omission. Two cases in particular stand out: the role of the United States in Indonesia's slaughter of 500,000–1,000,000 real or perceived Communists from 1965 to 1966 and the U.S. war on Vietnam. In the former case, the genocidal intent of the Indonesian planners and perpetrators is indisputable, as is the fact that the United States played a facilitating role. The only real question is whether the United States was complicit in the mass atrocities or actually conspired with Indonesia to kill Communists. In this regard, the only thing that separates Indonesia's crimes, and the shared responsibility for them of the United States, from genocide is the omission of political groups from the Genocide Convention.[67] In the latter case, the lack of protection for political groups and the Genocide Convention's explicit and specific intent requirement might be the only elements that separate the United States from responsibility for the commission of genocide in Vietnam.[68]

The Exclusion of Cultural Genocide

Under Article II of the Genocide Convention, the following acts are prohibited: killing members of the group; causing serious bodily or mental harm to members of the group; deliberately inflicting on the group conditions of life calculated to bring about its physical destruction in whole or in part; imposing measures intended to prevent births within the group; and forcibly transferring children of the group to another group.[69] Only the final element—the forcible transfer of children—relates in any way to Lemkin's concept of cultural genocide. Yet as it is included in the adopted text of the Genocide Convention, the forcible transfer of children is not viewed as an element of cultural genocide, but rather as a means of committing physical genocide by impeding members of a group from producing new members of the group.[70] Thus, while Article II protects the physical integrity of the groups under its protection, it does not protect their continued existence as such through the preservation of their cultures. The survival of some groups is predicated on the continued existence of their cultures: without their cultures, these groups would cease to exist. As Makau Mutua puts it, culture "represents the accumulation of a people's wisdom and thus their identity; it is real and without it a people is without a name, rudderless, and torn from its moorings."[71] However, under the legal definition of genocide, cultural genocide does not exist.

Adam Jones believes that cultural genocide was rightfully excluded from the Genocide Convention. He asks whether using means for the destruction of a group that are less than physically destroying it could constitute genocide: "The question remains, however, whether strategies of social and cultural 'destruction' should be considered genocidal *in the absence of systematic killing, or at least widespread physical attack*. I believe they should not be."[72] Conversely, Lippman argues for the importance of protecting cultures, stating that the crime of genocide "reflects a refusal to recognize the inalienable right of a collectivity to express its cultural identity and to contribute to the human mosaic. . . . The central purpose of the Genocide Convention is to preserve and promote pluralism in order to perpetuate the progress which historically has resulted from the clash of cultures."[73] Yet Lippman recognizes the controversial nature of cultural genocide. He notes that the crime of genocide "imposes unconscionable pain and suffering on its victims. The less dramatic impact is to prevent the perpetuation of a group's culture and to diminish demographic diversity."[74] Lippman opines that deliberate attacks on and destruction of cultural icons, libraries, and monuments could constitute genocide only when combined with physical acts of genocide.

Increasing attention to the history of settler-colonial states, the relationship between genocide and imperialism, and the long-term and ongoing effects of colonization on formerly colonized and indigenous peoples has brought with it greater recognition of the genocidal nature of cultural oppression and destruction.[75] For example, Julian Burger argues that colonial conquest inevitably leads to cultural genocide through the subjugation of the victims of colonial conquest and the marginalization of their cultures: "In such instances the marginalization of indigenous culture becomes cultural genocide or ethnocide. Ethnocide means that an ethnic group, collectively or individually, is denied its right to enjoy, develop and disseminate its own culture and language. Where indigenous peoples do not face physical destruction, they may nevertheless face disintegration as a distinct ethnic group through the destruction of their specific cultural characteristics."[76] Or, as Nersessian puts it, "By limiting genocide to its physical and biological manifestations, a group can be kept physically and biologically intact even as its collective identity suffers in a fundamental and irremediable manner. Put another way, the present understanding of genocide preserves the body of the group but allows its very soul to be destroyed."[77]

It is certainly arguable that physical acts of genocide ought to be differentiated from those meant to ultimately dissolve a group through the permanent removal of its cultural existence. However, differentiation is not the same as including one form of genocide while excluding the other. Threats to cultural groups extend beyond the group's physical integrity. Over a period of time, cultural groups can be destroyed through the prohibition of the use of the culture's language and the practice of the culture's religion, as well as the destruction of those attributes and artifacts that define a culture's uniqueness.

Like the omission of protection for political groups, the exclusion of cultural genocide from the adopted text of the Genocide Convention has had consequences that extend beyond the failure to protect groups and their cultural practices and identities. The exclusion of cultural genocide, in conjunction with the specific intent requirement, created an additional blind spot in the convention. It allows perpetrators to insist that the intent behind persecution and other violations of human rights, including the deprivation of life, is to remove the group and its culture from a given territory. In other words, a group's physical and cultural existence within a given territory can be erased without charges of genocide, so long as the means employed do not involve widespread killing of group members. Rather than genocide, this became known as ethnic cleansing. As chapter 4 shows in more detail, the exclusion of cultural genocide and the further disassociation of the legal definition of genocide from Lemkin's ideal were exploited by the P-5 to name violence, persecution, and destruction as ethnic cleansing rather than genocide.

Indeed, the term "ethnic cleansing" first became widely used during the Bosnian War (1992–1995) to describe the attempted eradication of all Muslims from Bosnia by the Bosnian Serbs and their benefactors in Serbia.[78] However, Martin Shaw argues that in some cases "ethnic cleansing" is a euphemism for genocide: "Because genocide has been narrowed down to Nazi-like extermination policies, few recent cases have been recognized.

Only that of Rwanda has been overwhelmingly accepted. . . . Before this, many commentators also saw Serbian nationalist campaigns in Croatia and Bosnia and Herzegovina as genocidal. Yet the phrase most widely used to describe them was 'ethnic cleansing', which quickly achieved an extraordinarily wide currency. Barely a year into the Yugoslav wars, it was 'adopted as part of the official vocabulary of UN Security Council documents and by other UN institutions and governmental and non-governmental international organizations.'"[79] Significantly, for Lemkin "ethnic cleansing" was more than a euphemism for genocide: he used the term "ethnocide" interchangeably with the term "genocide." As Ward Churchill points out, at the same time that Lemkin coined the term "genocide," he coined the term "ethnocide"—not (as it is used today) to describe actions different from genocide, but as a synonym for it.[80]

Like political groups, cultural genocide was included in the Secretariat and Ad Hoc Committee drafts of the Genocide Convention before being excluded from the text at the Sixth Committee. Article I of the Secretariat Draft defines cultural genocide as:

Destroying the specific characteristics of the group by:

(a) forcible transfer of children to another human group; or
(b) forced and systematic exile of individuals representing the culture of a group; or
(c) prohibition of the use of the national language even in private intercourse; or
(d) systematic destruction of books printed in the national language or of religious works or prohibition of new publications; or
(e) systematic destruction of historical or religious monuments or their diversion to alien uses, destruction or dispersion of documents and objects of historical, artistic, or religious value and of objects used in religious worship.[81] Article III of the Ad Hoc Committee Draft defines cultural genocide as:

1. Prohibiting the use of the language of the group in daily intercourse or in schools, or the printing and circulation of publications in the language of the group;
2. Destroying or preventing the use of libraries, museums, schools, historical monuments, places of worship or other cultural institutions and objects of the group.[82]

Despite this, cultural genocide was omitted from the adopted text.

Among the framers of the Secretariat Draft, Lemkin argued in favor of the inclusion of cultural genocide, while de Vabres and Pella argued for its exclusion. Lemkin insisted on the need for the protection against cultural genocide, arguing that the existence of a group required the preservation of "its spirit and moral unity."[83] In 1946, before the General Assembly passed its resolution affirming genocide to be a violation of international law, Lemkin wrote: "Our whole heritage is a product of the contributions of all nations. We can best understand this when we realize how impoverished our culture would be if the peoples doomed by Germany, such as the Jews, had not been permitted to create the Bible, or to give birth to an Einstein, a Spinoza; if the Poles had not had the opportunity to give to the world a Copernicus, a Chopin, a Curie; the Czechs, a Huss, a Dvorak; the Greeks, a Plato and a Socrates; the Russians, a Tolstoy and a Shostakovich."[84]

For Lemkin, the destruction of a group's culture would be just as effective in destroying a group's existence as the group's physical destruction would be. De Vabres and Pella disagreed not necessarily with Lemkin's concern but rather with whether a convention against genocide was the appropriate place to approach crimes against cultures. They saw the prohibition of cultural genocide as "an undue extension of the notion of genocide" to the protection of minorities "under cover of the term genocide."[85] As in the case of protection for political groups, the framers of the Secretariat Draft chose to respect the General Assembly's intention to include cultural genocide.

The Ad Hoc Committee voted six to one in favor of retaining the prohibition of cultural genocide. During negotiations at that Committee, two competing arguments were made concerning the extermination of a culture, which resulted in a compromise. One argument was that a group could be exterminated through either its physical destruction or the destruction of the culture that defines the group and with which the group's identity is entwined. The opposing argument was that a convention prohibiting genocide should be restricted to the most severe acts, and the protection of cultures and minority rights could be dealt with by U.N. organs concerned with human rights and discrimination against minority groups. The Ad Hoc Committee separated cultural genocide from physical and biological genocide, as suggested by the United States and France. The United States recommended the separation to "enable Governments to make reservations on a particular point of the Convention."[86] Cultural genocide was included in Article III in the Ad Hoc Committee Draft, while physical and biological genocide were included in Article II.

Despite the compromise, the lone dissenting vote was cast by the United States. According to the United States, "the decision to make genocide a new international crime was extremely serious, and the United States believed that the crime should be limited to barbarous acts committed against individuals, which, in the eyes of the public, constituted the basic concept of genocide."[87] Furthermore, the United States adopted a strategy similar to the one used by the Soviet Union in its opposition to the inclusion of political groups: "Were the Committee to attempt to cover too wide a field in the preparation of a draft convention for example, in attempting to define cultural genocide—however reprehensible that crime might be—it might well run the risk to find some States would refuse to ratify the convention."[88] The U.S. position toward the idea of cultural genocide became increasingly hostile even as its previous demands were met. Though the United States opposed the inclusion of cultural genocide from the start, together with France it proposed the terms of the compromise that led to the separation of cultural genocide from the other forms of genocide. This separation allowed the United States and other negotiating parties to submit a reservation to the article containing cultural genocide. Nonetheless, the United States argued that "some States" would not vote in favor of adopting the draft convention if cultural genocide was included.

The Ad Hoc Committee Draft was submitted for further debate to the Sixth Committee, where the question of cultural genocide was revisited. Pakistan was an impassioned supporter of the inclusion of cultural genocide, arguing that the physical destruction of a group and the destruction of a group's culture were inextricably intertwined. Pakistan stated that the motive for genocide was the destruction of the ideas and values of a group's culture and that physical destruction was just one means of achieving that end. According to Pakistan, "The chief motive of genocide was a blind rage to destroy the ideas, the values and the very soul of a national, racial or religious group, rather than its physical existence. Thus the end and the means were closely linked together; cultural genocide and physical genocide were indivisible."[89]

Later during the negotiations, Pakistan added, "To safeguard the physical existence of a group [of] human beings was a considerable achievement from a humanitarian point of view. But the mere physical existence of a group was of little value from the point of view of humanity, for a group deprived of the living springs of the spirit was only a body without a soul."[90] Pakistan also noted that Resolution 96(I) recognizes that genocide had inflicted "great losses on humanity in the form of cultural and other contributions."[91] Thus, Pakistan argued, the General Assembly had intended that cultures be protected. In response to those who brought up the importance of cultural assimilation, Pakistan noted that assimilation could be used as a "euphemism concealing measures of coercion designed to eliminate certain forms of culture."[92]

The United States and France, along with Denmark and the Netherlands, were vocal opponents of retaining cultural genocide during debates at the Sixth Committee. The United States argued that the convention should be limited to those acts that "shocked the conscience of mankind."[93] Meanwhile, France argued that protection of cultures was a human rights issue and, therefore, ought to be protected "within the framework of the international declaration on human rights."[94] Denmark argued that the inclusion of cultural genocide would relegate the convention to being "a tool for political propaganda instead of an international legal instrument."[95] Furthermore, and similar to comments by the United States, Denmark added that equating mass murder and the closing of libraries demonstrated a clear lack of logic and proportionality. Finally, the Netherlands argued that cultural genocide was too vague to be pinned down in a clear and concise definition. Furthermore, according to the Netherlands, it was questionable whether "all cultures, even the most barbarous, deserved protection, and whether the assimilation resulting from the civilizing action of a State also constituted genocide."[96]

The opponents of including cultural genocide in the Genocide Convention succeeded in having it omitted at the Sixth Committee by a vote of twenty-five to sixteen, with four abstentions. The Soviet Union made one last attempt to include cultural genocide at the General Assembly, prior to the official vote on the final adopted text. The proposed inclusion of cultural genocide was soundly defeated by a vote of thirty-one to fourteen, with ten abstentions.

As in the debate over protection for political groups, plausible arguments were made in support of and in opposition to the inclusion of cultural genocide. The importance of preserving cultures is difficult to understate. As Lemkin made clear, restrictions against members of a culture and their practices intended to erase the culture could deprive present and future generations of the contributions of the extinguished cultures. Pakistan was also correct to argue that physical genocide and cultural genocide were simply two different means to the same end. Protected groups could be destroyed through the annihilation of their cultures. Yet achieving the destruction of a group through prohibiting its cultural practices is vastly different from achieving the group's immediate physical destruction, which is why arguments against inclusion of cultural genocide might seem compelling. It is this latter point that was seized on by the United States, France, and Denmark in their opposition to the inclusion of cultural genocide. Yet Pakistan's argument that the extermination of a protected group could be achieved either through its immediate physical destruction or through a slower policy of eliminating all remnants of its cultural heritage is equally compelling.

The Politics of the Exclusion of Cultural Genocide

Despite being included in General Assembly Resolution 96(I), which authorized the creation of the Genocide Convention, and in the first two formal drafts of the treaty, cultural genocide was ultimately excluded from the adopted text. Both the arguments in support of and in opposition to the inclusion of cultural genocide were plausible. Proponents argued that the Genocide Convention should retain the spirit of Resolution 96(I) and that the cultural and physical methods of genocide were different means of achieving the same outcome: the destruction of a group as such. Therefore, it would not be justified to retain one while rejecting the other. Opponents essentially argued that acts constituting cultural genocide were not severe enough human rights violations to be incorporated into a treaty meant to prohibit genocide, sometimes referred to as the crime of crimes. They also argued that the inclusion of cultural genocide would be used politically to make trouble for certain states—which should be read to mean colonial powers.

It can be said with some certainty that concerns among the colonial powers that a Genocide Convention prohibiting cultural genocide would be used against them were warranted. This helps explain why these powers worked so aggressively to ensure that cultural genocide was excluded from the convention. The omission of political groups was part of the Soviet Union's path to impunity, and the exclusion of acts constituting cultural genocide was part of the same path for the colonial powers—in particular, the United States and France, along with the United Kingdom. However, as shown above, these P-5 members were not alone in wanting cultural genocide excluded from the convention. During the treaty negotiations, for example, the Netherlands was fighting to maintain its Indonesian colony. The Netherlands also maintained control over Suriname and the Netherlands Antilles. Meanwhile, the United States copied the Soviet Union's tactic, threatening to torpedo adoption of the draft convention if cultural genocide was included. Therefore, it is important to note that the most effective argument made by opponents of the inclusion of cultural genocide was that they would reject the adopted text if cultural genocide was included. Or, as Egypt put it in relation to the omission of political groups, cultural genocide was excluded primarily for practical reasons.

Though a relationship exists between colonization and cultural genocide, Kuper challenges the notion that the former inevitably leads to the latter by arguing that cultural genocide is not a universal feature of colonization.[97] One way he does so is by contrasting the voluntary borrowing of items of culture from the implementation of deliberate policies aimed at the elimination of a culture.[98] This is an important point because colonial policies varied among colonizers and colonies. Nonetheless, for the colonial powers to oppose the inclusion of cultural genocide, colonization need not be synonymous with cultural genocide. Nor did the potential for cultural genocide need to be present in every one of the colonial powers' colonies. For opposition to including cultural genocide in the Genocide Convention to be in the vested interest of colonizers, all that was necessary was that colonial policies in some colonies include elements of the crime of cultural genocide. Therefore, the question is not whether the colonial powers were committing cultural genocide beyond a shadow of a doubt before or during the Genocide Convention's negotiations or subsequent to its entry into force. Rather, the question is whether the colonial powers had reason for concern that they could be implicated in or accused of cultural genocide because of their colonial policies in one or more of the territories under their control or in their treatment of indigenous peoples within their own territories. If the colonial powers had reason for such concern, it would have been in their national interest to push for cultural genocide's omission. In particular, the United States, the United Kingdom, and France had the most to be concerned with based on their (mythical) positions as human rights leaders and their treatment of indigenous peoples (in the case of the United States) and their colonial empires (in the cases of the United Kingdom and France).

American Policies and Cultural Genocide

The role of the United States in the omission of cultural genocide from the Genocide Convention is especially significant, both because of its influence over the proceedings and because of its policies at the time of the convention's negotiations. Churchill describes the conduct of the United States during the negotiations as "subversive."[99] It is clear from the statements made and the votes cast that, unlike in the case of political groups, the United States was committed to the exclusion of cultural genocide from the start. U.S. statements made in opposition to the inclusion of cultural genocide were accompanied first by an effort to separate the crime of cultural genocide from the crimes of physical and biological genocide (to allow the United States to submit a reservation against the article containing the elements of cultural genocide), then by a vote against the inclusion of cultural genocide despite having succeeded in gaining its separation, and finally by a vow to undermine the adoption of the convention if it were to retain the crime of cultural genocide. Ultimately, the United States, along with other countries that voted for excluding cultural genocide, accomplished "a maneuver serving to exempt a range of its own dirty linen from scrutiny."[100] Churchill argues that, along with the Soviet Union, the United States was one of two countries with "sufficient clout to effect the sort of mutual exoneration from culpability through *a priori* alteration of law which ultimately prevailed."[101]

The U.S. opposition to the inclusion of cultural genocide in the Genocide Convention was at least in part based on concerns that the inclusion would leave the United States open to allegations of genocide due to its treatment of Native Americans.[102] According to Shamiran Mako, "Within North America, the American-Indian experience is one rooted in both physical and cultural dissipation. This becomes evident upon a closer examination of the way in which law and colonialism were instruments of genocide, both in the physical and cultural forms. . . . Beyond physical extermination, the State implemented policies of acculturalization by enacting laws that restricted land entitlements to Indians who had renounced tribal citizenship."[103]

As early as the 1870s, there were people in the United States who used their influence to lobby for a more cost-effective alternative to physical attacks for dealing with what was referred to as the Native problem—the complete elimination of native cultures through the coerced assimilation of the remaining Native American population.[104] Early in the twentieth century, Indian Commissioner Francis Leupp explained that it was possible to "kill the Indian, spare the man."[105] Charles Burke, Leupp's successor from 1921 to 1929, similarly stated, "It is not consistent with the general welfare to promote [American Indian national or cultural] characteristics and organization."[106] The means through which Native American cultures were to be eliminated were multiple. They included the outlawing of native spiritual traditions, the removal of Native American children from their homes to federally run boarding schools, and the forced dislocation of Native populations from their land.

In 1883, the Court of Indian Offenses was created to monitor the behaviors of Native Americans and punish those who committed "Indian offenses." Offenses included performing the "sun-dance," the "scalp-dance," and the "war-dance." The "usual practices" of medicine men were also designated as offenses.[107] The performance of important cultural traditions was punished by withholding of rations, exorbitant fines, and sentences of forced labor and jail time.[108] The sending of Native American children to boarding schools was clearly part of a long-term strategy aimed at the complete eradication of Native American cultures. Beginning in 1879, Native American children were sent to boarding schools far from their reservations. By the 1920s, there were seventy-seven such schools, "whose express purpose was the complete assimilation of Native American children, remolding their conception of life and their attitudes toward the land."[109] At these boarding schools, tribal religions were suppressed, use of the students' native tongue was physically punished, and students were taught to read and write English as well as to act and dress like white children.[110] One rationale behind the use of boarding schools was the need to "free" Native American children "from the language and habits of their untutored and often savage parents."[111] Laws were also passed that forced Native Americans to abandon their customary means of governance and adopt tribal governments, police forces, and judicial systems that emulated U.S. institutions.[112]

Churchill argues that the above policies, when combined with the forced removal of Native American populations from their land, can be described only as genocidal.[113] While the forced dislocation of Native Americans from their land had become policy well before the twentieth century, the policy was reestablished during a new period of assimilationist policies in the late 1940s.[114] In 1956, as part of a series of termination acts, Congress passed Public Law 959 (known as the Relocation Act) to "help adult Indians who reside on or near Indian reservations to obtain reasonable and satisfactory employment" through "vocational training that provides for vocational counseling or guidance, institutional training in any recognized vocation or trade, apprenticeship, and on the job training."[115] Despite the alleged noble intentions of this law, Churchill argues that the real goal was the permanent exodus of Native Americans from their land. More than "half the entire native population was dispersed from its own landbase into urban localities where it was mostly subsumed within 'mainstream' society by the 1980s."[116] Churchill also argues that there was a connection between the dislocation of Native Americans from their land and the disposition of their religious lands and shrines: "As to the disposition of American Indian religious shrines, one need only consider the creation of Mt. Rushmore National Monument and a correspondingly vast tourist industry in the Black Hills—the most sacred geography of the Lakotas, Cheyennes, and other peoples—to get the idea."[117]

It is clear that before and during the Genocide Convention's negotiations, as well as after its entry into force, the United States enacted policies that constituted cultural genocide. Thus, while the United States raised legitimate questions about whether the Genocide Convention was the appropriate place for the protection of minority cultural rights, it is clear that the United States had a vested interest in ensuring that cultural genocide was omitted from the convention for its own protection against being implicated in the commission of genocide.

French and British Policies and Cultural Genocide

During the Genocide Convention's negotiations, France and the United Kingdom maintained vast numbers of territories that were subject to U.N. trusteeship agreements or were listed by the United Nations General Assembly as non-self-governing territories. According to U.N. records, France maintained twenty-three such territories at the start of the convention's negotiations. Eight of those territories had a change in status during the negotiations. Meanwhile, the United Kingdom maintained forty-five such territories, all of which maintained their non-self-governing status throughout the negotiations.[118]

Whereas physical genocide seeks the near-immediate destruction of a targeted group, cultural genocide involves a process that would likely take generations before it could succeed in eliminating a group as such through the eradication of the group's culture. Thus, French and British education policies are critical to the examination of whether elements of the crime of cultural genocide were present in their non-self-governing territories before and during the Genocide Convention's negotiations, as well as after its entry into force. The most expeditious route to eliminating a culture would be through the indoctrination and assimilation of a group's children and future generations into the desired culture, with the best setting for such a venture being the classroom.

Numerous studies have attempted to delineate the differences in French and British education policies in Africa. Generally, French policies have been characterized as assimilationist "and aimed at the creation of an elite cherishing metropolitan values—Black Frenchmen."[119] British polices, in contrast, have been generally characterized as a form of "cultural adaptation" that seeks the adjustment of "metropolitan institutions to local political and social organizations and the creation of a group of educated Africans" who would be rooted in their own cultures.[120] Remi Clignet and Philip Foster argue that the purported differences in French and British policies have been exaggerated. According to the authors, both French and British policies were necessarily assimilationist because both France and the United Kingdom sought to adjust their local populations to the needs of the colonial elite.[121]

The finer details of French and British education policies were not necessarily consistent across African colonies or even within those colonies. However, there were some common features in the policies of the two countries in most, if not all, of their colonies. For France, these common features included: (1) teaching exclusively in French; (2) teaching directly and indirectly about the superiority of French culture; and (3) providing a secular education. Because this last feature is significant due to an absence from rather than a presence in French schools, it will be discussed along with the related British policy. For the United Kingdom, the common features included: (1) education in the native tongue; (2) promotion of the native culture; and (3) the importance of Christian religion to moral advancement.

When viewed through a wide lens, French and British education policies in Africa were not significantly different from those implemented in U.S. boarding schools for Native Americans. For example, Alf Heggoy argues emphatically that France attempted to "control Algeria through the assimilation of Algerians into French culture" through education.[122] According to Heggoy, "The imposition of French educational norms and the denial to the Algerian of his legitimate cultural identity through controls of language, curriculum, and methods of instruction revealed the colonialist policy in its most destructive aspect."[123] French assimilation, association, and integration policies, argues Heggoy, shared a justification for the domination of the Algerian population: to varying degrees, all policies aimed to create Frenchmen out of Algerians.[124] Derwent Whittlesey has a similar view of education policy in broader French Africa. He states that French schools in Africa were perhaps "the most vital cog in France's colonial administration."[125] French schools would consolidate control of France's African colonies through the conversion of Africans into Frenchmen. While African adults were fixed in their ways, African children were ripe for molding. According to Whittlesey, "With this goal in view, the African children are taught French . . . and they are steeped in French traditions."[126]

The number of students enrolled in French schools varied from colony to colony.[127] What was consistent, however, was the teaching of French from the first days of children's schooling.[128] French officials believed that educational advancement for Africans could be obtained through their learning French.[129] Albert Charton, inspector general of French West Africa in the 1930s, wrote of the "technical inferiority of the native worker" arising in part from "his ignorance of the [French] language."[130] The importance of a group's language to the preservation of its culture is undeniable. Interestingly, the British recognized this point. A 1953 report of the Nuffield Foundation and Colonial Office on British education policies in Africa stated, "To preserve the vernacular languages of Africa is to preserve the tribes that speak them."[131]

Georges Hardy, France's inspector general of education from 1912 to 1919, understood the relationship between a group's language and a group's culture. However, he did not view the imposition of French on Africans as a means of destroying them. Instead, he saw it as a way of lifting them up: "He could not possibly forget the good ideas that were introduced to him via this language: . . . these are our ideas, which constitute our moral, social and economic superiority, and little by little they will transform the barbarians of yesterday into disciples and assistants."[132] Hardy's reference to "disciples" is important. France had neither the infrastructure in Africa nor the personnel to teach every African child residing within its colonies in French schools. Therefore, it was important that the children of prominent members of the different communities be educated in the French schools, because they would likely have the most influence in the future. Raphael Antonetti, the governor-general of French Equatorial Africa from 1924 to 1934, stated:

"We can get to only a tiny minority of our native children. . . . It makes it imperative that we reserve the all too rare openings in our schools for those who are able to profit by our instruction."[133] Charton stated more clearly that the purpose of selecting students from the most influential African families was to educate those who would "form the backbone of the new native civilization."[134] In other words, France directly sought the participation of Africans in ensuring the demise of African cultures.

Education policies in British Africa contrasted with those in French Africa. Perhaps the most obvious difference is the language policy. Clignet and Foster note that "the use of vernacular languages in the first years of the primary school provided a radical contrast with French efforts."[135] They continue, "In spite of the formidable difficulties involved in using vernaculars, the British were more impressed by the handicaps imposed on the school child by requiring him to learn a foreign language than they were by the desirability of developing a lingua franca."[136] According to Whittlesey, in predominantly Muslim areas of British colonies, emirates maintained schools in which teaching was conducted in the country's language.[137] These observations were consistent with the professed values behind the policy. As noted above, the 1953 Nuffield Foundation and Colonial Office report on British education policies in Africa stated, "To preserve the vernacular languages of Africa is to preserve the tribes that speak them."

Just as the teaching of French correlated with France's wider perception of French and African cultures, the British policy of teaching in the local vernacular was also related to its wider cultural policies. British literature on education and culture tends to express an appreciation for local cultures and traditions.[138] The 1953 Nuffield Foundation and Colonial Office report supports this literature. It noted the importance of adapting education to the "traditions of the various peoples" and made suggestions for improvement, such as bringing in grandfathers from the local groups to tell stories as a way to teach students about their cultures while also teaching them how to better express themselves orally.[139] The report also suggested the recruitment of individuals from the students' own ethnic groups to teach them.[140]

Unlike France's secular approach to education, British policy was generally centered on the importance of religion to moral advancement. At the primary level especially, education in most of British Africa was left to missionaries.[141] The role missions played in British education policy was significant enough for the missions to be referred to as Britain's "unofficial partner."[142] The 1953 Nuffield Foundation and Colonial Office report offers many insights into British policy regarding the connection between religion and education. The report notes that the goal of education is enlightenment and that the path to greater enlightenment is paved by the truth that religion reveals.[143] More explicitly, the report encourages colonial administrators to "plainly declare their moral and material support for deep and sincere religious beliefs as the basis of all education."[144] Of course, as described by British administrators, missionary zeal reflected the best of intentions. Mutua—who was born in Kenya when it was a British colony—describes matters quite differently. According to him, "Inherent to any universalizing creed is an unyielding faith in the superiority of at least the beliefs of the proselytizer over those of the potential convert. The project of universality or proselytism seeks to remake the 'other' in the image of the converter."[145]

While French and British education policies in their African colonies diverged in some important ways, each set of policies contained elements that had the potential to significantly impact, if not irrevocably alter, local cultures. French schools required that African students be taught in French. There was a belief that with the teaching of French and, thus, the ability to read texts written in French, African students would learn about France's ideas, which constitute its "moral, social and economic superiority." Learning these ideas would "transform the barbarians of yesterday into disciples and assistants." These disciples were to be the means through which French language and culture would put down roots and would reach those Africans who were not educated in French schools. In British Africa, the role of religion in education infringed most intrusively on the local cultures. The British believed religion to be the foundation to all education. Importantly, both French and British policies were steeped in the rhetoric of cultural transformation. In other words, both sought to transform Africans individually and culturally.

It is important to note the context within which French and British policies, which clearly targeted elements of their colonies' local cultures, were employed: these policies targeted Africans living in Africa. Thus, France and the United Kingdom sought to assimilate Africans into at least some aspects of French and British cultures in their own homes. This is a very different act, and has a different intent, than attempts to assimilate African migrants into French and British cultures in France and the United Kingdom.

In determining whether to support or oppose the inclusion of cultural genocide in the Genocide Convention, France and the United Kingdom need only have had reason for concern that their policies in their colonies could potentially implicate them in the commission of cultural genocide. If there was reason for such concerns, it would have been in their national interest to support cultural genocide's omission from the Genocide Convention. Furthermore, the United States, perhaps the most influential negotiating party and an ally, had already emphatically stated its opposition to the inclusion of cultural genocide and its willingness to scuttle the convention's adoption if cultural genocide were included, thus providing additional cover for and cooperation with other countries in the pursuit of impunity against accountability for genocide.

CONCLUSION

In 1952, Hans Morgenthau wrote:

> Despite the profound changes which have occurred in the world, it still remains true, as it has always been true, that a nation confronted with the hostile aspirations of other nations has one prime obligation—to take care of its own interests. The moral justification for this prime duty of all nations—for it is not only a moral right but also a moral obligation—arises from the fact that if this particular nation does not take care of its interests, nobody else will. Hence the counsel that we ought to subordinate our national interest to some other standard is unworthy of a nation great in human civilization. A nation which would take that counsel and act consistently on it would commit suicide and become the prey and victim of other nations which know how to take care of their interests.[146]

Morgenthau's worldview held that states must prioritize their national interest over other morally worthy objectives when promoting those objectives, since such objectives—in this case, the prevention and punishment of genocide—could undermine the national interest. When combining Morgenthau's view of the supremacy of the national interest with Van Schaack's belief that the parties that negotiated the Genocide Convention were committed to a treaty under which they would not be implicated, the omission of political groups and the exclusion of cultural genocide were clearly in the national interests of, respectively, the Soviet Union and the triumvirate of the United States, the United Kingdom, and France.

Chapters 1 and 2 presented evidence showing how politics ruled the day throughout the drafting of the Genocide Convention. Though he did not do so without some consternation, Lemkin was at times a participant in these political machinations, even as negotiating parties unraveled his ideal conception of a treaty that would outlaw the crime whose name he created. Concerted efforts were made by the P-5 to ensure that their interests were protected. Repeatedly, provisions of the early drafts of the Genocide Convention that were viewed as unfavorable to the P-5 were negotiated out of the text, while others more favorable to them were retained or negotiated into it.

At times, criticism of the international community and the Security Council has been shortsighted in that it gives too much credit to states for drafting and ratifying the Genocide Convention. It assumes, at least for the most part, that the convention was actually negotiated in good faith with an accompanying commitment to its enforcement, when review of the negotiations reveals quite the opposite. This optimistic view is often divorced from the realities of the persistent interconnections between the politics of the law and the politics of its implementation and effectiveness. What is missing in such an analysis is the recognition that the treaty was designed to be ineffective, at least in relation to the specific interests of the P-5. Therefore, the fact that the Genocide Convention has proved ineffective is by design.

Chapter 3

The ICJ as Enabler of State Impunity for Genocide

The first two chapters showed how P-5 members worked to eliminate aspects of the Genocide Convention that could have implicated them in the commission of genocide and undermined their absolute control over their territory. Therefore, up to the point at which the Genocide Convention was adopted by the General Assembly and entered into force, the P-5 had successfully acquired the ability to act with almost full impunity as related to the law against genocide by ensuring territorial jurisdiction for the prevention of genocide, omitting political groups from protection, and excluding acts that constitute cultural genocide. However, the ability to submit reservations to the Genocide Convention is an often-overlooked additional key to state impunity. Article IX of the convention gives the ICJ jurisdiction to hear cases submitted to it by state parties concerning state responsibility for genocide. Therefore, a legal avenue to accountability for the commission of genocide survived the convention's drafting process.

P-5 members were not about to let this stand. The original solution to ICJ jurisdiction was the use of reservations to reject the ICJ's authority. However, such reservations were also objected to by other state parties to the Genocide Convention, thus raising questions about whether reservations should be permitted. For P-5 members seeking absolute state impunity, the right to submit reservations had to be protected. As this chapter shows, the United States and Soviet Union played essential roles in this regard.

Though the punitive purpose of the Genocide Convention has been the subject of an extensive body of literature and the focus of cases at the ad hoc International Criminal Tribunals for the former Yugoslavia and Rwanda, as well as at the International Criminal Court, state responsibility under the convention has been comparatively underexplored. As Anja Seibert-Fohr notes, "The acceleration of international criminal law with its focus on the individual perpetrator temporarily averted [attention] from the question of whether and to what extent states are responsible for violations of the

Convention on the Prevention and Punishment of the Crime of Genocide."[1] Under Article IX of the Genocide Convention, the ICJ can hear cases concerning the interpretation, application, and fulfillment of treaty obligations and prohibitions, including those relating to state responsibility for genocide and other ancillary acts listed under Article III. These other acts include conspiracy to commit genocide, direct and public incitement to commit genocide, attempt to commit genocide, and complicity in genocide.

In 1976, as part of an effort to further develop the concept of state responsibility, the ILC recognized the relationship between the capacity of individual actors to commit harmful acts and the state apparatuses through which they commit such acts.[2] In 2001, the ILC adopted its articles on the Responsibility of States for Internationally Wrongful Acts.[3] The ILC concluded that the commission of an "internationally wrongful act" by a state "entails the international responsibility" of that state. Furthermore, just as the Genocide Convention includes state responsibility for conspiracy to commit genocide and complicity in genocide, the ILC included an aspect of extraterritorial state responsibility for wrongful acts. According to Article 16, "A State which aids or assists another State in the commission of an internationally wrongful act by the latter is internationally responsible for doing so if: (a) that State does so with knowledge of the circumstances of the internationally wrongful act; and (b) the act would be internationally wrongful if committed by that State."

The concept of state responsibility for genocide was developed even further by the ICJ in the *Bosnia v. Serbia* case. In its 2007 ruling, the ICJ established what constitutes conspiracy in, complicity in, incitement to, and failure to prevent genocide.[4] Though the ruling has rightly been criticized, it nonetheless set a precedent and offers insight into the potential role of the ICJ in deterring states from committing genocide, as well as deterring other states from conspiring with genocidal states or facilitating conditions in which genocide becomes possible.[5]

Even more recently, the ICJ established that one state party to the Genocide Convention can submit a case against another state party, even when the applicant state has not been directly affected in any way by the actions of the respondent state. On November 11, 2019, The Gambia filed an application for proceedings at the ICJ, under Article IX, against Myanmar for alleged violations of the Genocide Convention committed against Myanmar's Rohingya population. On January 23, 2020, the ICJ accepted The Gambia's application, rejecting Myanmar's claim that The Gambia lacked standing to bring the case. In explaining its decision, the ICJ agreed with The Gambia's assertion that parties to the Genocide Convention hold obligations *erga omnes*, meaning obligations owed to all other parties to the convention. Therefore, each party has a legal interest in ensuring that all other parties uphold their obligations under the convention. For reasons discussed below in this chapter, it is worth quoting the ICJ's opinion at length:

> In view of their shared values, all the States parties to the Genocide Convention have a common interest to ensure that acts of genocide are prevented and that, if they occur, *their authors do not enjoy impunity* [emphasis added]. That common interest implies that the obligations in question are owed by any State party to all the other States parties to the Convention. . . . It follows that any State party to the Genocide Convention, and not only a specially affected State, may invoke the responsibility of another State party with a view to ascertaining the alleged failure to comply with its obligations *erga omnes*, and to bring that failure to an end.[6]

Together, Article IX of the Genocide Convention, the ILC's articles on the Responsibility of States for Internationally Wrongful Acts, and the ICJ's decisions in *Bosnia v. Serbia* and the Case Concerning the Application of the Convention on the Prevention and Punishment of the Crime of Genocide (The Gambia v. Myanmar) [herein after, *The Gambia v. Myanmar*] firmly establish that states can be held responsible for genocide and its ancillary acts.[7] This is true regardless of whether the case involves one state party contributing in some way to the commission of genocide within the territory of another state party (as in *Bosnia v. Serbia*) or involves one state party committing genocide against members of its own population without the participation in any form of an external state actor (as in *The Gambia v. Myanmar*). The significance of these developments should not be understated, because they have implications for interstate genocide, intrastate genocide, and intrastate genocide with interstate support.

Unfortunately, there is an "unfortunately." Despite the ICJ's assertion that all state parties to the Genocide Convention have a common interest in ensuring that states responsible for genocide "do not enjoy impunity," and despite the implicit recognition that the ICJ has a major role to play in combating state impunity, reservations made by state parties to Article IX of the Genocide Convention ensure the opposite: some state parties enjoy impunity for acts prohibited by the convention. Article IX reservations have taken one of two forms. In the absolutist form, state parties have rejected the ICJ's jurisdiction to hear cases involving the reserving states. In the softer form, which has the same practical effect, other state parties have required their prior consent on a case-by-case basis for the ICJ to have jurisdiction to hear cases involving these reserving states. Thus, the prospect remains that state parties that maintain Article IX reservations can commit genocide and contribute to the commission of genocide with impunity.

This did not need to be the case. The ICJ had an opportunity in 1951 to affirm its authority to hear all cases involving allegations of state responsibility for genocide by placing limitations on the permissibility of reservations. Instead, in its 1951 Advisory Opinion Concerning Reservations to the Convention on the Prevention and Punishment of the Crime of Genocide, the ICJ decided, for all intents and purposes, to give states the unilateral right to make reservations, including reservations that deny the ICJ the jurisdiction that Article IX of the Genocide Convention awarded exclusively to it.[8] Notably, in doing so, the ICJ can be seen as having been heavily influenced by two P-5 members (the United States and the Soviet Union), including by arguments each made while negotiating the text of the convention. The remainder of this chapter is divided into five sections. The first section provides the context in which the advisory opinion was requested and a summary of the majority opinion. The second section summarizes and analyzes the arguments made by states prior to the decision. The third section summarizes dissenting views from that of the majority of judges and proponent states. The fourth section demonstrates the practical implications of the ICJ's opinion for state impunity for genocide. Finally, the fifth section offers an alternative approach to reservations from that mandated by the ICJ and codified in the Vienna Convention of the Law of Treaties (VCLT).[9]

The ICJ and Reservations to the Genocide Convention

The Genocide Convention was unanimously adopted by the General Assembly on December 9, 1948. In Article XIII, the convention required that twenty states ratify or accede to the convention before it would enter into force. Though numerous states made reservations to the convention when they signed and ratified it, the reservations did not become a concern until the convention neared the requisite number of parties for entry into force. Thus, during 1949 and 1950, it was left unclear whether reservations to the convention were permitted. The convention does not contain an article that expressly prohibits reservations, but neither does it outline any procedures for determining whether a specific reservation is permissible and what the effect of a reservation is if other states object to it.

With the deposit of five new instruments of ratification on October 14, 1950, the number of state parties to the Genocide Convention reached twenty-two.[10] However, among these state parties, Bulgaria and Czechoslovakia made reservations to Articles IX and XII and the Philippines made reservations to Articles IV, VI, VII, and IX.[11] Meanwhile, Ecuador objected to Czechoslovakia's reservations on March 31, 1950, and to Bulgaria's on August 21.[12] Furthermore, if Ecuador's objection to Article IX reservations were to be considered absolute, the Philippines would join Czechoslovakia and Bulgaria as state parties to the Genocide Convention whose status as parties had been called into question, thus raising a question: can Czechoslovakia, Bulgaria, and the Philippines be considered parties to the Genocide Convention while maintaining reservations that had been objected to by another party to the treaty? If not, the Genocide Convention's twenty-party threshold would not have been met.[13]

On November 16, 1950, the General Assembly adopted Resolution 478(V), with forty-seven votes in favor of the resolution, five against, and five abstentions. The resolution requested that the ICJ answer a series of questions concerning reservations to the Genocide Convention. These questions can be summarized as:

(1) Can a state that has made a reservation to the Genocide Convention be regarded as a party to the treaty if the reservation is maintained and has been objected to by one or more, but not all, of the other parties?
(2) If a state that maintains a reservation that has been objected to can still be regarded as a party to the Genocide Convention, what is the effect of the reservation between the reserving state and the parties that have objected to it and the parties that have accepted it?
(3) What is the legal effect of an objection to a reservation made by a state that has not signed or acceded to the Genocide Convention, and a state that has signed, but not ratified the treaty?[14]

By the time the ICJ received written statements, heard oral statements, and made its decision, the urgency associated with deciding whether state parties that had made reservations to which objections had been raised were to be counted as parties had subsided. Laos became the twentieth party to the Genocide Convention, without reservation, on December 8, 1950. Nonetheless, the import of the questions put before the ICJ by the General Assembly remained. This was especially true concerning Article IX reservations.

Before delivering its majority opinion, the ICJ established the manner in which it would approach the questions put before it. Notably, the ICJ determined that the questions posed were "purely abstract in character," referring "neither to the reservations which have, in fact, been made . . . nor to the objections which have been made to such reservations."[15] Moreover, according to the ICJ, the questions did not refer to "reservations which may in future be made in respect of any particular article." The ICJ also emphasized that its mandate was "expressly limited by the terms of the Resolution of the General Assembly to the Convention on the Prevention and Punishment of the Crime of Genocide." Thus, based on this reading, the ICJ established at the outset that its task was not to decide whether it ought to be possible for states to make reservations, but rather whether a state party that has made a reservation "can, while still maintaining it, be regarded as being a party to the Convention, when there is a divergence of views between the contracting parties concerning this reservation, some accepting the reservation, others refusing to accept it."

On the surface, the ICJ's approach appears logical. The initial question submitted by the General Assembly does not ask the ICJ to consider the permissibility of reservations, but rather whether an objection to a reservation severs the reserving state's party status. Yet the question of whether reservations ought to be permitted at all is implied by the first question. To answer the question in the negative would mean that unanimous acceptance of all reservations would be required: a single objection would sever the reserving state's party status. The ICJ even pointed to the notion that the integrity of multilateral conventions is found within the four corners of what was adopted, meaning that no reservation could be valid unless accepted by every state party, without exception. Yet the likelihood of unanimous acceptance is slim, as is evidenced by the objections to reservations to the Genocide Convention that necessitated the ICJ's advisory opinion in the first place. Therefore, the ICJ essentially punted on the question of permissibility of reservations, instead accepting that reservations are permitted regardless of whether other state parties objected to them. As is shown below, the ICJ boxed itself in with this initial decision. Under this approach, reservations would have no impact on the relationship between the reserving state and the Genocide Convention: rather, the effect of a reservation would be limited to the relationship between reserving states and the objecting states.

In boxing itself in, the ICJ forced itself into contradictory justifications for its position. The ICJ justified permitting reservations because states could not be bound by international law without their expressed consent. Yet the ICJ also referred to the generally recognized principle that multilateral conventions like the Genocide Convention are the result of "an agreement freely concluded upon its clauses and that consequently none of the contracting parties is entitled to frustrate or impair, by means of unilateral decisions or particular agreements, the purpose and raison d'être of the convention."[16] Thus, the ICJ simultaneously held the following positions: the text of the Genocide Convention was freely concluded; when ratifying the convention, states express their consent to be bound by the law therein; and states can retract their consent to be bound by certain elements of the convention that were freely concluded, as long as doing so is not incompatible with the purpose of the convention.

To reconcile the contradictions in the majority opinion, the ICJ rebutted its own claim that the Genocide Convention was a freely concluded agreement, deciding that the convention must be viewed differently because, though unanimously approved at the General Assembly, its text was the result of a series of majority votes. Hence, according to the ICJ, "the majority principle, while facilitating the conclusion of multilateral conventions, may also make it necessary for certain States to make reservations."[17] In asserting that no state party has the right to "frustrate or impair . . . the purpose and *raison d'être* of the convention," the ICJ also introduced its "object and purpose" test for reservations. Accordingly, the true determinant of the permissibility of certain reservations is the compatibility of an individual reservation with the object and purpose of the Genocide Convention.

The ICJ identified the object of the Genocide Convention as twofold: humanitarian and civilizing. As the ICJ wrote in its advisory opinion: "It is indeed difficult to imagine a convention that might have this dual character to a greater degree, since its object on the one hand is to safeguard the very existence of certain human groups and on the other to confirm and endorse the most elementary principles of morality."[18] Importantly, confirmation and endorsement of the most elementary principles of morality was meant to be not relativistic but "universal in scope." Furthermore, according to the ICJ, state parties to the Genocide Convention "do not have any interests of their own; they merely have, one and all, a common interest, namely, the accomplishment of those high purposes which are the *raison d'être* of the convention." In this regard, the ICJ identified two potentially conflicting objects of the Genocide Convention. On the one hand, the ICJ needed to consider the integrity of the text of the convention as it pertains to the humanitarian purpose of the treaty. On the other hand, the ICJ determined that it was equally or more important that "as many States as possible should participate" as parties to the Genocide Convention, because the "complete exclusion from the Convention of one or more States would not only restrict the scope of its application, but would detract from the authority of the moral and humanitarian principles which are its basis."

Ultimately, in its majority opinion, the ICJ concluded that the purpose of the Genocide Convention could not be met if states that submit a "minor reservation" are excluded from the convention.[19] The ICJ also concluded that the purpose of the convention could not be met if states were permitted to make whatever reservations they see fit merely for the "vain desire to secure as many participants as possible." Therefore, the true determinant of the permissibility of individual reservations is the compatibility of reservations with the object and purpose of the convention.

In coming to this conclusion, the ICJ rejected the absolute sovereignty and orthodox approaches to reservations, instead opting for a variation of the Pan-American approach. According to the absolute sovereignty approach, states have a nonnegotiable right to make reservations upon signing and ratifying the Genocide Convention. In contrast, the orthodox approach permits only reservations that are unanimously accepted by all other state parties. Therefore, a single objection by one state party to a reservation made by another state party requires the reserving state to withdraw its reservation or lose its party status. Concerning its rejection of the absolute sovereignty approach, the ICJ explained, "It is obvious that so extreme an application of the idea of State sovereignty could lead to a complete disregard of the object and purpose of the Convention."[20] In rejecting the orthodox approach, the ICJ wrote that this view "rests essentially on a contractual conception of the absolute integrity of the convention as adopted. This view, however, cannot prevail if, having regard to the character of the convention, its purpose and its mode of adoption, it can be established that the parties intended to derogate from that rule by admitting the faculty to make reservations thereto."

It might be obvious from the above that the majority of ICJ judges answered the first question in the affirmative, asserting that "the appraisal of a reservation and the effect of objections that might be made to it depend upon the particular circumstances of each individual case."[21] Therefore, the ICJ determined that states that make reservations retain their status as parties to the Genocide Convention, regardless of the number of objections to the reservation, and even, potentially, if every other party objects to the reservation. How would this be possible? According to the ICJ majority opinion, "As no State can be bound by a reservation to which it has not consented, it necessarily follows that each State objecting to it will or will not, on the basis of its individual appraisal within the limits of the criterion of the object and purpose stated above, consider the reserving State to be a party to the Convention." In other words, the number of objections to a reservation is not important. Rather, what is important is the assessment by an objecting state of the relationship between the reserving state and the Genocide Convention. An objection alone, then, does not indicate that an objecting state does not accept a reserving state as a party to the convention.

According to the ICJ, the possibility of divergent views about reservations is mitigated by the object and purpose principle. Contracting states have a common duty to guide their judgment on reservations by basing whether they make reservations and whether they object to reservations made by other states on the "compatibility or incompatibility of the reservation with the object and purpose of the Convention."[22] Moreover, placing great faith in states with various interests, the ICJ wrote, "It must clearly be assumed that the contracting States are desirous of preserving intact at least what is essential to the object of the Convention; should this desire be absent, it is quite clear that the Convention itself would be impaired both in its principle and in its application." Finally, the ICJ raised the possibility that disputes concerning the admissibility of specific reservations, meaning whether individual reservations are compatible with the object and purpose of the Genocide Convention, could be settled by the ICJ under "the procedure laid down in Article IX of the Convention."

There is something interesting in the fact that the majority of ICJ judges pointed to the series of majority votes that resulted in the content of the Genocide Convention as a reason for why reservations must be permitted—especially when many of the votes on the specific language on the convention involved much larger majorities than that pertaining to the advisory opinion on reservations to multilateral treaties. Although five of the twelve judges (approximately 42 percent) dissented from the ICJ's majority opinion, the majority opinion determined the direction of international law on reservations.

Soviet and U.S. Support for Reservations: Working in Concert without Working Together

Though the ICJ received written statements from states and convened oral proceedings prior to delivering its majority opinion, it was important to present the majority opinion ahead of the arguments made by states to better highlight the arguments that seemingly determined the ICJ's decision. It is clear in the decision that the ICJ prioritized the maximization of state parties to the Genocide Convention over the convention's textual integrity, and to maximize the number of state parties, states must be permitted to make reservations. However, to avoid giving away the farm, the ICJ decided that reservations must be compatible with the object and purpose of the Genocide Convention.

In delivering its decision, the ICJ did not refer to the tactics displayed by the United States and Soviet Union while negotiating the content of the Genocide Convention. As chapter 2 showed, the Soviet Union threatened to undermine support for the convention if it protected political groups, and the United States threatened to erode support for the convention if acts constituting cultural genocide were not excluded. It can be speculated that their intransigence was influential in the ICJ's decision to seek to maximize the number of state parties, especially when considering the way in which the Soviet Union and United States reprised these roles during ICJ proceedings.

As noted above, the ICJ rejected the absolute sovereignty approach, opting instead for a version of the Pan-American approach. During the ICJ's written and oral proceedings, the Soviet Union argued for the former approach, while the United States supported the latter. Despite the different approaches taken by the two countries, both were seeking the same result: the uninhibited right to make reservations. The primary difference is one of perception. Whereas the Soviet Union took the hard-line position that states should have a nonnegotiable right to make reservations upon signing and ratifying the Genocide Convention based on the "inherent right of sovereignty,"[23] the United States framed its position as being pragmatically necessary and of little substantive consequence because "reservations may frequently be technical qualifications of a treaty rather than substantial limitations of its obligations."[24] Therefore, according to the United States, reservations that do not impact a state's substantive obligations should be permitted. Furthermore, the United States noted, the Genocide Convention is not an organizational treaty like the United Nations Charter. Therefore, the Genocide Convention need not be treated as an indivisible whole that must be maintained at all costs.

In their separate positions, it might appear as though the Soviet Union and United States were on different sides of the reservation debate. Indeed, the United States rejected what it referred to as the "sovereign power rule," arguing that "it hardly seems reasonable to say that each of those States has a basic sovereign right to make such modifications or amendments in the treaty as it desires, in the form of reservations, without regard to the right of the other States concerned to determine whether the treaty, so modified or amended, would be acceptable."[25] However, when considering the practical implications of the two approaches, it becomes evident that the two states were working in concert without working together. Both the absolute sovereignty approach and the Pan-American approach permit states to make reservations to the Genocide Convention. The former approach simply involves a blunter unilateral defense of the right to make reservations, while the latter dresses the right in a mirage of cooperation. The result of both approaches is the same: states have the right to make reservations and retain their status as parties to the Genocide Convention regardless of whether other states object to the reservations. Thus, writes Anton Weiss-Wendt, when the ICJ majority opinion was delivered, essentially instituting a version of the Pan-American approach, "The United States and the Soviet Union were both satisfied with the ruling: the states could from now on ratify the convention with reservations, whether they liked the specific clauses attached by others or not."[26]

In addition to advocating the Pan-American approach, the United States presented an argument cited by the ICJ in its majority opinion: a primary goal of the Genocide Convention is the maximization of state parties. The United States noted that state constitutions and other obstacles might make it impossible for some states to ratify the convention without permission to make reservations. Because it is desirable for the greatest possible number of states to become party to the convention, it is necessary for every state to be able to "give effect to the treaty even if it must make reservations which are not acceptable to some States although acceptable to other States."[27] The United States was supported in making this argument by the Organization of American States and Israel. According to the former, to achieve maximum participation, it must be taken into account that states have "fixed national policies in certain matters which they are not ready to abandon even for the sake of the adoption of a treaty which they may otherwise recognize as promoting the development of international law, or furthering their common political and economic interests. . . . To adopt a rigid rule prohibiting all reservations except those unanimously agreed to might defeat the adoption of the convention"[28] Similarly, Israel agreed that the "universal characteristics of the Genocide Convention" would be best promoted by the "maximum acceptance by the greatest possible number of States of the obligations defined by the Convention."[29] Maximization would also "give effect to the universal international desire to define clearly what genocide is and . . . to establish an obligation to co-operate in the prevention and punishment of the crime so defined."[30]

It is important to note that the defense of reservations summarized above employs the same abstract approach used by the ICJ. When the United States claims that "reservations may frequently be technical qualifications of a treaty rather than substantial limitations of its obligations," it does so while ignoring the fact that Article IX reservations are not mere technical qualifications, but rather a means by which to deny the ICJ the authority that had been conferred on it.[31] Article IX reservations deny the ICJ jurisdiction concerning state responsibility for genocide, pushing that responsibility into a legal vacuum for states that make such reservations.

DISSENTING OPINIONS: THE UNITED KINGDOM AND FIVE JUDGES

In its written and oral statements, the United Kingdom was the strongest proponent for the orthodox approach, which would have limited the permissibility of reservations to those that were unanimously accepted by all other state parties to the Genocide Convention. In arguing against the absolute sovereignty approach, the United Kingdom stated that such a system would allow states to unilaterally make and maintain reservations from which they stood to benefit without consequence, even when the reservations were objected to. In other words, states would be permitted to reject an element of the convention, thus unilaterally gaining some benefit from their reservations, while maintaining their full status as parties to the convention even when one or more of the other parties object to the reservation. The United Kingdom argued that to take the absolute sovereignty approach seriously would be to make a mockery of the process of treaty negotiation by allowing the work toward agreement to be undone. Yet the United Kingdom also asserted that the Pan-American approach would lead to the "re-introduction by the back-door of the absolute sovereignty conception" because the reserving state would be able to make any reservations it sees fit, "even if it were theoretically the position that (owing to these objections) the convention was not in force between the reserving State and the objecting State; for this position would be purely nominal, since the obligations of the objecting States would remain precisely the same."[32]

The United Kingdom's opposition to the absolute sovereignty and Pan-American approaches was grounded in the legal principle that contractual relationships cannot be altered without the consent of all parties involved. Therefore, when a state makes a reservation to the Genocide Convention, what it is doing is "suggesting the conclusion of a different and new contract."[33] The United Kingdom was also concerned that permitting reservations without the unanimous consent of all parties would transform the Genocide Convention into a series of bilateral agreements based on which states were making reservations and which states were objecting to or accepting reservations. According to the United Kingdom, "That kind of arrangement, as far as one can see, cannot establish a common standard for all the States parties to the convention. What it does is to set up as many separate standards as there happen to be reservations."[34] Relatedly, the United Kingdom questioned the utility of writing ambitious standards only to allow them to be transformed into mere "frauds and delusions."[35] In other words, when high-sounding standards are simply for show, since they will be chipped away at by state reservations, they are fraudulent in that there was never a possibility that they would be the actual standards to be met. The United Kingdom added that it would rather see a treaty to which states "can honestly adhere without reservations" than one "cast in over-ambitious terms to which States may be prepared to give lip-service . . . but to which they make reservations when it comes to the question of carrying out the obligations which have been agreed to."[36]

The United Kingdom also raised an issue of equity, asserting that there cannot be a fair system when parties to a convention are allowed to make reservations on substantive articles and receive the credit and advantages that derive from being a party to the convention, while also diminishing their obligations under the convention. Meanwhile, states that do not submit reservations receive the same credit as reserving states without the same advantages, because they assume the full set of obligations entailed in being a party to the convention.[37] Finally, the United Kingdom questioned the argument that reservations were necessary if not for substantive reasons then for ensuring the largest participation possible. The United Kingdom questioned the utility of a convention that has been allowed to be "emasculated" for the purpose of maximizing the number of states parties.[38] Indeed, in support of the orthodox view, the United Kingdom wrote, "Those holding this view considered that, regrettable though it might be that States should on occasion be unable to participate in a convention, this was a lesser evil than a position according to which there could never be any finality about the text of any convention, even when the process of its negotiation and drafting was supposed to be completed."[39]

In their joint dissenting opinion, ICJ judges Jose Gustavo Guerrero, Sir Arnold McNair, John Read, and Hsu Mo challenged two key elements of the majority opinion. First, they distinguished between the goals of the Genocide Convention and its primary objectives. Specifically, whereas the majority opinion claimed that maximization of states parties was a primary objective, the four dissenting judges instead described this as a goal, while maintaining the integrity of the convention could be seen as a primary objective. The dissenting judges wrote:

> We believe that the integrity of the terms of the Convention is of greater importance than mere universality in its acceptance. While is it undoubtedly true that the representatives of the governments, in drafting and adopting the Genocide Convention, wished to see as many States become parties to it as possible, it was certainly not their intention to achieve universality at any price. There is no evidence to show that they desired to secure wide acceptance of the Convention even at the expense of the integrity or uniformity of its terms, irrespective of the wishes of those States which have accepted all the obligations under it.[40]

Second, the dissenting judges challenged the idea that the series of majority votes that finalized the text of the Genocide Convention necessitated the right of states to make reservations. They noted that there had been an increasing tendency toward subverting some elements of sovereignty to promote "the common welfare of the international community. . . . So, when a common effort is made to promote a great humanitarian object, as in the case of the Genocide Convention, every interested State naturally expects every other interested State not to seek any individual advantage or convenience, but to carry out the measures resolved upon by common accord."[41] Therefore, the dissenting judges argued, "universality at any price" is not a primary objective, but "the acceptance of common obligations"[42] beneficial to all humanity is—meaning that reservations that undermine the integrity of the Genocide Convention require the consent of all parties to it.

Thus, the dissenting judges concluded, "In the interests of the international community, it would be better to lose as a party to the Convention a State which insists in face of objections on a modification of the terms of the Convention, than to permit it to become a party against the wish of a State or States which have irrevocably and unconditionally accepted all the obligations of the Convention."[43]

The remaining dissenting judge, Alejandro Alvarez, went a step further by challenging the idea that states would not join the Genocide Convention without the right to make reservations. Alvarez expressed his belief that states would have made reservations to the United Nations Charter and the ICJ statute if they had been permitted to do so. Nevertheless, states accepted the charter and statute because they did not have the choice to make reservations. Thus, Alvarez writes, "A psychological factor, in fact, comes into consideration in regard to these instruments: States are unwilling to remain aloof from these conventions, for, if they did so, they would find themselves in an awkward position in international society."[44] In other words, there are reputational benefits that come with being party to human rights treaties. Thus, the question remains whether permitting reservations is necessary to ensure participation. If permitting reservations does contribute to greater participation, it also allows states to have their cake and eat it too. As Heather McKibben and Shaina Western write, "Entering reservations therefore allows political elites to signal a commitment to co-operate by ratifying a treaty, while also allowing them to insulate domestic policies and practices that conflict with certain aspects of the treaty from challenges that could be raised by other political actors."[45] Importantly, reservations have consequences for what cooperation looks like in practice. In other words, states can point to their treaty membership as evidence of their commitment to cooperation, but the reservations (or the small print) are the more honest indicators of what a state is actually committing itself to. This highlights the significance of Article IX reservations, which shield the reserving states from being held responsible for the direct and indirect role they play in the commission of genocide by obstructing the ICJ's authority to hear cases against them.

The Practical Impact of Article IX Reservations

The practical implications of the ICJ decision on reservations belies the ICJ's own assertion that states that commit or facilitate genocide should not "enjoy impunity." In their dissenting opinions, Judges Guerrero, McNair, Read, and Mo asserted that the ICJ advisory opinion case was not actually "purely abstract," but rather involved concrete reservations already made by states that had signed and/or ratified the Genocide Convention.[46] The judges noted that eight states had collectively made or proposed eighteen reservations, with all eight making a reservation to Article IX of the Genocide Convention. The judges also noted that these reservations would preclude the ICJ from carrying out its function as the arbiter of disputes between state parties concerning state responsibility for genocide and its ancillary acts.

There is a plethora of evidence to support the claim that the combination of the ICJ advisory opinion and Article IX reservations fosters a culture of state impunity for genocide. On no less than four occasions, the ICJ has demonstrated deference to states that maintain Article IX reservations. In 1999, Serbia filed an application against ten North Atlantic Treaty Organization (NATO) states that were involved in the military intervention in Kosovo in that year. At the time, of the ten states, Spain and the United States maintained Article IX reservations.[47] Based on these reservations, the ICJ dismissed Serbia's claims against the two reserving states. In its response to Serbia's petition, the United States also attempted to head off the possibility that the ICJ might consider whether Article IX reservations are compatible with the object and purpose of the Genocide Convention. The United States asserted that Article IX reservations are compatible because the "possibility of recourse to this Court for settlement of disputes is not central to the overall system of the Convention, which has as its essential elements the definition of the crime of genocide and the creation of obligations to try and punish those responsible for genocide."[48]

In May 2002, the Democratic Republic of the Congo (DRC) filed an application with the ICJ, alleging that Rwanda was responsible for "massive, serious and flagrant violations of human rights and of international humanitarian law," and invoked Article IX as a source of ICJ jurisdiction regarding the dispute.[49] In its response, the ICJ dismissed the DRC's case, while affirming its decisions in the Spanish and U.S. cases and validating the U.S. argument on the compatibility of Article IX reservations with the object and purpose of the Genocide Convention. The ICJ found that Rwanda's Article IX reservation "bears on the jurisdiction of the Court" but does not "affect substantive obligations relating to acts of genocide themselves under that Convention." In other words, though Rwanda succeeded with its reservation in precluding the ICJ from hearing the DRC's complaint, this did not mean that the ICJ had cleared Rwanda of responsibility for the violations alleged by the DRC in its complaint. It was in this possibility of future settlement of the dispute that the ICJ also concluded that Article IX reservations are not incompatible with the object and purpose of the Genocide Convention, because such reservations are only "meant to exclude a particular method of settling a dispute relating to the interpretation, application or fulfilment of the Convention."

The ICJ also took into consideration Article IX reservations in Serbia's preliminary objections to ICJ jurisdiction in the separate cases filed against Serbia by Bosnia and Croatia. In both cases, Serbia pointed to the reservation it made to Article IX when it acceded to the Genocide Convention in 2001. Had Serbia's reservation been in effect at the time the crimes were committed, the ICJ would have dismissed Bosnia's and Croatia's cases. However, in 1992, the Permanent Mission of the FRY indicated to the U.N. secretary-general that the FRY considered itself to be the successor to the Socialist Federal Republic of Yugoslavia (SFRY) "on the basis of the continuing personality of Yugoslavia."[50] As the proclaimed legitimate successor, the FRY stated that it would "continue to fulfil all the rights conferred to, and obligations assumed by" the SFRY, "including its membership in all international organizations and participation in international treaties ratified or acceded to by Yugoslavia."[51] Thus, the ICJ determined that "Yugoslavia was bound by the provisions of the Convention on the date of the filing of the Application in the present case, namely, on 20 March 1993."[52]

The ICJ's validation of Article IX reservations by asserting that such reservations are only "meant to exclude a particular method of settling a dispute relating to the interpretation, application or fulfilment of the Convention" is problematic, both because the ICJ is the only existing forum for the settlement of disputes pertaining to state responsibility for genocide and because the ICJ was expressly given the authority by the Genocide Convention to arbitrate disputes pertaining to state responsibility for genocide. Relatedly, prior to the ICJ's delivery of its advisory opinion on reservations to the Genocide Convention, the United Kingdom identified Article IX as vital to the treaty because it "gives the Convention teeth."[53] John Quigley believes that Article IX reservations are incompatible with the object and purpose of the Genocide Convention: "Subjecting states to accountability was a central feature of the Genocide Convention. The fact that a number of states have withdrawn their reservations to Article IX has lessened the problem, yet the number of reservations remains sufficiently high to threaten the ability of the ICJ to enforce the Genocide Convention."[54]

The ILC also foresaw the possibility that states might be able to act with impunity. In its commentary on its articles on the Responsibility of States for Internationally Wrongful Acts, the ILC wrote, "States are entitled to assert complicity in the wrongful conduct of another State even though no international court may have jurisdiction to rule on the charge, at all or in the absence of the other State."[55] In a way, this highlights the problem with Article IX reservations. In the case of genocide, there is an international court that has jurisdiction to rule on allegations concerning state responsibility. Yet Article IX reservations allow states to reject this jurisdiction. Such reservations push genocide back into the domain of customary law, even though the Genocide Convention has been codified—which involves treaty-based obligations that extend beyond customary international legal obligations. As a peremptory norm under customary international law, genocide is universally prohibited. Therefore, becoming a state party to the Genocide Convention is not required for the prohibition of genocide to apply to each individual state. However, writes Quigley, "the obligation to submit to the court's jurisdiction, which is not found in customary law, is the critical element of the Convention."[56] Thus, becoming a party to the Genocide Convention ought to mean something more than the mere positive acknowledgment by state parties that genocide is in fact a crime under international law. The purpose of the Genocide Convention is the prevention and punishment of the crime. One aspect of this dual function is state responsibility for genocide. Reservations to Article IX have the effect of defeating the purpose of the convention by obstructing the authority of the ICJ to determine when a state is responsible for the commission of genocide or any of its ancillary acts.

The United States and China: Article IX Reservations and State Impunity for Genocide

Since the Genocide Convention was opened for signature and ratification in December 1948, twenty-nine states have made reservations to Article IX. Twelve states have since withdrawn their reservations, leaving seventeen states that maintain reservations.[57] Most notable among these seventeen are the United States and China. In *The United States and Genocide: (Re)Defining the Relationship*, I use what I refer to as the *Bosnia v. Serbia* precedent as a framework to analyze the historical relationships of the United States with states that have committed genocide. These include relationships with Indonesia when it committed genocide in 1965, Pakistan when it committed genocide in 1971, Guatemala when it committed genocide in the early 1980s, and Iraq when it committed genocide in 1988.[58] The United States had the requisite influence to incur an obligation to make an effort to deter the governments of each of the four states from committing genocide.

However, the United States' responsibility does not end there. As I write in the conclusion of *The United States and Genocide*: "The US conspired with Indonesia to commit genocide against members of Indonesia's Communist political group. . . . The US supplied Indonesia with covert support, including communications equipment, small arms, and the names of 5,000 communists, while sharing Indonesia's genocidal intent. The US was complicit in genocide in Bangladesh, Guatemala, and Iraq. In each of these cases, the US provided the genocidal governments with material aid and diplomatic support."[59] Of course, the United States did not ratify the

Genocide Convention until 1988, but that is beside the point. What is important here is that, with its Article IX reservation, had the United States ratified the Genocide Convention prior to any of these cases, no state would have been able to do what The Gambia has done with Myanmar—that is, bring a case to the ICJ against the United States for failing to prevent genocide, conspiring to commit genocide, or complicity in the commission of genocide. Furthermore, United States' shared responsibility for crimes committed by other states is not a thing of the past. In "A 'Synchronized Attack' on Life: The Saudi-Led Coalition's 'Hidden and Holistic' Genocide in Yemen and the Shared Responsibility of the US and UK," I argue not only that the Saudi-led coalition is responsible for genocide in Yemen, but also that the United States and the United Kingdom are complicit in the genocide based on their continued provision of material and logistical support with the knowledge that the Saudi-led coalition was committing numerous crimes against the Yemeni people.[60] Even an end to the conflict in Yemen and a transition to a government seeking accountability for the death, suffering, and destruction will not be able to reach the United States, in no small part thanks to the impunity with which it operates based on its Article IX reservation.

Because China was working alongside the United States in protecting Pakistan when it committed genocide in 1971, the same charge of failing to prevent genocide, if not complicity in genocide, could similarly be levied at China. However, the benefits China receives extend beyond its impunity for responsibility that it shares for genocide committed by other states. In March 2021, the Newlines Institute for Strategy and Policy published a report titled "The Uyghur Genocide: An Examination of China's Breaches of the 1948 Genocide Convention." The authors conclude that all five of the acts of genocide listed in Article II of the Genocide Convention have been violated by China. These acts are killing members of the group, causing serious bodily or mental harm to members of the group, deliberately inflicting on the group conditions of life calculated to bring about its physical destruction in whole or in part, imposing measures intended to prevent births within the group, and forcibly transferring children of the group to another group. Therefore, when China's policies and practices toward Uyghurs are viewed in their totality, they amount "to an intent to destroy the Uyghurs as a group, in whole or in substantial part, as such."[61] Furthermore, according to the report, "The persons and entities perpetrating the above-indicated acts of genocide are all State agents or organs—acting under the effective control of the State—manifesting an intent to destroy the Uyghurs as a group within the meaning of Article II of the Genocide Convention. This report therefore concludes that China bears State responsibility for an ongoing genocide against the Uyghurs, in breach of the Genocide Convention."[62]

As with allegations against the United States, whether the allegations against China would hold up at the ICJ is not important here. What matters is that China's Article IX reservation precludes even the possibility that China can be held legally responsible for genocide.

Impediments to the Purpose of the Genocide Convention: An Alternative Approach to the Compatibility Test

All five of the dissenting ICJ judges questioned the majority opinion concerning the compatibility test for determining the permissibility of specific reservations. Judge Alvarez argued that compatibility is a subjective standard of assessment, one in which the reserving state can claim compatibility and the objecting state can assert the opposite. In their joint dissent, the other four judges rejected the compatibility test for two reasons. First, accepting that there are compatible and incompatible reservations would involve also accepting that there are two categories of provisions in the Genocide Convention—those of minor and those of major importance. Reservations to the former would be permissible, while reservations to the latter would be prohibited. Second, the dissenting judges expressed doubt that the doctrine could work. For example, the judges write that if each party is left to individually appraise a reservation and come to its own conclusion, "a reserving State may or may not be a party to the Convention according to the different viewpoints of States which have already become parties. Under such a system, it is obvious that there will be no finality or certainty as to the status of the reserving State as a party as long as the admissibility of any reservation that has been objected to is left to subjective determination by individual States."[63]

Despite concerns about reservations, Madeline Morris writes that it is best to employ an inclusive approach, as opposed to a restrictive one. If a state ratifies a treaty but because of reservations does not work to achieve all of a treaty's purposes, this does not necessarily conflict with the treaty's object and purpose. Morris writes, "There is a difference between frustrating the purposes of a treaty and fulfilling some, but not all, of its purposes."[64] This "flexible reservations regime" is meant to maximize the number of treaty parties with various circumstances while "retaining the integrity of the treaties sufficiently for them to be meaningful and effective."[65] Of course, this is a theory of reservations, one that seems willing to accept the ideas that treaty integrity can, in fact, persevere despite the array of reservations made against it and that reservations that irrevocably damage treaty integrity will not have legal effect.

Dan Hammer argues that the benefits of allowing reservations, including those to the ICJ's jurisdiction, outweigh the costs to the integrity of the treaty.[66] Specifically, Hammer argues that "the damage of one or two states that violate the Convention and cannot be held to account is outweighed by the potential of many more states following the Convention and the resulting changes in normative international law." Such a rationale would seem to accept that more damage would be done by compelling states like the United States and China to accept the ICJ's jurisdiction (thus allowing cases to be brought against them by directly injured states, as well as by states based on a common interest in preventing genocide) than by allowing the United States and China to subvert the purpose of the Genocide Convention (the prevention of genocide and accountability for those that commit or contribute to the commission of genocide).

Mark Gibney and Kasey McCall-Smith offer alternative guidance for how to approach reservations. For Gibney, "the key is to compare state behavior against the object and purpose of the Convention."[67] McCall-Smith writes, "If the object and purpose test remains as the ultimate test of reservations permissibility, the end product of a decision using the test must be objectively identifiable."[68] A more objective system for determining the permissibility of a reservation would move away from the compatibility test to a test based on a fairly simple question: does a reservation impede fulfillment of the purpose of the Genocide Convention? Since the purpose of the convention is to prevent the crime of genocide and punish those responsible for its commission, the question then becomes: are there objectively identifiable reservations that impede the purpose of the convention by allowing state (and individual) behaviors to go unchecked? Article IX reservations unequivocally impede the prevention of genocide and shield responsible states from accountability. These reservations do so by allowing reserving states to reject the ICJ's jurisdiction over disputes concerning the responsibility of reserving states for the commission of genocide and any of its ancillary acts found in Article III. The practical impact of these reservations is clear in the impunity with which the United States and China are able to act relating to the crime of genocide.

Conclusion

Chapters 1 and 2 showed how changes made to the Genocide Convention at the behest of P-5 members have contributed to a culture of state impunity concerning the crime of genocide. The changes do so in two ways. First, the institutionalization of territorial jurisdiction for the prevention of genocide treats genocide as an internal matter for a state as long as genocide is contained within the state's territorial borders. As discussed in chapter 1, based on the ICJ's decision in *Bosnia v. Serbia*, responsibility for prevention of genocide may extend to an external state when this state wields political, financial, and/or military influence over those responsible for genocide. However, the ICJ limited preventive action to appropriate means under international law, such as withdrawing material and nonmaterial forms of support that could facilitate the commission of genocide. Second, as discussed in chapter 2, the omission of political groups from the Genocide Convention's protection and the exclusion of acts constituting cultural genocide from those prohibited made it less likely that P-5 members would be implicated in the commission of genocide. The omission of political groups and the exclusion of cultural genocide were of such significance that the Soviet Union (in the case of the former) and the United States (in the case of the latter) threatened to undermine the viability of a convention against genocide by withdrawing their support for it.

The Soviet Union and the United States continued to wield their influence over the law of genocide, with each making a case to the ICJ for why states must be permitted to make reservations to the Genocide Convention. Meanwhile, the United Kingdom made a strong case for limiting the permissibility of reservations to those that achieve unanimous acceptance. In the ICJ's majority opinion, it is abundantly clear that even among the P-5, the positions of some members carry more weight than others. This is especially true of the United States, as is evident in the fact that seven of the twelve judges who delivered the majority opinion incorporated the U.S. argument that reservations were necessary to maximize the number of state parties to the Genocide Convention.

It is noteworthy that both the Soviet Union and China (and, later, the United States) made Article IX reservations.[69] Thus, in the ICJ's advisory opinion, Article IX reservations were central. Nonetheless, in the majority opinion, ICJ judges approached the question of the permissibility of reservations as an abstract one. In explaining the majority decision to permit reservations to the Genocide Convention, the ICJ emphasized the need to allow reservations to ensure maximum state participation in the convention. The ICJ delivered this decision even though in doing so it gave states the power to opt out of the system of accountability for state responsibility for genocide established by Article IX of the Genocide Convention.

Permitting Article IX reservations conflicts with the ICJ's own claim that "parties to the Genocide Convention have a common interest to ensure that acts of genocide are prevented and that, if they occur, their authors do not enjoy impunity." The ICJ's jurisdiction is typically limited to disputes between two or more states—that is, interstate disputes between two or more states. However, because the Genocide Convention gives the ICJ jurisdiction over disputes pertaining to state responsibility for genocide and because the convention includes obligations owed to the international community as a whole, cases can be brought to the ICJ based on a common interest in the prevention and punishment of genocide, rather than based on being a directly injured party. *Bosnia v. Serbia* and *The Gambia v. Myanmar* show the potential for holding states accountable as external actors facilitating genocide and actors committing genocide against their own people. Yet neither of these cases would have been possible had Serbia and Myanmar made Article IX reservations. Thus, while it cannot be said that the United States, China, and the Soviet Union (prior to withdrawing its reservation) are the only states that enjoy impunity from responsibility for genocide and its ancillary acts, it is evident that, through their own policies and their relationships with other states, they disproportionately benefit from the permissibility of reservations to the Genocide Convention.

Chapter 4

The P-5 and Discretionary Nonapplication of the Genocide Convention

Security Council deliberations play a unique role in defining the events under that body's consideration. How events are defined at the Security Council also determines what, if any, U.N. response there will be. As discussed in previous chapters, this is because the Security Council holds the authority under Chapters VI and VII of the United Nations Charter to decide what noncoercive and coercive measures are suitable for responding to the events in question. Moreover, the P-5 exert a level of influence over Security Council deliberations unmatched by that of the nonpermanent members through the soft power they wield, as well as through their capacity to veto measures they oppose (there is no real check on this power). Hence, the P-5 also have the capacity to exercise unmatched influence over the discretionary application and nonapplication of the law as embodied by the Genocide Convention. Importantly, this control over the application and nonapplication of the Genocide Convention also has implications in terms of states responsibility for genocide and its ancillary acts. Though states need not wait for an official recognition of genocide at the Security Council to submit a case to the ICJ for adjudication, Security Council recognition would no doubt offer the ICJ political support.

In this regard, definitions matter not simply in themselves, but also because how things are defined have implications for practice. Thus, we can evaluate the changes made to the Genocide Convention discussed in chapters 1 and 2 as harmful textual deficiencies that place the power of genocide prevention in the foxes' hands and limit the legal definition to a particular set of acts against a specific set of groups, and we can stop there. Or we can consider the ways in which these changes—all of which can be traced back to the inequitable influence of P-5 members—have been exploited by the P-5 to shape events in ways that conform to their desired policy outcomes.

As the introduction briefly discusses, through their influence as permanent members and their veto power, the P-5 are able to control the narratives that form the official Security Council record of events before it. This allows the P-5 to frame events in ways that will promote or reject particular outcomes. This is especially true when it comes to suspected cases of genocide, because the Genocide Convention is a legal text that defines a crime much more limited in scope than other mass atrocity crimes—such as crimes against humanity and war crimes. Thus, when framing events, the P-5 are likely to select and highlight some facets of the events "to promote a particular interpretation, evaluation, and/or solution."[1] In other words, the P-5 will seek to situate events either within or outside the scope of the Genocide Convention, as determined by their interests. As Dirk Moses writes "Such is the genocide concept's stigmatic aura that states are reluctant to name conflicts as genocide if they are disinclined to intervene, if their clients are the perpetrators, if their enemies' clients are the victims, or if it is otherwise diplomatically inconvenient."[2] Moses continues, "The political problem is founded on a conceptual one: distinguishing genocide from non-international armed conflict (civil war: rebellion, insurgency, and belligerency) and international armed conflict (interstate war)."[3] This reframing of genocide as something other than genocide need not be a complex endeavor. Indeed, the process may be as simple as deliberately choosing not to label the events as "genocide." However, in avoiding that word, alternative labels, names, and descriptions have been used in its place.

As discussed in this book's introduction, Michel-Rolph Trouillot highlights the significance of naming events by noting that the "Castilian invasion of the Bahamas" more accurately describes the "discovery of America."[4] The former describes the uninvited and unwelcomed arrival of a group that, upon its arrival, attacks the land's inhabitants, whereas the latter portrays the arrival of a group to a land on which no human has previously set foot. Thus, Trouillot writes, "The naming of the 'fact' is itself a narrative power disguised as innocence. . . . Naming the fact thus already imposes a reading and many historical controversies boil down to who has the power to name what."[5] Comparable to the "innocence" Trouillot refers to is the idea that the Security Council's P-5 operate in good faith when naming the events that come before them. Importantly, as analysis of Security Council deliberations will show, there is no rule that precludes false depictions from having real world consequences. As David Carr aptly puts it, "some histories may be inaccurate and some stories *invraisemblable*, but nothing in principle prevents such narratives from succeeding at their aim."[6]

This chapter demonstrates connections between the power to write the content of the Genocide Convention and narrate events so as to remove them from the convention's scope. At the Security Council, the P-5 have succeeded in this by constructing narratives and using frames and names that detract from the possibility that genocide is being committed. In doing so, the P-5 have exploited the very changes they imposed on the Genocide Convention, sometimes in surprising ways. Indeed, in some cases powerful states that opposed a change to the content of the Genocide Convention have taken advantage of that change for their political benefit, while states that advocated for a change have found that the arguments they made in support of it are now being used against them.

Evidence of exploitation is located in the official record of Security Council meetings that were held to discuss cases that have since been recognized as genocide. This analysis will be primarily limited to the positions taken and the arguments made by the P-5, both because of the significant role these states played in writing the textual deficiencies described above and because they dictate what, if any, response will be taken. Of course, it is important to acknowledge that there is a constructivist element to what I am describing here that one might perceive as inconsistent with the realist position central to the preceding chapters. However, the narrative politics central to this chapter is not an alternative to the realist position, but rather an adaptation that is necessary because the P-5 cannot wholly control what events land on their doorstep. The Security Council has a mandate to maintain international peace and security. Threats thereto can easily find their way onto the Security Council's agenda. The Secretariat may include specific concerns when it prepares its tentative monthly forecast of the work for the Security Council president (a position that rotates monthly). The president, as well as other Security Council members, can also influence the body's agenda. Moreover, emergency sessions may be called as circumstances dictate. Therefore, the P-5 do not have the luxury of simply ignoring cases of genocide, as dictated by their individual interests, even when they would prefer to do so. Naming events and narrative construction, then, act as ways for the P-5 to assert their national interests within the confines of their roles as permanent Security Council members.

Before turning to case analyses, a brief summary of the changes made to the Genocide Convention during the drafting process is in order. Using their significant influence, P-5 members succeeded in establishing a form of territorial jurisdiction for genocide prevention, omitting protection for political groups, and excluding acts that constitute cultural genocide. Political alignment was not as dichotomous when it came to arguments about preventive jurisdiction as it was during debate about methods of genocide and groups protected. Territorial jurisdiction for the prevention of genocide was largely supported, including by the United States and Soviet

Union. However, the United States, France, and United Kingdom favored protection for political groups and opposed the inclusion of cultural genocide, while the Soviet Union held the opposite positions. As Hirad Abtahi and Philippa Webb note, "The rest of the UN member states followed one or the other of the above groups depending, generally, on their affiliation to them."[7]

To demonstrate the ways in which the P-5 have used the textual deficiencies negotiated into the Genocide Convention, three cases will be analyzed: Pakistan (1971), Rwanda (1994), and Bosnia (1991–1995). It should be noted that the purpose here is neither to go into substantial detail about the cases (there is a vast literature on each, especially Rwanda and Bosnia), nor to imply that the P-5 response to a case of genocide committed during the Cold War can be compared "apples to apples" to the P-5 responses to cases after the Cold War. Rather, these cases were chosen because there is a general consensus among genocide scholars that genocide, *stricto sensu*, was committed in them. Evidence of this consensus can be found in my correspondence with four scholars, my review of two other scholars' publications, and Alex Hinton's genocide studies canon.[8] These cases were also chosen because Security Council deliberations on each produced a record extensive enough for analysis.

East Pakistan: Narrating Political Conflict and Aggression

Pakistan's genocide in East Pakistan began in March 1971 and was brought to an end in December 1971.[9] Genocide was committed after contentious elections that saw candidates based in East Pakistan win the majority of seats in Pakistan's parliament. President Yahya Kahn refused to seat the new government, leading to talk of the prospect of East Pakistan's secession. On March 25, 1971, Pakistan launched Operation Searchlight. During the next eight-plus months, upward of one million people were killed, between 200,000 and 400,000 women were raped, and another ten million people were forced to seek refuge in India.[10] Kaylan Chaudhuri estimates the number of people killed as 1,247,000, based on figures for property damage, slaughterhouses, mass graves, sexually assaulted women, and skeletons found in the worst affected areas.[11] The ten million refugees, mostly Hindu, who were able to escape the violence faced "conditions of extreme hardship, and with an appalling death rate."[12] After nearly nine months, India's unilateral intervention in East Pakistan, without Security Council authorization, ended the genocidal campaign and pushed back West Pakistani forces. Pakistan surrendered in less than two weeks, signing an instrument of surrender in Dacca on December 16, 1971.

On March 28, 1971, only three days after Pakistan launched Operation Searchlight, Archer Blood, U.S. consul general in Dacca, wrote in a cable with the subject line "Selective Genocide" that Pakistan's military was "systematically eliminating" Awami League supporters "by seeking them out in their homes and shooting them down."[13] On April 6, having not received a response to his March 28 cable, Blood sent what became known as the "Blood Telegram." In it he chastised his own government for failing to take forceful measures to stop the atrocities and accused it of "bending over backwards to placate the West Pak[istan] dominated government."[14] Instead, wrote Blood, "we have chosen not to intervene, even morally, on the grounds that the Awami conflict, in which unfortunately the overworked term genocide is applicable, is purely an internal matter of a sovereign state."[15]

While Blood first used the term "genocide" to describe Pakistan's violence in East Pakistan three days after the start of Operation Searchlight, the Security Council did not meet to deliberate the case for more than eight months. The first meeting to consider "the recent deteriorating situation which has led to armed clashes between India and Pakistan" occurred on December 4, 1971.[16] In the debate, the Security Council was essentially divided into two factions: the United States and China aligned with Pakistan, and the Soviet Union aligned with India. Notably, the grounds on which Blood criticized the U.S. response highlights the practical implications of the efforts during the Genocide Convention negotiations to prevent genocide from being defined as an inherent threat to international peace and security. Blood's criticism is also applicable to the positions taken by China and Pakistan during Security Council deliberations. Furthermore, the omission of political groups from the Genocide Convention's protection (something the United States opposed and the Soviet Union supported) would also play a key part in narrating the violence in East Pakistan beyond the scope of the Genocide Convention.

Security Council Deliberations and Changes to the Genocide Convention

During Security Council deliberations, two changes that were made during the drafting of the Genocide Convention were particularly relevant. First, the failure to define genocide as an inherent threat to international peace and security, along with the rejection of the Soviet Union's argument that all suspected cases of genocide ought to be brought to the Security Council, made it easy for Pakistan, the United States, and China to repeatedly refer to the genocide (without referring to it as "genocide") as an internal matter. Second, the omission of political groups from the Genocide Convention made it easy to transform the genocide into a civil conflict in which Pakistan had responded legitimately to subversive elements based in East Pakistan. Put another way, the United States and China exploited the changes made to the Genocide Convention to pursue their interests by avoiding naming events "genocide" when one of their client states was the perpetrator.

During its participation in Security Council meetings, Pakistan sought to focus attention on the political nature of the violence, justifying its use of force in East Pakistan in ways that mirrored an argument made by Venezuela at the Ad Hoc Committee. Venezuela had argued that the inclusion of political groups in the Genocide Convention would hamper the ability of states to take "action against domestic subversive movements by possibly exposing them to unjustified accusations."[17] Pakistan claimed that it was the victim of subversive acts by armed bands and, therefore, was "entitled to take all reasonable and adequate steps to safeguard its existence and its institutions."[18] Furthermore, Pakistan asserted that it had "by no means exceeded this right in suppressing armed and terrorist bands which aimed to bring about a dismemberment of the State."[19] A direct correlation of Pakistan's framing its violence as a legitimate and proportionate response to subversives and terrorists acting within its territory is that the conflict was an internal matter. Pakistan stated this explicitly: "The nature of Pakistan's internal crisis is outside the Security Council's concern. . . . The Security Council is concerned with international peace, not with the internal peace and political life of a Member State."[20]

The United States and China similarly framed Pakistan's violence in East Pakistan as part of a civil conflict and then used India's intervention to shift the focus to India's violation of Pakistan's sovereignty. For example, the United States identified the violence in East Pakistan as "civil strife" originating in "political problems" that require a "political solution."[21] In doing so, the United States chose not to recognize genocide in East Pakistan, or even the possibility that Pakistan was committing unlawful acts other than genocide. Instead, the United States referred to a "guerrilla war" from within East Pakistan and a cross-border war between India and Pakistan. By framing violence in East Pakistan essentially as between Pakistan and both an internal insurrection and an external aggressor, the United States was able to propose that India and Pakistan "terminate their military confrontation by agreeing to an immediate cease-fire and to the immediate withdrawal of forces from foreign territories."[22] The United States also dismissed suggestions that it was taking a one-sided approach to the violence, arguing: "This has been a full-scale invasion in East Pakistan and it must stop. If people say we are favouring one side over another, they are wrong. But if they say that we insist that these invading forces go back to their own borders, they are correct."[23]

Like the United States, China referred to the political opposition in East Pakistan as "rebellious elements" and argued that allowing representatives of East Pakistan to participate in Security Council meetings "would be tantamount to asking the Security Council to interfere in the internal affairs of a sovereign State, Pakistan."[24] China also invoked the United Nations Charter, arguing that "the Security Council should surely condemn the acts of aggression by the Government of India and demand that the Indian Government immediately and unconditionally withdraw all its armed forces from Pakistan."[25] Though it played a smaller role than the United States or China during these deliberations, France also framed the violence in East Pakistan as being both a "civil war" and "a war between nations."[26] Regarding the "civil war," France said that the Security Council was faced with a dilemma. If the Security Council considered only the intrastate violence, any action it took would risk "being considered as interference in internal affairs, and we appreciate the fact that Pakistan is attached both to its sovereignty and its integrity."[27]

In its condemnation of Pakistan and its support of India, the Soviet Union simultaneously recognized the atrocities committed by Pakistan in East Pakistan and pointed to the movement of refugees from East Pakistan into India as the primary justification for India's use of force. The Soviet Union also claimed that Pakistan's and China's use of the word "rebels" to describe the population of East Pakistan was a ploy to legitimize Pakistan's violence against them.[28] Key to the Soviet position was the argument that the root causes of all the violence were Pakistan's refusal to respect the 1970 election results and its actions against the population of East Pakistan. This can be seen clearly in the following Soviet statement:

> Several speakers here have tried to convince us that it would be "unprecedented" for the Security Council to deal with this main and real cause of the conflict. Attempts have also been made to take cover behind the clause regarding so-called "non-intervention in the domestic affairs of other States". And yet it does not take much work or effort to understand quite clearly that this very phenomenon—the flight of almost 10 million people from their own country to another country in order to save their lives—is in itself an unprecedented event, and, what is more, this unprecedented event has had serious international consequences.[29]

It is evident that according to the Soviet position, Pakistan's violence was unjustified and India's intervention was justified not directly by Pakistan's violence, but by the massive flow of refugees from East Pakistan into India caused by Pakistan's violence.

India attributed to Pakistan, the United States, and China much of the blame for the failure to prevent genocide in East Pakistan. India strongly criticized the United States and China for seeking the withdrawal of Indian forces from East Pakistan. Their proposal would have required Pakistan and India to withdraw "armed personnel present on the territory of the other to their own side of the India-Pakistan borders."[30] Thus, the proposed withdrawal would have forced India to vacate East Pakistan while allowing Pakistan to maintain its presence there, as East Pakistan was still a recognized part of Pakistan and, therefore, within Pakistan's sovereign territory. India rightfully argued that such a requirement would only aid Pakistan in its violent repression of the population of East Pakistan. India asked: "A cease-fire between whom and whom? Shall we release the Pakistan soldiers by a so-called cease-fire so that they can go on a rampage and kill the civilians in Dacca, in Chittagong, and in other places?"[31]

By seeking to highlight the conflict between India and Pakistan, India accused the United States and China of attempting to "internationalize the problem" by making it an "Indo-Pakistan dispute."[32] According to India, "once it turned into an Indo-Pakistan dispute, people will forget what the Pakistan army is doing in East Pakistan."[33] India also made clear what it believed the Pakistani army was doing in East Pakistan: committing genocide. During Security Council deliberations, India accused Pakistan of genocide no less than six times and chastised the Security Council for allowing the "policy of repression and genocide" to continue "unabated over the last nine months," stating that it was "a matter of great surprise and infinite regret to us that when so many men, women and children were butchered, raped, [or] massacred, no action was taken."[34] During the Security Council's initial meeting on December 4, as the United States and China attempted to limit the discussion to the conflict between India and Pakistan, India asked, "What happened to the campaign of genocide?"[35]

Even more pertinent to this analysis of how changes to the Genocide Convention have been exploited, India suggested that Pakistan, the United States, and China selectively invoked some core principles while ignoring others: "This debate has shown that selectivity is the order of the day. Now, several principles have been quoted by various delegations: sovereignty, territorial integrity, noninterference in other peoples' affairs, and so on. But I wonder why we should be shy about speaking of human rights. What happened to the Convention on genocide?"[36] What happened to the Genocide Convention was that it had been changed in ways that made it easy for cases of genocide like the one in East Pakistan to be pushed into blind spots and loopholes that were created during the evolution of the convention's text. For example, the failure to define all cases of genocide as threats to international peace and security created a push-pull scenario. India and the Soviet Union repeatedly sought to push the violence in East Pakistan within the U.N. mandate by referring to the movement of refugees from East Pakistan into India as destabilizing and, therefore, a threat to peace. Meanwhile, Pakistan, the United States, and China similarly attempted to internationalize the violence, but for opposite reasons: they sought to paint India as an aggressor that was interfering in Pakistan's internal matters. Thus, they pulled back against Indian and Soviet efforts to fit India's intervention within the right to self-defense.

Pakistan, the United States, and China were further aided in their efforts to frame violence in East Pakistan as a civil conflict and internal matter by the omission of political groups from the Genocide Convention. It is somewhat ironic that the United States sought to exploit the omission of political groups, considering how strongly it had advocated for their inclusion during the convention's drafting process. In its attacks on the people of East Pakistan, Pakistan's military murdered members of the Awami League political group, Bengali ethnolinguistic group, and Hindu cultural-religious group.[37] The facts that a portion of the targeted individuals were members of a political group and that all the killings took place in the context of a territorially bound civil conflict created the space needed for Pakistan and its American and Chinese allies to frame genocide in Pakistan as a civil conflict that remained strictly in the realm of Pakistan's internal affairs.

This case is an example of one that inevitably found its way onto the Security Council agenda, despite there being P-5 members that would have preferred that it did not. The United States and China had vested interests in ensuring that Pakistan's actions in East Pakistan be treated as an internal matter, free of interference from the Security Council as well as India. Yet this case also demonstrates the ways in which P-5 members can adapt to the situation while continuing to pursue their narrow interests. Given the Genocide Convention's reinforcement of state sovereignty and territorial jurisdiction, the task of pushing Pakistan's genocide into the treaty's blind spot was an easy one. By failing to define genocide as an inherent threat to international peace and security, and by omitting protection for political groups, intrastate cases of genocide like that in East Pakistan can be framed as justifiable responses to political turmoil. As chapter 2 explained, the efficacy of creating false narratives finds its strength in the partial truth that the narratives contain. Furthermore, the inclusion of political groups in the Genocide Convention would have protected members of such groups (such as Awami League supporters) and made it more difficult to hide the genocide of groups protected under the Genocide Convention (such as Hindus and Bengalis) behind a narrative of civil conflict by diminishing the effectiveness of creating false narratives aimed at pushing a targeted group beyond the scope of the Genocide Convention.

Ultimately, the case of genocide in East Pakistan shows how P-5 members were able to (1) exploit the limited scope of the Genocide Convention; (2) discretionarily avoid applying the convention to Pakistan's actions in

East Pakistan; (3) work in concert when doing so was beneficial for two or more P-5 members; and (4) implicitly identify India, not Pakistan, as the rogue or outlaw state, with the latter acting on its right to defend itself against internal insurrection and external aggression and the former acting as the aggressor.

Rwanda: A Civil War with Some "Acts of Genocide"

Considering the scale of the violence in Rwanda, it is somewhat remarkable that the Security Council met as many times to discuss Pakistan and India from December 4 to December 21, 1971, as it did to discuss Rwanda from April 7 to July 14, 1994. There were ten meetings on the former case during seventeen days and ten meetings on the latter case in a period lasting more than four months. As is clear from the number of meetings and the periods of time during which the meetings were held, there were times during the genocide in Rwanda when the Security Council did not discuss it for weeks. The two longest stretches between meetings occurred from April 30 to May 16 and from May 16 to June 8. It is estimated that 157,000 people were killed in the first stretch and as many as 275,000 people were killed in the second.[38] Put differently, if the killings had taken place only during these two periods, each period would have still amounted to genocide.

The lack of Security Council engagement during the genocide in Rwanda is evidenced in more than the comparatively few meetings held on the subject. It can also be found in the length of the meetings and in the minimal participation of the P-5. Though not a perfect measure, Security Council meeting records from December 4 to December 21, 1971, fill 231 pages of text, for an average of 23.1 pages per meeting. In contrast, the ten meetings on Rwanda from April 7 to July 14, 1994, span 66 pages, or 6.6 pages per meeting. Furthermore, it was not until the fourth meeting in 1994, on May 16, that China, Russia, the United Kingdom, and the United States made their first official statements concerning Rwanda. In addition, during the meetings on Pakistan, U.S. participation filled 19.00 columns of text, compared to 6.25 columns during the meetings on Rwanda. The numbers of columns were 14.00 versus 5.00 for China, 54.25 versus 4.25 for the Soviet Union or Russia, 8.75 versus 11.00 for France, and 3.75 versus 5.00 for the United Kingdom. Indeed, even while Rwanda was on the Security Council agenda, the P-5 acted on behalf of their individual interests through a near-absolute lack of engagement, until they were no longer able to ignore what was happening.

During the ten Security Council meetings on Rwanda, six resolutions were adopted and three presidential statements authorized. Though there were differences in the details that formed P-5 positions, those positions varied little in overall substance. There was a concerted effort among the P-5 to identify what was happening in Rwanda as a civil war and to situate the deaths of hundreds of thousands of people within the context of this war—not as victims of genocide, but rather as victims of violation of the laws of war. In doing so, P-5 members framed the violence in Rwanda either implicitly or explicitly as an internal matter, a political conflict requiring a political solution, and one that involved violations of international humanitarian law. This persisted to a certain degree even after P-5 members finally labeled the atrocities as "acts of genocide" on June 8.[39]

In 1994, Rwanda was a nonpermanent member of the Security Council and therefore was able to participate in the deliberations concerning the violence in that country. Though the focus here is on the P-5, it is important to note that how members of the P-5 framed the violence was fairly consistent with the way Rwanda's U.N. representative (Augustin Bizimana) framed it. For example, in January 1994, Bizimana told the Security Council that the "entire Rwandese people have pinned their hopes on the mandate of UNAMIR [United Nations Assistance Mission for Rwanda] to put an end to the appalling war that has raged since 1 October 1990."[40] Two weeks into the genocide, on April 21, Bizimana spoke of "the resumption of hostilities" and "armed attacks" following the assassination of President Juvenal Habyarimana.[41] At this meeting, Bizimana referred to "hostilities" six times. When he referred to "massacres," he did so within the context of the civil war and as committed by the Rwandese Patriotic Front (RPF).[42] Nearly four weeks later, on May 16, Bizimana again referred to the "resumption of hostilities" and "resumption of war," and framed the massacres as the result of an "inter-ethnic war of unbelievable cruelty."[43] He added that the perpetrators of massacres throughout the "entire duration of the war, that is, since 1 October 1990," must be "identified and punished."[44]

How the P-5 would frame the violence in Rwanda became clear beginning with the second Security Council meeting on the subject, on April 21. At this meeting, France declared that there could be "no military solution" to the violence and that the Peace Agreement between the Government of the Republic of Rwanda and the Rwandan Patriotic Front [hereinafter, the Arusha Accords] remained "the only legitimate framework for seeking a political solution to the problem in Rwanda."[45] This was reflected in Resolution 912, which was unanimously adopted at the same meeting. The resolution demanded "an immediate cessation of hostilities between the forces of the Government of Rwanda and the Rwandese Patriotic Front and for an end to the mindless violence and carnage which are engulfing Rwanda."[46]

On April 30, more than three weeks into the genocide, the Security Council authorized a presidential statement that acknowledged the "slaughter of innocent civilians," but nonetheless it situated the violence as being within the war rather than outside of it by condemning "all these breaches of international humanitarian law in Rwanda, particularly those perpetrated against the civilian population."[47] The significance of this cannot be overstated. Invoking international humanitarian law makes clear how the P-5 were viewing the violence against civilian populations. International humanitarian law constitutes *lex specialis*, meaning that its specific purpose is to regulate the use of force in war and armed conflict situations. The Genocide Convention contributes to human rights law even though genocide can be committed in times of peace or war. What is important here is that, unlike war crimes, genocide is not a violation of international humanitarian law. Thus, by invoking international humanitarian law, it is clear the P-5 were not even entertaining the possibility that genocide was being committed, at least not within the Security Council.

Primarily at the behest of New Zealand, which was president of the Security Council in April 1994, the council added that "in this context," meaning violations of international humanitarian law, "the killing of members of an ethnic group with the intention of destroying such a group in whole or in part constitutes a crime punishable under international law."[48] New Zealand intended for the term "genocide" to be used here, but it had to accept the definition of genocide without use of the actual term because of P-5 pressure. Moreover, the Security Council referred to breaches of international humanitarian law, while merely recalling that killing members of a group with genocidal intent is a crime. Moving immediately away from implicit recognition of genocide, the presidential statement reiterated the Security Council's demand "for an immediate cease-fire and cessation of hostilities between the forces of the interim Government of Rwanda and the Rwandese Patriotic Front."[49]

The Security Council again invoked international humanitarian law on May 16, nearly a month and a half after the genocide began, with an estimated 325,000 people having been killed.[50] In Resolution 918, which was unanimously adopted, the Security Council expressed alarm about the reports of "systematic, widespread and flagrant violations of international humanitarian law in Rwanda, as well as other violations of the rights to life and property."[51] The resolution also mirrored the previous resolution by including the definition of genocide without using the term.[52] Despite this implicit reference to genocide, the resolution's operative clauses demanded that "all parties to the conflict immediately cease hostilities, agree to a cease-fire, and bring an end to the mindless violence and carnage engulfing Rwanda" and requested that the secretary-general "present a report as soon as possible on the investigation of serious violations of international humanitarian law committed in Rwanda during the conflict."[53] With more than 300,000 people killed, the P-5 still opted to invoke international humanitarian law rather than the Genocide Convention.

As noted above, it was not until the Security Council met on May 16 that China, Russia, the United Kingdom, and the United States made their first official statements concerning Rwanda. At this meeting and successive ones, China made clear that its position was that violence in Rwanda was part of a civil war, making it an internal matter—and thus only a political solution between the warring parties could end the violence. For example, at the May 16 meeting, China spoke of a "civil war engulfing the whole country."[54] China added that bringing the civil war to an end and implementing the Arusha Accords together was the only way for there to be a "peaceful settlement of the conflict" and restoration of "peace and stability."[55]

At the next meeting, on June 8—by when approximately 400,000–600,000 people had been killed[56] and during which a resolution was unanimously passed that referred to "acts of genocide" for the first time[57]—China continued to frame the violence as something that could be ended by reaching "a cease-fire at an early date and to bring about national reconciliation within the framework of the Arusha Peace Agreement [Arusha Accords]."[58] Additionally, China directly targeted the loophole included in the Genocide Convention that, by design, situated the convention within the existing international system based on territorial jurisdiction. According to China, "The United Nations Charter contains explicit provisions on the mandates of the Security Council. . . . The Security Council should therefore refrain from involvement in activities that go beyond its mandate. It is our consistent position that the Security Council should work in line with the purposes and principles of the United Nations Charter and with the relevant mandates."[59] Even on June 22, by which point there is little doubt that more than 600,000 people had been killed, China referred to the need for an "early settlement of the question of Rwanda" and called for an immediate "cease-fire."[60] For China, then, the situation in Rwanda should not have been on the Security Council agenda. Nonetheless, China adapted to its inclusion by naming and framing the events as shown.

Until the Security Council authorized France to intervene in Rwanda on June 22, the U.S. approach mirrored that of China (though not its directness) when it came to the role of the Security Council. In its first statement on the violence in Rwanda, made on May 16, the United States asserted that "whatever efforts the United Nations may undertake, the true key to the problems in Rwanda is in the hands of the Rwandese people."[61] The United States added that "the killing—by all parties—must stop"—not only the killing being committed "between armed combatants" but also that being committed against "unarmed civilians."[62] It can be inferred from this reference to these two types of killing that the United States was still framing the violence in Rwanda as being governed by international humanitarian law. When the Security Council reconvened to discuss Rwanda on June 8, not much had changed in the U.S. position. With more than 600,000 people having been killed, the United States referred to "thousands upon thousands who have died"; declared its hope that international efforts would stop the killings, protect "innocent civilians," and bring "the belligerent parties to a cease-fire"; and urged "a resumption of negotiations and speeding delivery of humanitarian assistance."[63]

When the United States did refer to "genocide," it did so in the same manner as was used in Resolution 925, which was passed at the meeting on June 8. The resolution and the United States both referred to "acts of genocide reported in Rwanda."[64] This is, of course, a passive way to first use the term "genocide" to describe the violence in Rwanda. One might expect this passive use to normalize the term's use at successive meetings. Yet on June 22, when France's use of force in Rwanda was authorized by the Security Council, the United States declared: "It is not necessary to catalogue once again the horrors of what has been taking place [in Rwanda], the tales of butchery, of slain orphans, nuns, mothers, hospital patients, innocent victims; it becomes almost mind-numbing. . . . Despite the demands that the killing stop, despite the expressions of outrage, reports of continuing atrocities still reach our ears."[65] Noticeably missing is the term "genocide."

When France first weighed in on the violence in Rwanda, on May 16, it called for the Government of Rwanda and the RPF to "conclude a cease-fire and to cooperate with UNAMIR to restore peace to the country."[66] On June 8, France used the term "genocide" for the first time in the Security Council's discussions of Rwanda, joining the United States. However, whereas the United States referred to "acts of genocide reported in Rwanda," France referred to massacres as being "what can only be described as genocide."[67] This, too, is a passive way to refer to genocide. Moreover, France still stressed that there could be "no military solution" and that "only a political solution can restore lasting peace and stability to Rwanda." Thus, what was necessary to end what could only have been described as genocide was "a cease-fire agreement and to resume the dialogue that must lead to national reconciliation."[68] It was not until June 22, when France received authorization to use force in Rwanda, that France observed that "one no longer hesitates to describe [the massacres] as genocide."[69]

Like the other P-5 members, the United Kingdom made its first official statement at the Security Council on May 16. When it did so, it too called for a "cease-fire" and a return to the "peace process."[70] At the next meeting, on June 8, the United Kingdom spoke in what were unequivocally understatements, referring to the "humanitarian situation" in Rwanda as "terrible" and the "crisis . . . huge," with "over a quarter of Rwanda's population . . . affected."[71] To its credit, the United Kingdom moved beyond international humanitarian law by invoking human rights, but again it understated the nature of the violations by referring to "human rights abuses in Rwanda." Even when joining the United States and France in using the term "genocide," the United Kingdom did not come to its own conclusion but rather noted "the Secretary-General's conclusion."[72] Also, like the United States, when the United Kingdom voted on June 22 to authorize France's use of force in Rwanda, the United Kingdom reverted to leaving the term "genocide" out of its description of the violence. Instead, the United Kingdom appealed to the Government of Rwanda and the RPF to "stop the fighting and seek a negotiated solution, within the framework of the Arusha agreement, to the terrible conflict which has engulfed their country."[73]

Notably, though quietly, Russia seemed in some ways to take a more assertive approach than did other P-5 members. For example, on June 8, while China was invoking the United Nations Charter, the United States was referring to "the thousands upon thousands who have died," and the United Kingdom observed that "over a quarter of Rwanda's population is affected," Russia expressed profound concern at the "killing of hundreds of thousands of people and the tragic lot of 1.5 million displaced persons and refugees."[74] Though it did not use the term "genocide," Russia also referred to "the deliberate mass extermination of innocent people."[75] Furthermore, Russia stated that "the ongoing human tragedy of Rwanda and its unprecedented scale require that the international community take urgent and effective action."[76]

According to a Rwandan proverb: "Power that does not kill, that does not seek vengeance, is, like a gourd, a fragile power."[77] "In other words," Susan Thomson writes, "a zero-sum political game does not allow for power sharing—there can only be one winner."[78] The political characteristics of the genocide in Rwanda should not be overlooked. Those characteristics aided the P-5 in their narratives that repeatedly framed the violence in Rwanda as a civil war governed by international humanitarian law. The fact that the genocide in Rwanda was intrastate further situated the violence as an internal matter.

In this regard, there are parallels between how P-5 members responded to genocide in Pakistan and Rwanda. In both cases, genocide was committed during times of political turmoil and instability. In the case of Pakistan, genocide was committed after elections in which the Awami League, located in East Pakistan, won the majority of parliamentary seats. In the case of Rwanda, the Arusha Accords represented a power-sharing agreement that required a political transition. Thus, in Pakistan and Rwanda, genocide was perpetrated by governments that were not willing to share power, whether such sharing was mandated by election or by agreement. Once again, and more in concert than in the case of Pakistan, the P-5 narrated a civil war, implicitly framed the massive number of people killed as the result of war crimes, and emphasized the violence as an internal matter that could be solved only politically. In conclusion, the P-5 adapted to Rwanda's being on the Security Council agenda by successfully using the Genocide Convention's blind spots and loopholes (which they were partly responsible for writing into the convention) to name the genocide as something else until they could no longer avoid the label—thus offering another example of the discretionary nonapplication of the law. They also succeeded in working in concert to promote their narrow and, in some cases, overlapping interests.

Bosnia: The P-5 and "Cleansing" Genocide

In March 1992, Bosnians voted overwhelmingly—though without the vote of most Bosnian Serbs, who boycotted the referendum—to secede from the former Yugoslavia. Approximately one week later, the European Union recognized Bosnia's independence. Soon thereafter, Bosnian Serbs (under the leadership of Radovan Karadžić) began a siege of Sarajevo and other cities in Bosnia. Despite the popular decision to secede, Bosnian Muslims were systematically murdered or deported in an attempt to "cleanse" Bosnian territory of anyone but Serbs as part of an effort to create a "Greater Serbia."[79] From 1992 to 1995, as many as 200,000 Muslims were killed by Bosnian Serb forces. It was not until approximately 7,000–10,000 Muslim men and boys were massacred at Srebrenica in July 1995 that a robust intervention was carried out by NATO, forcing Slobodan Milošević to sign the Dayton Peace Accords.[80]

The Security Council met regularly during the duration of the violence in the Balkans. Between 1992 and 1995, the council passed nearly sixty resolutions on the former Yugoslavia and Bosnia without a single mention of genocide. In the same period, none of the P-5 used the term "genocide" to describe the treatment of Bosnia's Muslim population. Instead, the Security Council maintained a significant imbalance of power between the aggressors (the Bosnian Serbs) and the victims (the Bosnian Muslims). Due to the already ongoing hostilities and tensions in the former Yugoslavia, the Security Council had passed an arms embargo in 1991,[81] thus ensuring a gross imbalance in military capacity between Bosnian Serbs and Muslims because the Serbs were receiving weapons from their benefactors in Serbia.[82]

So far, this chapter has shown how the omission of political groups from the Genocide Convention's protection and the failure to define all cases of genocide as inherent threats to international peace and security, when combined, have facilitated the framing of violence constituting genocide as legitimate responses to insurrection, as characteristic of violence in civil wars, and/or as internal matters of a state. However, these tactics have not been the only ones used by the P-5 in pursuit of their national interests. The exclusion of acts constituting cultural genocide also created space for the same P-5 members to avoid using the term "genocide," instead using "ethnic cleansing" to describe the violence and persecution perpetrated by Bosnian Serbs against Bosnian Muslims.

Though during the genocide in Bosnia P-5 members used some language that was similar to that in the cases discussed above, such as calling for respect for international humanitarian law and insisting that only a political settlement could end the violence, what is most interesting is how P-5 members used "ethnic cleansing" and its associated acts to avoid naming the violence and persecution in Bosnia as genocide. A U.N. commission of experts, whose creation was mandated in 1992 by the secretary-general via a Security Council resolution, defined "ethnic cleansing" initially as "rendering an area ethnically homogeneous by using force or intimidation to remove persons of given groups from the area"[83] and later as "a purposeful policy designed by one ethnic or religious group to remove by violent and terror-inspiring means the civilian population of another ethnic or religious group from certain geographic areas."[84] In terms of specific acts and coercive practices aimed at removing a population from an area, the commission of experts included murder; torture; arbitrary arrest and detention; extrajudicial executions; rape and sexual assaults; severe physical injury to civilians; confinement of civilian population in ghetto areas; forcible removal, displacement, and deportation of civilian population; deliberate military attacks or threats of attacks on civilians and civilian areas; use of civilians as human shields; destruction of property; and robbery of personal property.[85]

A comparison of the definition of "ethnic cleansing" to Raphael Lemkin's concept of genocide and the definitions of "cultural genocide" included in the Secretariat and Ad Hoc Committee Drafts of the Genocide Convention is instructive. Lemkin wrote: "Genocide has two phases: one, destruction of the national pattern of the oppressed group; the other, the imposition of the national pattern of the oppressor. This imposition, in turn, may be made upon the oppressed population which is allowed to remain or upon the territory alone, after removal of the population and the colonization by the oppressor's own nationals."[86] In Lemkin's description, an area may not necessarily be rendered entirely "ethnically homogeneous," but the objective remains the same: the taking over of an area, resettling it with the oppressor's nationals, and imposing the practices and institutions of the oppressor. As discussed above, Lemkin also played a key role in writing the Secretariat Draft of the Genocide Convention. Acts of cultural genocide in that draft included confiscation of property; forced exile of individuals representing a group's culture; systematic destruction of religious works and books printed in the group's national language; and systematic destruction of historical monuments, religious monuments, and objects of historical, artistic, or religious value. Similarly, the Ad Hoc Committee Draft of the Genocide Convention included as acts of cultural genocide the destruction or prevention of the use of libraries, museums, schools, historical monuments, places of worship, or other cultural institutions and objects of the group. These acts of cultural genocide overlap with acts of "ethnic cleansing," including forcible removal, displacement, and deportation of civilian population; destruction of property; and robbery of personal property. Thus, as shown below through an analysis of Security Council deliberations, writing cultural genocide out of the Genocide Convention and the broader disassociation of the legal definition of "genocide" from that forwarded by Lemkin (the term's creator) made it possible for the P-5 to employ the term "ethnic cleansing" rather than identify what was happening in Bosnia as what it was—genocide.

During Security Council meetings on Bosnia, "ethnic cleansing" was used hundreds of times to describe what was happening in Bosnia. It was used by every P-5 member other than China, and it was used in Security Council presidential statements and resolutions. Of course, "ethnic cleansing" is an imprecise term. It encompasses a range of acts, from direct violence against individuals' physical integrity to destruction of property. A key characteristic, as with genocide, is the group-based nature of the acts.

In addition to the repeated use of "ethnic cleansing" to describe what was happening in Bosnia, P-5 members had three other commonalities in their reaction to the situation: they all condemned the forcible removal of Bosnian Muslims from areas of Bosnia, the acquisition of territory by force, and intentional and indiscriminate attacks against civilians. The forcible removal of Bosnian Muslims was described in different, though certainly comparable, ways. For example, the United Kingdom spoke of the "forcible removal of civilian populations"[87] and France of the "forced displacement of populations."[88] The United States asserted, quoting the International Committee of the Red Cross, that detention of Bosnian Muslims was "part of a policy of forced population transfers carried out on a massive scale and marked by the systematic use of brutality."[89] Security Council resolutions also referred to "forcible expulsions and attempts to change the ethnic composition of the population"[90] and "mass forcible expulsion and deportation of civilians."[91] Most benignly, China referred multiple times simply to "displaced persons."[92]

The forced removal of Bosnian Muslims was interconnected with the acquisition of territory. The United States condemned attempts at "territorial conquest."[93] The United Kingdom similarly condemned "acquisition of territory" by force, while adding to this "alteration of borders."[94] France did the same for "military attacks" aimed at the "acquisition of territory,"[95] but it went further by expressing concern that territorial conquest could lead to "the disappearance, pure and simple," of Bosnia.[96] Presidential statements reaffirmed Bosnia's "sovereignty, territorial integrity and independence"[97] and condemned efforts toward "territorial aggrandizement"[98] or "any dissolution of the Republic of Bosnia and Herzegovina."[99]

Notably, even when attacks against civilians were recognized, it was primarily in the context of "cleansing" Bosnian areas of Muslims. For example, the United States argued: "These wanton attacks on civilians have no military justification. Their purpose is to terrorize the people of Gorazde into leaving their homes and their city. Their purpose is 'ethnic cleansing.'"[100] It is also important to note that on more than one occasion, China spoke of "huge losses of life and property."[101] Thus, as opposed to a campaign of genocide, Bosnian Serbs were using intentional and indiscriminate force not to destroy Bosnian Muslims, but rather to leave them with no choice except to leave their homes and entire areas of Bosnia. In this regard, according to the "ethnic cleansing" framing, the violence, forced removal of Muslims, destruction of property, and territorial conquest were all inextricably connected. The intent was not genocidal but territorial.

The P-5 did not name what was happening in Bosnia as genocide even though they unanimously voted to establish the International Criminal Tribunal for the Former Yugoslavia (ICTY) on May 25, 1993.[102] For two and a half years after providing the ICTY with the necessary jurisdiction to try individuals for genocide, the term "genocide" was not spoken by any of the P-5 at the Security Council. Even after the massacre at Srebrenica, the term was not used by the P-5 during the remainder of the conflict. Of course, as defined by the commission of experts and in subsequent legal proceedings, the forcible removal of a group from areas, territorial conquest, attacks against civilians (including rape), and destruction of property are all elements of ethnic cleansing. However, they also add up to genocide, especially when acts that constitute cultural genocide and Lemkin's concept of genocide are included. This was not lost on Judge Elihu Lauterpacht, who wrote in his *Bosnia v. Serbia* dissenting opinion:

> The evidence . . . indicates plainly that, in particular, the forced migration of civilians, more commonly known as "ethnic cleansing", is, in truth, part of a deliberate campaign by the Serbs to eliminate Muslim control of, and presence in, substantial parts of Bosnia-Herzegovina.

> Such being the case, it is difficult to regard the Serbian acts as other than acts of genocide in that . . . they are clearly directed against an ethnical or religious group as such, and they are intended to destroy that group, if not in whole certainly in part, to the extent necessary to ensure that that group no longer occupies the parts of Bosnia-Herzegovina coveted by the Serbs.[103]

Once again, the role the P-5 played in writing the Genocide Convention had practical implications. Cultural destruction has occurred in numerous other conflicts, but this destruction in Bosnia, combined with forced deportation of Bosnian Muslims, draws especially clear parallels to Lemkin's two phases of genocide and his concept of cultural genocide, which was reproduced in the Secretariat Draft of the Genocide Convention and, to a lesser extent, the Ad Hoc Committee Draft before being removed from the text.[104] Thus, with the exclusion of cultural genocide and the disassociation of the legal definition of genocide from Lemkin's definition, the P-5 were able to create narratives that framed the violence and persecution in Bosnia as ethnic cleansing and thus to avoid applying the law of genocide.

Perhaps more than any other, the Bosnian case also shows how the names, labels, frames, and narratives the P-5 employ are the determinant ones, even when counternarratives are widely endorsed. Put differently, the power of the P-5 is exemplified in the Bosnian case by the way in which the P-5 withstood concerted efforts by other states to change the narrative and, potentially, the outcome. Indeed, though Bosnia appeared regularly on the Security Council agenda, the P-5 were able to use their power to fend off what was a steady barrage of genocide accusations made against Bosnian Serbs. While the P-5 refused to recognize genocide in Bosnia throughout the duration of the violence, the label of genocide was repeatedly applied by nonpermanent members of the Security Council, by other states invited to hearings as nonvoting participants, and in letters addressed to the secretary-general and the president of the Security Council. Nonetheless, as the following details show, these efforts did not change the outcome.

In 1992, the P-5 were joined by nonpermanent members Austria, Belgium, Cape Verde, Ecuador, Hungary, India, Japan, Morocco, Venezuela, and Zimbabwe. In a letter dated May 20, 1992, Egypt became the first state to name what was happening in Bosnia as genocide.[105] Bosnia was next, in a letter dated May 27, 1992.[106] The first reference to events in Bosnia as genocide by nonpermanent members of the Security Council came on October 6, 1992, when both Hungary and Venezuela used the term.[107] As nonvoting participants in the discussion, Turkey,[108] Bangladesh,[109] Albania,[110] Iran,[111] and the United Arab Emirates (UAE)[112] followed Hungary and Venezuela in recognizing genocide. Specifically, the UAE called upon the Security Council to "oppose the plan of genocide and extermination,"[113] and Bangladesh said that the Security Council was allowing its decisions to be flouted by Serbia's "persisting in its policies of aggrandizement and genocide."[114]

In 1993, Austria, Belgium, Ecuador, India, and Zimbabwe were replaced by Brazil, Djibouti, New Zealand, Pakistan, and Spain as nonpermanent members of the Security Council. On May 25, Venezuela reiterated its position that Bosnian Muslims were victims of genocide.[115] Pakistan joined Venezuela in this assessment.[116] Numerous formal letters were also addressed to the Security Council by Bosnia's president and its permanent representative to the United Nations. On May 30, Bosnia's permanent representative wrote to the Security Council president: "They [the Serbian leadership] fear no reprisal from the international community. . . . . We call upon the United Nations Security Council and relevant Member States to take the 'necessary measures' to challenge and stop this latest act of aggression and genocide."[117]

In 1994, the Security Council nonpermanent members were Argentina, Brazil, the Czech Republic, Djibouti, New Zealand, Nigeria, Oman, Pakistan, Rwanda, and Spain. Though genocide was mentioned in previous Bosnian communiques to the Security Council in 1994, its letter of March 30 of that year was especially damning. It stated, "The international community has been a passive observer of the genocide, unprecedented by its scope and cruelty of its perpetration in the entire period of global peace."[118] The members of the Security Council were joined in its April 21 meeting (at its request) by representatives of Afghanistan, Albania, Algeria, Austria, Bosnia, Bulgaria, Croatia, Egypt, Finland, Greece, Hungary, Indonesia, Iran, Jordan, Malaysia, Morocco, Norway, Poland, Qatar, Saudi Arabia, Senegal, Slovenia, Sweden, Tunisia, Turkey, and the UAE. At this meeting, Afghanistan, Algeria, Bosnia, Egypt, Iran, Malaysia, Senegal, Slovenia, Tunisia, and Turkey all referred to genocide in Bosnia.[119] Bosnia urged the Security Council to stop calling for more talks, because the talks were being used as "a weapon of genocide" rather than as "a tool of peace."[120] Turkey castigated the Security Council: "On several occasions, we have voiced before this body our deep anguish over the inability of the Security Council to protect the Bosnians from genocide. . . . It is precisely the lack of such decisive action that has sent wrong signals to the aggressors that they might push the imperiled Bosnian people into practical extinction."[121] Perhaps the strongest statement came from Iran: "The fact that the Security Council has not shouldered its responsibilities in the face of continued Serbian aggression cannot be brushed aside. . . . Had the Security Council reacted promptly and vigorously when its first resolution was violated by the Serbs, the people of Bosnia and Herzegovina would not have had to face the present situation."[122]

Throughout the rest of 1994, those Security Council members and nonvoting participants that had already labeled the crimes being committed in Bosnia as genocide were joined by Pakistan,[123] Djibouti,[124] India,[125] Croatia,[126] Bangladesh,[127] Afghanistan,[128] Senegal,[129] Pakistan (again),[130] Iran,[131] and Turkey.[132] Especially strong statements emanated from Pakistan and Egypt. Pakistan stated: "Our people ask: how is it that we have allowed this genocide to be committed against defenseless Muslims? They ask: what are we doing to punish those responsible for the rape of 40,000 thousand Muslim women and young girls in Bosnia and Herzegovina?"[133] Egypt said: "This is in fact a flagrant manifestation of genocide, undertaken by the aggressor State—which enjoys significant military superiority over its neighbor. . . . The Security Council has adopted a number of resolutions under Chapter VII of the Charter. But today the problem has reached a climax, for what is at stake here is the credibility of the Council."[134]

Argentina, Brazil, the Czech Republic, Djibouti, New Zealand, Nigeria, Oman, Pakistan, Rwanda, and Spain made up the nonpermanent members of the Security Council in 1995. Of the nonpermanent members, Oman and Pakistan referred to genocide in Bosnia. They were joined in this naming by the following nonvoting participants: Bosnia,[135] Egypt,[136] Turkey,[137] and Morocco.[138] Also in 1995, Bosnia expressed its increasing desperation and its frustration with the Security Council. On March 31, Bosnia stated, "It has become a substitute for real peacemaking. After three years of this imposed rule, UNPROFOR [United Nations Protection Force] . . . must be judged a failure. Moreover, those behind the strategy of usurping UNPROFOR for the purpose of substituting it for peacemaking must be judged guilty also of allowing aggression and genocide to continue, of endangering international peace and security, and of betraying their responsibilities to this institution, the United Nations."[139] And on June 16, it stated:

> As a sovereign country facing a most brutal aggression and endeavouring to defend our peoples from premeditated genocide, we have welcomed the assistance of the United Nations mission in our Republic. Yes, this assistance was largely symptomatic relief and, as a whole, has been a poor substitute for a real remedy addressing our victimization at the hands of a relentless aggressor. . . . Maybe by rejecting those half-measures, by demanding our full rights and by calling upon the world Powers to meet their clear responsibilities in the face of aggression and genocide, we would have ultimately forced a true remedy.[140]

From 1992 to 1995, no fewer than twenty-two states named the violence and persecution inflicted in Bosnia as genocide during Security Council deliberations and proceedings. Yet not a single P-5 member did so, even as a parade of other states repeatedly used the term "genocide" in their presence. And it was the lack of use of the term by the P-5, rather than the use of it by so many other states, that drove the Security Council's agenda concerning genocide in Bosnia.

Conclusion

This chapter has demonstrated how the legal loopholes and blind spots written into the Genocide Convention by P-5 members have been exploited by the P-5 to narrate, frame, and name violence in ways that situate it outside the scope of the convention when they are unable to avoid addressing it altogether. In particular, by defining genocide as an internal matter when the crime does not cross state borders, omitting protection for political groups, and excluding acts constituting cultural genocide, the P-5 were able to frame genocide in Pakistan, Rwanda, and Bosnia as armed conflicts, thus invoking international humanitarian law as opposed to the law of genocide and implicitly naming violations of the law as aggression, war crimes, and ethnic cleansing.

Furthermore, in the cases of Pakistan and Rwanda, the political origins of the violence and the omission of political groups from the Genocide Convention created space in which P-5 members were able to emphasize the need for political settlements. Meanwhile, in the case of Bosnia, the P-5 used the fact that Bosnian Serbs were not targeting all Bosnian Muslims with direct physical violence, instead forcibly expelling significant numbers of people, to name the violence and persecution ethnic cleansing.

Together, these cases highlight the practical implications of P-5 influence over the writing and discretionary nonapplication of the Genocide Convention. It also shows how P-5 members will work in concert when their interests align. As Moses notes, at times the P-5 may be disinclined to intervene. At other times, a client state might be the perpetrator, or an enemy might be the victim. And at still other times, recognizing genocide might simply be diplomatically inconvenient.[141] Often, there will be some combination of these factors among the different P-5 members, which respond according to their individual narrow interests when cases of genocide find their way onto the Security Council's agenda. As chapter 5 shows, though the responsibility to protect doctrine addresses many of the Genocide Convention's exploited deficiencies, the ability of the P-5 to define events and the politics among P-5 members (especially with the United States, the United Kingdom, and France on one side and Russia and China on the other) continue to drive discretionary nonapplication of the responsibility to protect, except under particular circumstances.

Chapter 5

The Responsibility to Protect and P-5 Impunity

Chapters 1 and 2 showed how P-5 members ensured that elements included in the early drafts of the Genocide Convention that were counter to their interests were excluded from the text adopted by the General Assembly in December 1948. Using their significant influence, the United States and the Soviet Union took different, though parallel, tracks to ensure that the prevention of genocide rested exclusively with the state on whose territory the crime was being committed. In addition to territorial jurisdiction, the United States and the Soviet Union also worked to ensure that the types of genocide they had committed, were committing, and/or were most likely to commit in the future were erased from the text of the Genocide Convention, even going so far as to threaten to scuttle the convention if their concerns were not addressed. Along with its fellow P-5 colonial powers France and the United Kingdom, the United States succeeded in removing acts that constitute cultural genocide from the convention, and the Soviet Union succeeded in eliminating protection for political groups.

Chapter 3 showed how the ICJ bent, even if indirectly, to the threats the United States and the Soviet Union had made previously against the Genocide Convention by advising that states should be permitted to unilaterally make reservations, including those that obstruct the only enforcement measure that was firmly in place (the ICJ's authority to determine state responsibility for genocide), for the purpose of maximizing the number of state parties to the convention. Finally, chapter 4 showed how P-5 members were able to exploit the deficiencies negotiated into the Genocide Convention when their interests alone could not dictate the Security Council's agenda, by framing the Pakistan, Rwanda, and Bosnia cases in ways that situated the violence, persecution, and destruction outside the scope of the convention. When essentially forced to discuss cases that fell outside their narrow interests, P-5 members exhibited a willingness to resort to the use of alternative narratives, frames, and names to describe events in ways that avoided conflicts with their interests.

This chapter builds on the previous chapters by identifying the ways in which R2P addresses many of the deficiencies that were negotiated into the final text of the Genocide Convention. Yet the chapter also shows that, despite the efforts of the International Commission on Intervention and State Sovereignty (ICISS) to grapple with "the whole range of questions,"[1] including political ones, it is the national interests of the P-5, and not humanitarian impulses, that have determined (and will continue to do so) whether and how R2P is applied, on a case-by-case basis. Therefore, R2P is and will always be a political doctrine that cannot be salvaged even by the best of intentions, unless we are to be satisfied by yet another development that fails to challenge P-5 impunity.

This chapter begins by demonstrating how R2P fills in the Genocide Convention's gaps. It then shows how R2P is destined to be used as a political tool that is invoked in ways that create a two-track narrative. According to that narrative, the United States and the West more broadly are positioned as R2P's champions, even as they primarily invoke R2P only when doing so corresponds with their interests, while Russia and China are positioned as the villains that have constrained R2P's transformative potential. Notably, the "hero" and "villain" tracks both lead to P-5 impunity.

R2P AND THE GENOCIDE CONVENTION

Dirk Moses highlights the hierarchy of international criminal behavior, with genocide situated at the top of this hierarchy as the "crime of crimes": "Politically rather than racially defined victims are effectively assigned a lower status in the hierarchy of criminality. International law and popular culture regard genocide—and its archetype, the Holocaust—as the ultimate violation. The result is not only to trivialize war crimes and crimes against humanity, but also to exclude the aerial bombing of civilians, which likewise violates the principle of distinction, and is often deadlier."[2] As chapter 4 showed, obvious crimes that were treated as being less than genocide elicited little preventive urgency among the P-5. This is at least in part because, as Moses asserts, "The distinction between genocide and political violence blinds us to civilian destruction in general and the circumstances that produce it."[3]

In December 2001, a little more than fifty years after the Genocide Convention entered into force, the ICISS issued its report on R2P. R2P seeks to address many of the problems described in previous chapters (including territorial preventive jurisdiction, the omission of political groups, and the exclusion of cultural genocide, as well as the politics of framing and naming at the Security Council) by seeking to diminish their effectiveness. Concerning politics at the Security Council and genocide prevention, Kofi Annan—the U.N. secretary-general who issued the call to reconcile state rights with the need to protect individuals and groups against egregious human rights violations—wrote in the *Economist*:

> The tragedy of East Timor, coming so soon after that of Kosovo, has focused attention once again on the need for timely intervention by the international community when death and suffering are being inflicted on large numbers of people, and when the state nominally in charge is unable or unwilling to stop it. In Kosovo a group of states intervened without seeking authority from the United Nations Security Council. In Timor the council has now authorized intervention, but only after obtaining an invitation from Indonesia. We all hope that this will rapidly stabilize the situation, but many hundreds—probably thousands—of innocent people have already perished. As in Rwanda five years ago, the international community stands accused of doing too little, too late.[4]

Annan challenged the international community to reach a consensus on how to promote and protect state sovereignty without impeding intervention for the protection of the citizens of the world from the most severe human rights violations. In response to Annan's challenge, the Canadian government, along with a group of major foundations, established the ICISS. The ICISS wrestled "with the whole range of questions—legal, moral, operational and political—rolled up in this debate" and consulted "with the widest possible range of opinion around the world" before completing its report on the responsibility to protect.[5]

A few years later, R2P moved from a new framework to an emerging doctrine. In 2005, 150 heads of state and 41 other dignitaries, representing each of the then 191 U.N. members, convened for the World Summit in New York City to follow up on the 2000 Millennium Summit. Progress made during the 2005 summit was summarized in the World Summit Outcome Document, which was adopted by the General Assembly later in that year. Two of the articles included in the document pertained to R2P. According to Article 138, "Each individual State has the responsibility to protect its populations from genocide, war crimes, ethnic cleansing and crimes against humanity. This responsibility entails the prevention of such crimes, including their incitement, through appropriate and necessary means."[6] With their support for Article 138, members of the international community endorsed the reconceptualization of sovereignty from the unconditional right of states to enact policies free of external interference to the responsibility of states to protect their populations from crimes such as genocide. Article 139 states:

> The international community, through the United Nations, also has the responsibility to use appropriate diplomatic, humanitarian and other peaceful means, in accordance with Chapters VI and VIII of the Charter, to help protect populations from genocide, war crimes, ethnic cleansing and crimes against humanity. In this context, we are prepared to take collective action, in a timely and decisive manner, through the Security Council, in accordance with the Charter, including Chapter VII, on a case-by-case basis and in cooperation with relevant regional organizations as appropriate, should peaceful means be inadequate and national authorities are manifestly failing to protect their populations from genocide, war crimes, ethnic cleansing and crimes against humanity.[7]

With their support for Article 139, members of the international community also endorsed the responsibility of the international community to use diplomatic and other means to protect populations from genocide and other egregious violations of human rights law and humanitarian law.

Unlike the Genocide Convention, which is considered a two-pronged treaty because of its preventive and punitive elements, R2P is primarily focused on preventing genocide, as well as other mass atrocities. Thus, R2P does not need to contend with a specific intent requirement and other elements of criminal law. Additionally and relatedly, R2P was not constrained by the legal definition of genocide included in the Genocide Convention, which had a limiting effect on the definition included in the International Criminal Court's Rome Statute. Indeed, the ICISS was writing not law, but rather a report with potential normative implications. This provided the ICISS with space to develop an approach to preventing mass atrocities free of the direct influence of states motivated by their own interests. With this freedom, the ICISS closed many of the loopholes and eliminated many of the blind spots that had been negotiated into the Genocide Convention. This is most evident in R2P's grouping of genocide with other international criminal acts—specifically, crimes against humanity, war crimes, and ethnic cleansing. In doing so, at least on paper and for preventative purposes, R2P dismantles some elements of the hierarchy of international crimes.

R2P and Genocide's Status in International Law

In the preamble to the Secretariat Draft of the Genocide Convention, genocide was identified as a threat to "international order and peace" that required its prevention and punishment.[8] As chapter 1 noted, international order and peace is synonymous with international peace and security. Thus, had international order and peace been retained in the subsequent drafts of the Genocide Convention, all cases of genocide, including those committed intrastate, would have fallen within the Security Council's explicit mandate to maintain international peace and security. If we put the politics of this body aside for the moment, we can see that states committing genocide against their own populations would not have been able to claim that their acts were an internal matter, though they would certainly have argued that they were not committing genocide.[9] Instead, in the adopted text of the Genocide Convention, genocide was identified as a violation of international law, but not necessarily a threat to international peace and security. Because of this and because cases of intrastate genocide, by definition, do not constitute a threat to international peace and security, such cases remained within the exclusive jurisdiction of the territorial authority.

There were additional attempts during the Genocide Convention's negotiations to bring all cases of genocide within the Security Council's purview. Recall from chapter 1 that the Soviet Union sought to include in the convention a requirement that all suspected cases of genocide be recognized as threats to international peace and security and dealt with by the Security Council under its Chapter VI and VII powers.[10] Though the Soviet proposal was amended twice (first by France and then by Iran), the triple amendment that would have placed the General Assembly alongside the Security Council as a body to which genocide could be referred was rejected at the General Assembly's Sixth Committee by a vote of twenty-seven to thirteen, with five abstentions.

R2P closes the preventive jurisdiction loophole that was left open by the Genocide Convention's negotiating parties by grouping genocide with other mass atrocities. Like genocide, other mass atrocity crimes—such as crimes against humanity, war crimes, and ethnic cleansing—can be committed by a state against members of its own population. In addition, R2P states explicitly that "the primary responsibility for the protection of its people lies with the state itself" and that "where a population is suffering serious harm . . . and the state in question is unwilling or unable to halt or avert it, the principle of non-intervention yields to the international responsibility to protect."[11] Thus, under R2P, genocide and other mass atrocities are not internal matters: instead, they fall within the Security Council's mandate to maintain international peace and security.

R2P and the Genocide Convention's Specific Intent Requirement

Though it was not a primary focus of the first two chapters, the Genocide Convention's rigid specific intent requirement acts as another potential impediment to preventing and punishing genocide. Related to what was discussed in chapters 2 and 4, the specific intent requirement allows genocidal states to push genocide into the "shadow of war." It also allows states to ascribe a political motive to acts of genocide, thus positioning what would otherwise be genocide outside the scope of the Genocide Convention.

Arguments in support of the specific intent requirement have generally focused on the importance of mens rea for judicial proceedings. Because the Genocide Convention is both preventive and punitive, and because it was created to differentiate genocide from other crimes against humanity, the specific intent requirement is arguably essential. Adam Jones notes that most scholars and legal theorists agree that genocidal intent is an indispensable element of the crime of genocide.[12] John Quigley explains that genocidal intent is the feature that distinguishes genocide from other serious offenses: "Acts directed against human beings must be committed with an intent to destroy a group to which the immediate victims belong. . . . The act against the immediate victims must reflect a culpable state of mind in regard to the group. Thus, genocide encompasses a dual mental element: one directed against the immediate victims, and a second against the group."[13]

Josef Kunz simultaneously recognizes the difficulty in proving specific genocidal intent and its necessity. He writes, "It has been said that this specific criminal intent makes the Convention useless; that governments, less stupid than that of National Socialist Germany, will never admit the intent to destroy a group as such, but will tell the world that they are acting against traitors and so on."[14] Despite the potential difficulty of proving specific intent, Kunz argues that a specific intent requirement is necessary to distinguish genocide from other international criminal acts. Matthew Lippman echoes Kunz's sentiment but advances Kunz's recognition of the potential difficulty in proving specific intent to its logical conclusion: some planners and perpetrators of genocide will not be punished because of a failure to prove an intent to destroy the protected group. According to Lippman, "The intent requirement is thought to be essential in order to distinguish genocide from homicide. Critics complain, however, that the intent standard permits those who commit genocide to claim that they lacked the intent to exterminate the group."[15] Lippman also notes that the Genocide Convention's specific intent requirement "means that some manifestations of mass violence against some protected groups do not fall within the terms of the Treaty."[16]

Lippman's recognition that some manifestations of mass violence that satisfy the Genocide Convention's *actus reus* will fall outside the scope of the Genocide Convention is an important one when considering the impact that the specific intent requirement could have on the failure to prevent genocide. Yet Lippman does not connect the difficulty in proving specific intent for the purpose of punishing perpetrators of genocide to the purpose of preventing genocide. Lawrence LeBlanc similarly recognizes that when considering alleged cases of genocide, "arguments are likely to concentrate on the need to prove intent."[17] He continues, "This is a serious problem in applying the Convention even if . . . the number of victims may be of evidentiary value with respect to proving the necessary intent."[18]

Like Lippman, LeBlanc focuses on the problems associated with the specific intent requirement for the Genocide Convention's punishment function, but LeBlanc also makes an important point concerning the specific intent requirement and the prevention of genocide. The fact that proving intent is problematic even after many people have already been killed exemplifies how the specific intent requirement could impede recognition of genocide for the purpose of its prevention before irreparable harm has already been committed. How can the Genocide Convention be expected to be successful in achieving its purpose when such a significant impediment to genocide prevention is built into its text? Imagine a situation in which acts of genocidal violence with genocidal intent are being perpetrated against a defenseless group protected under the Genocide Convention but preventive action continues to go unauthorized because it cannot be proven that the perpetrators intend to destroy the group in whole or in part. Consider further that even if prosecutors in a criminal trial were unable to prove genocidal intent retroactively against those who perpetrated the violence, the perpetrators could still be punished for crimes against humanity. While based on the hierarchy of international crimes, the punishment would not entirely fit the crime due to the inability to prove intent, the perpetrators would nonetheless be punished. Those killed, however, would remain victims of genocide that could have been more easily prevented had the Genocide Convention included a separate intent requirement for its preventive and punitive functions.

Frank Chalk, Kurt Jonassohn, and Helen Fein have criticized the specific intent requirement because of its potential to impede the fulfillment of the Genocide Convention's preventive purpose. As they have noted, genocidal regimes are more aware now than they once were of the legal provisions of the Genocide Convention, including the specific intent requirement. The results of the Nuremberg trials provided a stark warning against maintaining a record of genocidal plans and making overt and explicit statements of intent. Jonassohn and Chalk argue that the specific intent requirement can be satisfied without explicit statements or documentation. They ask, "What elements do we look for in evaluating situations and events to determine whether we are dealing with a case of genocide?"[19] Jonassohn's and Chalk's criteria include "evidence, even if only circumstantial, of the intent of the perpetrator."[20] Their creation of a lesser intent requirement illustrates how difficult it is to conclusively prove specific intent. Jonassohn and Chalk believe that the problem of intent resolves itself using their criteria. They argue that once reliable and accurate information about the killing operations has been obtained, it can be treated as circumstantial evidence of the perpetrator's genocidal planning and intent. Jonassohn and Chalk state emphatically, "It is not plausible that a group of some considerable size is victimized by man-made means without anyone meaning to do it!"[21] Similarly, Fein writes, "I am now convinced one can demonstrate intent by showing a pattern of purposeful action, constructing a plausible prima facie case for genocide in terms of the Convention."[22]

The belief of these authors that specific intent can be proved through circumstantial evidence was later strengthened by the International Criminal Tribunal for Rwanda (ICTR). The ICTR ruled in a number of cases that circumstantial evidence can be used to prove specific intent. For example, in 2008 the ICTR's Appeals Chamber stated, "Genocide is a crime requiring specific intent, and . . . this intent may be proven through inference from the facts and circumstances of a case."[23] The ICTR also established a list of factors to be assessed when considering circumstantial evidence of specific intent. The Appeals Chamber wrote:

> The Trial Chamber, in line with the Appeals Chamber's previous holdings, stated that "the specific intent of genocide may be inferred from certain facts or indicia, including but not limited to (a) the general context of the perpetration of other culpable acts systematically directed against that same group, whether these acts were committed by the same offender or by others, (b) the scale of atrocities committed, (c) their general nature, (d) their execution in a region or a country, (e) the fact that the victims were deliberately and systematically chosen on account of their membership of a particular group, (f) the exclusion, in this regard, of members of other groups, (g) the political doctrine which gave rise to the acts referred to, (h) the repetition of destructive and discriminatory acts and (i) the perpetration of acts which violate the very foundation of the group or considered as such by their perpetrators."[24]

Allowing the use of circumstantial evidence to prove specific intent offers an improvement over rigid specific intent, especially for the purpose of punishment. It is an improvement for the purpose of punishing those suspected of planning and perpetrating genocide because it allows the trial chambers to use the scale of the atrocities committed after they have been committed as circumstantial evidence of specific intent. Therefore, for the purpose of punishment, permitting the use of circumstantial evidence to satisfy the specific intent requirement makes it more difficult for planners and perpetrators of genocide to avoid punishment by avoiding explicitly stating their intent or keeping records of it. Yet for the purpose of prevention of genocide, the essential problem related to the specific intent requirement remains. It is more difficult to prove that Group A intends to exterminate the members of Group B in whole or in part than it is to prove that Group A is acting in ways that threaten the lives of members of Group B. Thus, the specific intent requirement creates an extra burden that could impede the effective prevention of genocide. Furthermore, using circumstantial evidence to prove specific intent essentially requires that members of the targeted group be killed on a massive scale for there to be evidence of specific intent. Such irreparable harm is what the adoption of the Genocide Convention was supposedly meant to prevent.

While the Genocide Convention essentially incorporates one specific intent requirement for its dual purposes of prevention and punishment, the ICISS did not need to concern itself with international criminal law. This allowed the ICISS to focus on what ought to be the criteria for prevention without taking into consideration what impact this might have on punishment. Therefore, R2P was able to incorporate a less burdensome intent requirement without needing to separate it from the intent requirement for the purpose of punishing the crimes it seeks to prevent. R2P's intent requirement is included in its principle of a just cause threshold. This principle states: "Military intervention for human protection purposes is an exceptional and extraordinary measure. To be warranted, there must be serious and irreparable harm occurring to human beings, or imminently likely to occur, of the following kind: large scale loss of life, actual or apprehended, *with genocidal intent or not*, which is the product either of deliberate state action, or state neglect or inability to act, or a failed state situation" (emphasis added).[25]

R2P expressly eliminates the specific intent requirement present in the Genocide Convention. R2P's just cause threshold states that military intervention for human protection is warranted when there is "large scale loss of life, actual or apprehended, with genocidal intent or not." Therefore, establishing specific genocidal intent prior to taking preventive action is not a requirement under R2P.

R2P and the Genocide Convention's Omission of Political Groups

In chapters 2 and 4, I argued that the omission of political groups from the Genocide Convention's protection created a blind spot into which genocidal acts perpetrated against those groups protected by the convention can be pushed. The perpetrators of genocide can take advantage of this blind spot by creating misleading narratives that frame the deaths resulting from a policy of genocide as unfortunate collateral damage caused by politically motivated violence. As chapter 4 demonstrated, when forced to address situations that fall outside their narrow interests, the P-5 can also use this blind spot if they prefer not to recognize a case of genocide.

R2P eliminates the blind spot created by the omission of political groups from the Genocide Convention. As just noted, according to R2P's just cause threshold, military intervention for human protection is warranted when there is "large scale loss of life, actual or apprehended, with genocidal intent or not, which is the product either of deliberate state action, or state neglect or inability to act, or a failed state situation." The 2005 World Summit Outcome Document adds specificity to the ambiguous "large scale loss of life." Article 139 includes genocide, crimes against humanity, war crimes, and ethnic cleansing as acts that could involve such loss. While ethnic cleansing includes a defined group component, crimes against humanity and war crimes do not. Therefore, by grouping genocide with these crimes, the omission of political groups is addressed.

To understand this point, it is instructive to consider the Rome Statute of the International Criminal Court's definition of crimes against humanity and war crimes. The Rome Statute defines crimes against humanity as acts committed "as part of a widespread or systematic attack directed against *any* civilian population" (emphasis added).[26] Acts that constitute both crimes against humanity and acts of genocide under the Genocide Convention include murder, extermination, and enforced sterilization. Furthermore, the Rome Statute includes the following as a crime against humanity: "Persecution against any identifiable group or collectivity on political, racial, national, ethnic, cultural, religious, gender as defined in paragraph 3, or other grounds that are universally recognized as impermissible under international law, in connection with any act referred to in this paragraph or any crime within the jurisdiction of the Court."[27] Any of the acts that constitute genocide committed against any identifiable group or collectivity amount to crimes against humanity.

The Rome Statute defines war crimes as "grave breaches of the Geneva Conventions of 12 August 1949," particularly when "committed as part of a plan or policy or as part of a large-scale commission of such crimes."[28] Acts that constitute war crimes that are relevant to the crime of genocide include "willful killing," "intentionally directing attacks against the civilian population as such or against individual civilians not taking direct part in hostilities," and "intentionally using starvation of civilians as a method of warfare by depriving them of objects indispensable to their survival, including willfully impeding relief supplies as provided for under the Geneva Conventions."[29] Furthermore, the Rome Statute's definition of war crimes includes acts that constitute genocide under the Genocide Convention with no limitation on who is protected against these acts. Therefore, for the purpose of prevention, under R2P it is no longer necessary to prove that the group is protected by the Genocide Convention, thus potentially limiting the effectiveness of creating false or misleading narratives.

R2P and the Genocide Convention's Omission of Cultural Genocide

Like the omission of political groups, the exclusion of cultural genocide from the Genocide Convention created a blind spot into which cases of genocide can be pushed. The perpetrators of genocide can insist that the intent behind their human rights violations is the removal of a group and its cultural presence from a given territory. This is generally referred to as ethnic cleansing. Attempts to describe violence, persecution, and destruction as ethnic cleansing, as opposed to genocide, are addressed by R2P's just cause threshold, which includes "large scale 'ethnic cleansing', actual or apprehended, whether carried out by killing, forced expulsion, acts of terror or rape."[30] By including ethnic cleansing among those crimes that R2P aims to prevent, the omission of cultural genocide is partially corrected for by impeding the purposeful use of the crime of ethnic cleansing to avoid the application of the Genocide Convention.

The inclusion of genocide alongside crimes against humanity and war crimes completes the correction of the exclusion of cultural genocide. The Secretariat Draft defined cultural genocide as:

> Destroying the specific characteristics of the group by:
> (a) forcible transfer of children to another human group; or
> (b) forced and systematic exile of individuals representing the culture of a group; or
> (c) prohibition of the use of the national language even in private intercourse; or
> (d) systematic destruction of books printed in the national language or of religious works or prohibition of new publications; or
> (e) systematic destruction of historical or religious monuments or their diversion to alien uses, destruction or dispersion of documents and objects of historical, artistic, or religious value and of objects used in religious worship.[31]

Under the Rome Statute's definition of crimes against humanity, the deportation or transfer of populations is prohibited, as are enforced disappearances. Actions related to cultural genocide that constitute war crimes under the Rome Statute include destruction and appropriation of property not of a military necessity, unlawful deportation or transfer of persons, the transfer "by the Occupying Power of parts of its own civilian population into the territory it occupies, or the deportation or transfer of all or parts of the population of the occupied territory within or outside this territory," and "intentionally directing attacks against buildings dedicated to religion, education, art, science or charitable purposes, historic monuments . . . provided they are not military objectives."[32] As noted above concerning political groups, for the purpose of prevention, the omission of cultural genocide is addressed by R2P.

R2P and the Limitations of Territorial Preventive Jurisdiction

In chapter 1, I identified territorial jurisdiction for the prevention of genocide as a deficiency in the Genocide Convention because it makes it more difficult to prevent cases of intrastate genocide. By awarding the territorial authority with jurisdiction over the prevention of genocide within its territory, the convention tasked the authority likely to commit genocide with preventing it. R2P addresses this issue in its two core principles: "state sovereignty implies responsibility, and the primary responsibility for the protection of its people lies with the state itself," and "where a population is suffering serious harm, as a result of internal war, insurgency, repression or state failure, and the state in question is unwilling or unable to halt or avert it, the principle of non-intervention yields to the international responsibility to protect."[33]

The first principle recognizes the sovereign right of states to govern their territories, but it includes a caveat not found in the concept of sovereignty in the United Nations Charter. Under the charter, the United Nations is an organization of states "based on the principle of the sovereign equality of all its Members" and its Members "shall refrain in their international relations from the threat or use of force against the territorial integrity or political independence of any state, or in any other manner inconsistent with the Purposes of the United Nations."[34] Meanwhile, R2P's conception of sovereignty emphasizes the responsibility of the governing authority for the welfare of its population.

The second principle essentially establishes a form of subsidiary preventive jurisdiction for the enforcement of human rights protection against violations that cause severe human suffering. Together, the basic principles form the idea of an international system grounded in complementarity, meaning that the right to govern and the responsibility for a given territory rests first with the government of that territory. However, if the authority governing a given territory fails to defend and/or protect its people, the responsibility for their protection falls to the international community.

The basic principles represent two significant achievements. The first principle, by incorporating elements of social contract theory, challenges the previous conception of sovereignty: that state sovereignty equates to the right of states both to enact policies they deem necessary and to do so without external interference. Sovereignty is instead derived from the consent of the citizenry of the state and the recognition of sovereignty by the other members of the international community. The failure of a government to protect its population from serious human suffering caused by genocide or other mass atrocity crimes constitutes a breach of the contract between the state and its citizens.

The second principle is the logical extension of the first. Whereas sovereignty involves responsibility for the well-being of the people living within the sovereign territory, with the failure to protect the people due to direct state action, state negligence, or the state's inability to provide a remedy, the international community temporarily assumes responsibility for the protection of the people. Thus, R2P addresses the limitations of territorial preventive jurisdiction included in the Genocide Convention through its reconceptualization of state sovereignty and the responsibilities of the members of the international community. Furthermore, by including genocide alongside crimes against humanity, war crimes, and ethnic cleansing, all of which can be perpetrated within territorial borders, R2P indicates that it does not matter if acts of genocide are intrastate or interstate.

R2P's Practical Limitations

Those who have celebrated R2P have had reason for doing so. As shown above, R2P successfully addresses numerous deficiencies in the Genocide Convention. R2P was also incorporated into the 2005 World Summit Outcome Document, with heads of state endorsing key elements of R2P. Therefore, it is not an exaggeration to say that on paper, R2P makes it easier to act to prevent genocide. This is because R2P has pushed the evolution of our understanding of state sovereignty away from sovereignty as absolute and toward sovereignty as somewhat contingent, while also creating space in which genocide need not be recognized as such for preventive action to be taken. However, changes in discourse are not accompanied in all cases by changes in practice. Thus, the changes ushered in by R2P may not have led to changes in how the international community in general, and the P-5 in particular, respond to genocide and other mass atrocities. This raises a question: does R2P provide actual benefits when it comes to the prevention of genocide and atrocities?

As the remainder of this chapter discusses, the short answer to the above question is "no." R2P retains and even explicitly authorizes the use of practical impediments to genocide prevention. Under its principle of right authority, R2P states, "The Permanent Five members of the Security Council should agree not to apply their veto power, in matters where their vital state interests are not involved, to obstruct the passage of resolutions authorizing military intervention for human protection purposes for which there is otherwise majority support."[35]

R2P's position on the veto power exemplifies how little R2P changes the political realm, which is where decisions are made. What happens within the borders of P-5 states is vital to their interests. R2P explicitly justifies the use of the veto by the P-5 to thwart preventive action against any one of them. More important, vital state interests do not end at P-5 borders. Therefore, R2P justifies the use of the veto to preclude preventive measures against any other state that falls within the vital interests of the P-5. Thus, from the start, R2P is limited in the extent of its realistic application.

It is also important to recall the text of Article 139 of the 2005 World Summit Outcome Document. The heads of state in attendance at the 2005 World Summit explicitly endorsed a policy of genocide prevention that acknowledges beforehand that some cases of genocide will receive an effective response, while others will not. The article states, "In this context, we are prepared to take collective action, in a timely and decisive manner, through the Security Council, in accordance with the Charter, including Chapter VII, *on a case-by-case basis* . . . should peaceful means be inadequate and national authorities are manifestly failing to protect their populations from genocide, war crimes, ethnic cleansing and crimes against humanity" (emphasis added).

Despite the obvious political constraints associated with R2P and the likelihood that it will be selectively invoked, the diplomatic support that it has received has been used to make grandiose proclamations about its achievements. For example, in the context of the intervention in Libya, Alex Stark described R2P as the policy realization of the promise of "never again."[36] In contrast, Aidan Hehir questions why other cases that have warranted external intervention of some kind, such as Sri Lanka, Darfur, and the DRC, did not receive it. Hehir concludes: "If R2P meant something and had real influence, why was this? Supporters argue that R2P constitutes more than military intervention and such action is not always prudent. A more accurate explanation, however, is that the response of the 'international community' remains dependent on the interests of the P-5."[37]

Selective intervention undermines R2P and raises questions about the intent of the intervention, especially when it occurs in crises of less necessity relative to other ongoing crises. R2P is further undermined when intervention takes place against those states with poor relationships with some members of the international community but not against those states with good relationships with the same members. Yet this outcome is built into R2P and the system endorsed in 2005. Thus, while R2P did succeed in reconceptualizing sovereignty, covering all groups of peoples, removing the impediment of establishing intent prior to taking preventive action, and establishing a form of subsidiary preventive jurisdiction, it did not reform the procedures by which decision making for the purpose of preventing genocide occurs. Hehir provides an apt conclusion: "The problem with R2P is precisely that which rendered 'Never Again!' and the Genocide Convention impotent, namely that its enforcement is predicated on the assent of the Security Council. . . . Only the very naïve imagine that the P5 honour Article 24.1 of the Charter and act on behalf of UN member states; each state's respective national interest determines their position on a particular issue much more so than their commitment to legal or moral principles."[38]

Beyond Selectivity: R2P and P-5 Impunity

I noted at the beginning of this chapter that it would not only build on previous chapters by identifying the ways in which R2P addresses deficiencies in the Genocide Convention, but it would also show how R2P reinforces the ability of P-5 members to control when R2P is applied, just as P-5 members have been able to use narratives, names, and frames to control the (non)application of the Genocide Convention in ways that protect their various interests. In some ways, this is a more challenging endeavor because, as presented above in this chapter, R2P fills gaps in the Genocide Convention by situating genocide alongside rather than above other mass atrocity crimes. Yet R2P has also been used to promote a specific narrative that situates the United States, the United Kingdom, and France as upstanders, meaning states that seek to take action to prevent genocide, and Russia and China as spoilers, meaning states that seek to impede preventive action. Russia and China are typically held up as obstacles to R2P implementation. This is easily achieved both because it is typical for them to emphasize the importance of state sovereignty and because they have wielded their vetoes to block passage of resolutions invoking R2P, most notably as they relate to Syria.[39] Yet as will be shown below, it is their decision to avoid invoking R2P that contributes to their impunity, by making sure that R2P is not invoked against them. This decision also contributes to impunity for the United States, the United Kingdom, and France because they are not prone to implicating themselves.

Russia and China give narrative control to their fellow P-5 members by essentially excluding the phrase "responsibility to protect" from their vocabulary. Meanwhile, as R2P advocates, the United States, the United Kingdom, and France control the application of R2P in cases in which they have an interest. Put differently, the problem is not simply that R2P is selectively applied, but that R2P is directed toward and away from cases based on the interests of these three Western powers. Evidence of this can be found in Security Council resolutions passed between 2007 and 2020 that contained either direct or slightly fragmented reference to R2P.[40] During this period, the Security Council passed 138 resolutions that included R2P references, and 122 of those resolutions passed unanimously.[41] Neither Russia nor China authored or sponsored any of the 138 resolutions. However, Russia abstained from voting on 13 of them, and China abstained from voting on 10. Meanwhile, France drafted or sponsored 92 of the 138 resolutions. The United States did the same for 72 of the resolutions, and the United Kingdom did so for 64 of them.[42]

Clearly, France, the United States, and the United Kingdom control the R2P narrative through their overwhelming participation in dictating when R2P is invoked, coupled with the lack of participation from Russia and China beyond their Security Council votes. Because France, the United States, and the United Kingdom control the application of R2P, it is also worth noting where they have applied the doctrine. In alphabetical order, and with the number of resolutions passed in parentheses, R2P has been invoked against Burundi (five), the Central African Republic (sixteen), Chad (one), Côte d'Ivoire (nine), the DRC (twenty-eight), The Gambia (one), Guinea-Bissau (one), Lebanon (four), Liberia (eight), Libya (five), Mali (ten), Somalia (fifteen), South Sudan (seventeen), Sudan (ten), Syria (seven), and Yemen (one). Every one of these sixteen states is in the Middle East or Africa. This ought to be astounding, yet it is completely unsurprising. Invoking R2P offers moral signaling without threatening French, American, or British interests. And as long as invoking R2P does not threaten Russia's or China's interests or authorize military intervention, these resolutions are likely to pass.

Importantly, an additional element is at play. It matters not only against which states R2P is invoked, but also which states avoid having R2P invoked against them. Not a single resolution was passed against a state in a way that implicates any of the P-5 members for their actions. For example, none of the seven resolutions passed on Syria mentioned Russia or the United States, and the Yemen resolution was passed four years prior to the Saudi-led coalition's bombardment of Yemen, which has enjoyed the direct material and logistical support of the United States and the United Kingdom, among others.[43] What R2P amounts to, then, is a tool that is not only selectively brandished by three of the P-5 members but one that is also brandished only in ways that either coincide with or do not conflict with the interests of these members. Indeed, the selectivity debate fails to recognize that there might be situations in which R2P could rightfully be applied against the same three P-5 members that invoke R2P against others. Yet this possibility is foreclosed.

According to Moses, "The genocide keyword is . . . conscripted into a civilizing mission for the Global North to spread to the Global South."[44] The same can be said for R2P. Though some choose to avoid explicitly acknowledging the practical reality, it is clear that R2P is a doctrine to be invoked by the West against the rest—in particular, against states in the Global South. The idea that Global North states commit crimes that also fall within R2P's scope is an afterthought at best, despite there being obvious and documented evidence. Indeed, violence in pursuit of what Moses describes as "liberal permanent security" tends to be either legitimized or ignored, with R2P being wielded primarily against states pursuing "illiberal permanent security."[45]

As implied above, academic scholarship, including work in genocide studies, is not immune from the politics of genocide. As Moses writes, "a prominent Genocide Studies academic can reassure his readers that 'genocide contradicts traditional Western norms and approaches to law and morals,' thereby projecting criminal mass violence outward."[46] Further evidence of this can be found in my examination of cases studied by genocide scholars that have been published in *Genocide Studies and Prevention* and the *Journal of Genocide Research*. I reviewed every original research article on specific cases of genocide that had been published in the *Journal of Genocide Research* from 1999 to 2018 and in *Genocide Studies and Prevention* from 2006 to 2018. I found that 61.9 percent of the cases studied in the former periodical and 61.3 percent of the cases studied in the latter had been committed by governments that are commonly classified as authoritarian or totalitarian.[47] It goes without saying where such governments are located.

Conclusion

It is worth returning here to the question of whether R2P provides tangible benefits when it comes to genocide and atrocity prevention. As this chapter demonstrates, the potential for tangible benefits is eroded by the P-5's pursuit of their own narrow interests and their associated ability to act with impunity. Though R2P addresses many of the deficiencies that were negotiated into the final text of the Genocide Convention, its effectiveness is constrained by the politics that preceded it and that continue unabated. The doctrine does not have the capacity to remove the impunity with which the P-5 are able to operate. R2P does not alter the international system as it stood prior to the development of the doctrine. Thus, procedures for its implementation remain within a system in which the Security Council has the primary responsibility for maintaining international peace and security, recognizing threats to peace and security, and determining what kind of response (if any) will be authorized on a case-by-case basis. As Julia Hoffmann and André Nollkaemper write, "there is considerable overlap between RtoP and the Security Council agenda items relating to 'protection of civilians', conflict prevention, the peacekeeping operations obligations of third states under international humanitarian law, the Genocide

Convention and the law of international responsibility. These overlaps are not a coincidence."[48]

These overlaps have been a cause for concern for some African states. Ademola Abass writes that the opposition of African states to the Security Council's being the "right authority" to determine R2P cases and determine what response is warranted "derives from a history of costly disappointments and betrayals suffered by Africa, inflicted by the notoriously selective collective security of the UN."[49] The state subjects of R2P resolutions provide evidence that such concerns are warranted. Nonetheless, Hoffmann and Nollkaemper are optimistic that R2P "may help to enforce the normative acknowledgement that outright arbitrariness and the cynicism of selective compassion with victims of state-sponsored or tolerated mass atrocity is no longer a policy option."[50] Therefore, R2P "may lead to a strengthened effort to ground the political powers in law to incrementally remove the arbitrariness of their use."[51] While pointing out that selective application and abuse will need to be addressed, Hoffman and Nollkaemper add that the United Nations is not capable of protecting everyone everywhere. Therefore, in cases for which R2P is applicable, "some form of transparency and predictability as to when action is and is not taken is necessary."[52]

Unfortunately, discussions of selective and arbitrary application, along with the need for greater transparency, remain grounded in an outward gaze emanating primarily from the United States, the United Kingdom, and France. R2P will be applied by the P-5 only against states as determined by these three states. Thus, even if it was possible to remove the element of selectivity, doing so would not change the reality that R2P will never be invoked against these three states. As a result, the overarching R2P narrative will continue to be one in which R2P applies only to other states. Indeed, the narrative will continue not to be one in which the United States, the United Kingdom, and France are condemned for their own R2P-implicating actions, but one in which those states are condemned for not doing more to protect the populations of other states—specifically, Global South states in which they do not share responsibility for the atrocities.[53] Of course, for political reasons, Russia and China are likely to escape R2P as well. If the United States, the United Kingdom, or France were to invoke R2P against either Russia or China, they would risk the reciprocal application of R2P on them by Russia and China.[54] Thus, R2P further highlights P-5 impunity as it relates to genocide and other mass atrocity crimes. Though her account does not perfectly sum things up, Heather Roff aptly writes: "The R2P doctrine, as the UN is currently practicing it, will continue to yield unsatisfying results. States will continue to choose when to intervene selectively, and power politics and political machinations will be the order of the day."[55]

Conclusion

THE PERSISTENT OUTLAW, PERPETUAL IMPUNITY, AND THE FIELD OF GENOCIDE STUDIES

AT THE BEGINNING OF THIS BOOK, I provided a description of an ideal genocide convention based on the work of Raphael Lemkin, one with the potential to protect social collectivities in all their forms, prohibit all acts that undermine foundations of life, and universally suppress genocide by preventing and punishing the crime. I also posited that the P-5 actively worked to undermine the creation of such an ideal convention to ensure their ability to operate with impunity as concerns the crime of genocide, and that they have done the same concerning subsequent legal and normative developments. Then, throughout the five main chapters of this book, I showed how P-5 members, working sometimes in concert and at other times in conflict, (1) replaced universal preventive jurisdiction in the Genocide Convention with territorial jurisdiction, (2) omitted protection for political groups and excluded cultural genocide from the convention, (3) ensured the permissibility of Article IX reservations, (4) exploited the deficiencies they had negotiated into the convention to control its application and nonapplication, and (5) invoked R2P only when doing so did not threaten their interests. Taken cumulatively, it is clear the P-5 have pursued and largely achieved state impunity for genocide.

The implications of P-5 impunity are significant. It impacts everything from genocide prevention and punishment to justice, accountability, and historical memory. Moreover, the implications are self-perpetuating. This is especially true for the United States. When the United States escapes being subjected to the same scrutiny and accountability as those states that lack impunity, it can maintain its mythical stature as the upholder of human rights and the moral authority for determining when other states must be stopped and held to account for their actions.

THE MAKING OF OUTLAW STATES

The above myth is unmistakably present in the literature on so-called outlaw states. For example, Louis Henkin makes a number of bold and myopic proclamations. He claims that the United States "does not lightly violate accepted norms, customary or conventional," and therefore the United States has rarely committed major violations of international law.[1] As evidence of this assertion, Henkin writes, "It [the United States] did not threaten the political independence or territorial integrity of others, even while it had a monopoly of atomic power."[2] Immediately following these easily refuted claims, Henkin brings up "the deposition of President Arbenz of Guatemala," the "overthrow of Allende in Chile," the "intervention in the Dominican Republic," and the U.S. "actions in Vietnam and Cambodia."[3] Yet he does not think it necessary to reconcile these seemingly contradictory bits of information. Furthermore, these are just a few examples, and they are largely understated. Henkin omits other incidences such as the role of the United States in Indonesia's genocide and its occupation of East Timor. Nonetheless, he celebrates the U.S. respect for international law: "Particular national values and traditions will mold attitudes toward law or a particular law or obligation. Western-style democracies have tended to observe international law more than do others."[4] As José Alvarez writes in "Do Liberal States Behave Better?," "For many in the West the answer to the question posed in the title of this essay is only too obvious."[5]

Embedded in Henkin's pronouncements is the idea that liberal democracies are more observant of international law because they have respectable domestic values and institutions. Anne-Marie Slaughter makes a similar case: "Agreements concluded among liberal States are more likely to be concluded in an atmosphere of mutual trust, a precondition that will facilitate any kind of enforcement."[6] This trust emanates from the "domestic constraints"[7] placed on liberal states. Such constraints include limits on government power by domestic courts, separation of powers, the guaranteed rights of individuals, and a commitment to transparency.[8] This predominant focus on domestic institutions obscures the ways in which liberal democracies have repeatedly harmed people residing outside their territorial borders, and it shifts "attention away from the scale, character and sources of deprivation, oppression and conflict in the contemporary world."[9]

Nonetheless, this limited, if not false, conception of liberal democracies as law-abiding at home and abroad is largely the source of the idea that such states have a moral authority to intervene in illiberal states. This is exemplified in David Luban's "Just War and Human Rights."[10] At the core of Luban's conception of legitimate war for human rights is the idea that, based on their treatment of their citizens, some states lose their legitimacy and therefore their sovereignty. Meanwhile, other states retain their legitimacy by treating their citizens well. It is these latter states (that is, liberal democracies) that have the moral authority necessary to determine when other states have lost their legitimacy and require intervention by legitimate states for the protection of the illegitimate states' populations. Luban's ideas about just war for human rights can be found in R2P. They can also be found in what Benjamin Meiches refers to as the hegemonic understanding of genocide—an understanding that excludes some forms of violence, such as those that tend to be associated with settler and imperialist Western states, and instead focuses on forms of violence which are more likely to be associated with authoritarian forms of government.[11] Of course, such tunnel vision is required for liberal democracies to be viewed the way they are in many circles.

The idea that liberal democracies are in a position not only to judge but also to act against illiberal states is central to what Gerry Simpson refers to as "liberal anti-pluralism"[12]—a form of liberalism "endowed with a sort of moralistic fervor, a conviction and, at times, an intolerance of the illiberal."[13] Simpson writes that anti-pluralism is manifested in the works of Fernando Tesón, Michael Reisman, Thomas Franck, John Rawls, and Slaughter, works in which "the internal characteristics of a state has [*sic*] the potential to determine the state's standing in the Family of Nations."[14] For example, Slaughter notes that liberal theory "permits more general distinctions among different categories of states based on domestic regime types."[15] This emphasis on state compliance with or adherence to individual human rights regimes and international norms is also reflected in the concept of the outlaw state.

The criteria for an outlaw state are composed almost exclusively of ways in which states violate the rights of members of their own populations. Outlaw states, also referred to as rogue states and renegade regimes, have been identified based on their deviance from accepted international laws and norms. For example, Wolfgang Wagner, Wouter Werner, and Michal Onderco note that the "persistent deviance of 'rogue states' . . . is to a large extent defined in terms of international law, in particular the vocabulary of human rights, humanitarian law and the prohibition of aggression."[16] Meanwhile, James Christensen describes an outlaw state as "an oppressive regime that violates the basic rights of its own citizens, or an aggressive regime that wrongfully threatens the security of outsiders."[17]

Miroslav Nincic writes that international deviance "refers to a flouting of key norms of conduct espoused by the global community" and that an "international consensus has emerged on a core of inviolate human rights and on the need to restrict the concept of sovereignty . . . so as to remove a shield behind which egregious violations of human rights can hide."[18] The idea that the outlaw state uses a shield (which must be removed) is key to the traditional understanding of outlawry. States that disregard or defy the law must be compelled, by force if necessary, to comply with the law. Relatedly, John Rawls defines outlaw states as those with "regimes" that "refuse to comply with a reasonable Law of Peoples."[19] By "Law of Peoples," Rawls means "a particular political conception of right and justice that applies to the principles and norms of international law and practice."[20] For Rawls, universal human rights are intrinsic to the Law of Peoples, and outlaw states that violate human rights may be subjected to external intervention to force them to change. Jack Donnelly makes a similar case while discussing sovereign inequalities. He argues that some states are unequal sovereigns because they are outlaws, and he defines outlaw states as those that violate international norms, placing themselves outside the law and therefore becoming "liable to legitimate limitations on the exercise or enjoyment of their sovereign rights."[21] Donnelly offers Iraq and Serbia in the 1990s as examples of states whose sovereignty was legally restricted based on their criminal behavior.

The idea that outlaw states place themselves outside the law by failing to comply with it is another key element in the idea of the outlaw state. Failure to comply with some aspects of the law can result in a loss of legal protections afforded to states that maintain their compliance with the law. Taken together, states that violate international laws and norms are outlaw states. Outlaw states place themselves outside the law by these violations. States that place themselves outside the law relinquish legal protections. This is the condition of the outlaw state. However, two questions remain: who determines when a state has become an outlaw, and what should be done to force outlaws back into compliance with the law? According to Anthony Lake, the United States, as the "sole superpower," has a "special responsibility for developing a strategy to neutralize, contain and, through selective pressure, perhaps eventually transform" outlaw states into "constructive members of the international community."[22]

The lists of commonly identified outlaw states is a who's who of illiberal states. In 1994, Lake (then assistant to the president for national security affairs in the administration of President Bill Clinton) described Cuba, North Korea, Iran, Iraq, and Libya as a group of "recalcitrant and outlaw states."[23] Lake's criteria are similar to those used by others: Lake considered these five states as outlaws because of their "aggressive and defiant"[24] behavior and their attempts to thwart global progress or quarantine themselves from it. There were additional commonalities among the outlaws: (1) they were "ruled by cliques that control power through coercion"; (2) they "suppress basic human rights and promote radical ideologies"; (3) they have leaders who "share a common antipathy toward popular participation that might undermine the existing regimes"; (4) they "exhibit a chronic inability to engage constructively with the outside world"; (5) they "do not function effectively in alliances"; and (6) they "share a siege mentality."[25]

Cuba,[26] North Korea,[27] Iran,[28] Iraq,[29] and Libya[30]—along with Sudan[31] and Syria[32]—are commonly featured on lists of outlaw states. However, some lists are even more expansive, using different levels of outlawry. For example, in 2004, Robert Rotberg identified the following as the "most repressive states in the world": Belarus, Burma, Equatorial Guinea, Iran, North Korea, Saudi Arabia, Syria, Togo, Tunisia, Turkmenistan, Uzbekistan, and Zimbabwe.[33] However, Rotberg writes that "among those dangerous and despicable states," North Korea and Iran sit at the top in terms of aggression. Saudi Arabia, Uzbekistan, and Zimbabwe sit below them. Meanwhile, Belarus, Burma, Equatorial Guinea, Togo, Tunisia, and Turkmenistan "threaten their own nationals much more than they currently undermine world order." Like others, Rotberg asserts that the United States has a "responsibility to protect the weak and the preyed upon" in rogue states.[34]

The cumulative list of outlaw states makes clear that outlawry is associated with states that episodically or persistently engage in acts that violate some elements of international law. Common criteria include aggression, the sponsorship of terrorism, proliferation of weapons of mass destruction, antidemocratic governance, and lack of respect for human rights.[35] According to Donnelly, outlaw states place themselves outside the law by their noncompliance with it.[36] This is similar to the idea of the outlaw individual and their relation to the state in which they reside. As Elizabeth Anderson writes, "Traditionally, the outlaw was someone cast outside the protections of the law. . . . Modern outlawry, while not so extreme, creates classes of persons from whom some of the ordinary protections and benefits of the law are withheld or who are subject to private punishment in virtue of their membership in an outlaw class."[37]

The Persistent Outlaw as an Outlaw State

The conventional understanding of what constitutes an outlaw state is limited by its failure to look beyond behavior that violates international laws and norms to the act by some states of systematically and completely removing themselves from the reach of these same laws and norms, thus fully insulating themselves from meaningful accountability for their actions. What is described here is a persistent outlawry that few states are capable of achieving. Persistent outlawry is limited specifically to powerful states (for example, the United States and China), and it is a specific type of outlaw behavior in which the outlaws are not cast outside the protection of law by law-abiding states but rather one in which the outlaws cast the law aside.

On the face of it, casting the law aside might sound similar to Rawls's description of outlaw states as those that disregard or defy the law. The difference is the persistent outlaw does not merely ignore the law episodically, no matter how long such episodes might last. Rather, for the persistent outlaw, the law is irrelevant. According to the conventional understanding, the outlaw state can and ought to be compelled, if necessary through various coercive means, to comply with the law. However, according to this concept of a persistent outlaw, the outlaw cannot be compelled to comply with the law. Persistent outlaws act outside the reach of the law: they act with perpetual impunity.

Persistent outlawry is not defined by perpetual engagement in illegal activities, such as genocide. Rather, persistent outlawry is defined by the perpetual impunity with which persistent outlaws act domestically and/or internationally. To the persistent outlaw, the law has no real practical meaning. At times, the persistent outlaw's behavior may conform to legal standards. At other times, its behavior will offend legal standards. What is important is not compliance and noncompliance, but whether the law has any practical impact on compliance. In other words, persistent outlaws may conform their behavior to the law at times, but this is not because they are law-fearing and law-abiding states. Rather, it is because they do not deem it necessary in such times to violate the law. There are times when their goals can be achieved in ways that comply with the law, and there are other times when their goals can be achieved only in ways that violate the law. The persistent outlaw has the ability and the willingness to achieve its goals (whether by compliance or noncompliance), with the knowledge that it has insulated itself against accountability whichever route it takes.

A persistent outlaw, then, can be defined as a state that has insulated itself from the reach of the law, thus allowing it to act with impunity by violating the law at will without any fear of legal consequence. Time and again, this book has shown how the P-5 have awarded themselves various levels of impunity for genocide. However, because the United Kingdom, France, and Russia accept the ICJ's jurisdiction for cases involving allegations of state responsibility for genocide, the label of persistent outlaw best applies to the United States and China. What makes the United States unique in this regard, though, is the active role it has played in developing the laws and norms that it then exploits for its own protection from accountability.

Perpetual U.S. Impunity and the Field of Genocide Studies

The impunity with which the United States acts extends beyond the international political arena to large swaths of the field of genocide studies. This impunity is perpetuated by three mutually reinforcing elements. First, as Dirk Moses writes, the language of transgression is used by liberal states to place the "objects of condemnation beyond the realm of humanity, as 'barbarians,' 'savages,' and 'enemies of humanity,' to justify the permanent extension of their power to oppose and even eliminate them."[38] This binary language of barbarians and civilized peoples is codified in the language of the Genocide Convention: genocide is "contrary to the spirit and aims of the United Nations and condemned by the civilized world."[39] As Alexander Hinton writes, this language "implies that genocide is only carried out by barbarians and savages" and contributes to "metanarratives of progress and civilization" that "might also structure our thinking, directing our gaze to genocidal despots (Hitler, Pol Pot, Milošević, al-Bashir) and authoritarian regimes."[40] "Thus," Moses writes, "a prominent Genocide Studies academic can reassure his readers that 'genocide contradicts traditional Western norms and approaches to law and morals,' thereby projecting criminal mass violence outward."[41]

Second, when criminal violence is projected outward, some cases of genocide are foregrounded while others are backgrounded or ignored. Hinton argues that there has been a bias in genocide studies toward a genocide studies canon, formed by a disproportionate focus on cases that he labels the twentieth-century core. These include the Holocaust, Armenians, Cambodia, Rwanda, Bosnia, Darfur (in the twenty-first century), and Indigenous peoples (taken as a whole).[42] My research into which cases are the predominant focus of genocide studies scholars reinforces Hinton's canon. I found that the twentieth-century core accounted for 50 percent of cases studied in the *Journal of Genocide Research* and more than 65 percent of cases studied in *Genocide Studies and Prevention*.[43] This means that seven cases have been weighed as equal to or greater than the bottom half of the genocide studies canon, which includes fifteen specific cases as well as all Soviet cases, individual indigenous cases, settler cases, cases of antiquity, and the innumerable forgotten cases.[44] Furthermore, as I noted in chapter 5, I also found that 61.9 percent of cases studied in the *Journal of Genocide Research* and 61.3 percent of cases studied in *Genocide Studies and Prevention* were committed by governments that are commonly classified as authoritarian or totalitarian.[45]

Third, because genocide is largely committed by authoritarian or totalitarian governments, as compared to democracies or republics—which leads to a focus on a particular set of cases and the general exclusion of others—the worst that can be said about the United States is that it has not done enough to stop these authoritarian regimes from committing genocide. This is evident in the dominant narrative in genocide studies that portrays the United States as a generally well-meaning actor that needs to do more to prevent genocide by mustering the political will and leadership to act in the face of genocide and, relatedly, by making human protection a central component of its national interest. This narrative is critical of the U.S. inaction to prevent genocide but optimistic based on instances in which the United States has exhibited its leadership, as well as on the country's supposed core values. In this common narrative, the United States is portrayed as if on a continuum, moving between being a force for good in the world at one end and being a bystander to genocide at the other.

In *The United States and Genocide: (Re)Defining the Relationship*, I describe the ubiquity of this narrative as the "Samantha Power Effect."[46] In *"A Problem from Hell": America and the Age of Genocide* (which won multiple awards), Power writes,

> People have explained U.S. failures to respond to specific cases of genocide by claiming that the United States didn't know what was happening, that it knew but didn't care, or that regardless of what it knew, there was nothing useful to be done. I have found that in fact U.S. policymakers knew a great deal about the crimes being perpetrated. Some Americans cared and fought for action, making considerable personal and professional sacrifices. And the United States did have countless opportunities to mitigate and prevent slaughter. But time and again, decent men and women chose to look away. We have all been bystanders to genocide.[47]

According to Power, the absence of leadership and the political will to act to prevent genocide has left the United States "slow to muster the imagination needed to reckon with evil."[48] She makes a connection between the language of transgression, the projection of criminal violence outward, and the United States as a bystander that does not do enough to stop others from committing genocide.

Of course, Power is not alone. Madeleine Albright and William Cohen write, "As Americans consider our country's role in the world in the years to come, we are convinced that the U.S. government can and must do more to prevent genocide, a crime that threatens not only our values, but our national interests."[49] The authors argue that "America's standing in the world—and our ability to lead—is eroded when we are perceived as bystanders to genocide."[50] Hence, "A core challenge for American leaders is to persuade others—in the U.S. government, across the United States, and around the world—that preventing genocide is more than just a humanitarian aspiration; it is a national and global imperative."[51] Once again, criminal violence is projected outward, and the United States is guilty of nothing more than neglecting its good Samaritan role.

There is also a connection between the specific cases that receive disproportionate focus in genocide studies and the perpetual impunity of the United States. For example, take the cases included in Power's *"A Problem from Hell*." Power could have selected cases in which the United States wielded significant influence over states that have perpetrated genocide (such as the cases of Indonesia [1965–1966], Pakistan [1971], and Guatemala [1981–1983]), cases in which the term "bystander" does not sufficiently cover the role of the United States. Instead, Power chose to focus on cases for which the United States primarily failed to act or acted belatedly, including Cambodia [1975–1979], Rwanda [1994], and Bosnia [1995]. In doing so, Power included cases firmly situated in the twentieth-century core, while ignoring cases in the second circle (Pakistan and Guatemala) and the periphery (Indonesia).[52] This demonstrates the influence the genocide studies canon can have on how we think about and understand the role certain states play in the commission and facilitation of genocide. As Hinton argues, canonization is not value neutral but "linked to issues of power and knowledge."[53]

Significantly, Power downplays the role of the United States even in the cases she includes—such as the rise of the Khmer Rouge in Cambodia and Iraq's Kurdish genocide, which she treats as a case in which the "Reagan administration punted on genocide,"[54] thereby understating the U.S. relationship with Iraq before, during, and after the genocide. As I write in *The United States and Genocide*, the way Power describes this relationship "whitewashes the essential role the US has played in facilitating the conditions in which genocide has been committed and ignores entirely the possibility that the US could be directly responsible for the commission of genocide."[55] Indeed, using the ICJ's precedent-setting decision in *Bosnia v. Serbia* as a framework, I argue that the United States conspired in Indonesia's genocide and was complicit in Pakistan's, Guatemala's, and Iraq's.[56]

For Power and some other contributors to genocide studies, the standing of the United States in the world is affected not by what it does but by what it does not do. Thus, it is up to the United States to stop being a bystander to genocide and to bring the rest of the world along with it. Importantly, the bystander narrative has corollary implications. If the United States is merely a bystander to genocide, there is no need to contemplate the ways in which the United States has been insulated from accountability for its actions as they relate to the crime of genocide. Put differently, the portrayal of the United States as a benign bystander is not only inaccurate, but it also erases any need to consider the ways in which the United States has worked to ensure that it can act with complete impunity. If bystanding is the worst of U.S. transgressions, correction and repair does not require a reckoning via accountability for historical and, in some cases, ongoing violence at home and abroad. Instead, what is needed is a concerted effort to reshape the U.S. prevention policy. The possibility that others must be protected from the United States and that the United States must be held accountable not for its inaction but rather for its actions is rarely addressed because it has been made unthinkable.[57] Therefore, the ways in which the United States has insulated itself from accountability and continues to do so can be overlooked because the country stands beyond even the periphery of what is being studied.

For genocide studies to evolve in a progressive direction, the special status that has been awarded the United States (and states in the Global North more broadly) must be removed. Failure to do so may have three implications. First, violence committed and facilitated by the United States will fail to receive the recognition it deserves. This failure of recognition is not limited to omission from books, book chapters, and articles. There are policy implications of the work that scholars do. If scholarship that focuses on the role of the United States in genocide is treated as radical or political, it can easily be dismissed. Second, violence committed and facilitated by the United States will continue to go unprevented. The prevention of genocide is core to genocide studies. Therefore, allowing the United States to operate with impunity within the study of genocide is antithetical to the objectives of genocide studies scholars. In this regard, the first two implications work together. If genocide studies can influence policy through greater recognition of the role of the United States in committing and facilitating genocidal violence, this could increase the likelihood of preventive action being taken, if not directly against the United States but perhaps against its clients. Third, violence committed and facilitated by the United States will continue to go unpunished. This, too, is antithetical to the purpose of genocide studies. Not only will most of the individuals responsible for the violence escape prosecution, but other forms of justice will be foreclosed. This has potential implications for historical memory and related trauma. Thus, for past, present, and future generations, it is essential that genocide studies scholars do all that we can to end impunity for genocide.

Acknowledgments

Thanks to everyone at Rutgers University Press, including Alex Hinton and Nela Navarro, editors of the Genocide, Political Violence, Human Rights Series, for helping this book come to fruition.

The kind of support that is needed to complete a book project comes in many forms and from many different directions, ranging from family and friends to peers, colleagues, and students. I want to thank especially Michael Tolley, Stephen Nathanson, Denise Lapon, Eve Darian-Smith, Adam Jones, Dirk Moses, and Alex Hinton for their mentoring and support. I also want to thank Maureen Hiebert both for supporting my project when it was in its early stages by providing a favorable review of my sample chapters and for the feedback she provided that helped me improve these chapters and better situate the book in the field.

Special thanks, of course, go to my wife, Jeannie; my mom and dad; and my sisters, Jenn and Jodie.

Notes

Introduction

Epigraph: Wole Soyinka, *The Burden of Memory, the Muse of Forgiveness* (Oxford: Oxford University Press, 1999), 81–82.

1. According to Lassa Oppenheim, "States are by their nature certainly not equal as regards power, extent, constitution, and the like. But as members of the community of nations they are equals, whatever differences between them may otherwise exist" (*International Law: A Treatise*, vol. 1, 2nd ed. [London: Longmans, Green & Co., 1912], 20). This may be true to the extent that states with unequal qualities similarly find themselves in arenas of accountability. However, this is an unlikely scenario.
2. Albert Venter, "Reform of the United Nations Security Council: A Comment on the South African Position," *International Journal on World Peace* 20, no. 4 (2003): 31; Osita G. Afoaku and Okechukwu Ukaga, "United Nations Security Council Reform: A Critical Analysis of Enlargement Options," *Journal of Third World Studies* 18, no. 2 (2001): 152.
3. Venter, "Reform of the United Nations Security Council," 31.
4. From 1946 to 2020, the Soviet Union or its successor, Russia, has used its veto 118 times (90 times for the Soviet Union and 28 times for Russia), and the United States has used its veto 82 times. They are followed by the United Kingdom (29 times) and then France and China (16 times each). For an excellent study of the Security Council, see David Bosco, *Five to Rule Them All: The UN Security Council and the Making of the Modern World* (Oxford: Oxford University Press, 2009).
5. United Nations, United Nations Charter, 1945, https://www.un.org/en/about-us/un-charter/full-text.
6. See, among others, Jeffrey S. Bachman, *The United States and Genocide: (Re)Defining the Relationship* (London: Routledge, 2017); Adam Jones, *Genocide, War Crimes and the West: History and Complicity* (London: Zed Books, 2004); Marnia Lazreg, *Torture and the Twilight of Empire: From Algiers to Baghdad* (Princeton, NJ: Princeton University Press, 2016); Norman Naimark, *Stalin's Genocides* (Princeton, NJ: Princeton University Press, 2010); Sean R. Roberts, *The War on the Uyghurs: China's Internal Campaign against a Muslim Minority* (Princeton, NJ: Princeton University Press, 2020).
7. Soyinka, *The Burden of Memory, the Muse of Forgiveness*, 81–82
8. Lassa Oppenheim, *International Law*, vol. 1—Peace, 8th ed. by Hersch Lauterpacht (London: Longmans, Green & Co., 1955), 751.
9. Barry Schiller, "Life in a Symbolic Universe: Comments on the Genocide Convention and International Law," *Southwestern University Law Review* 9, no. 1, (1977): 47.

10. Payam Akhavan and René Provost, "Moving from Repression to Prevention of Genocide," in *Confronting Genocide*, ed. Payam Akhavan and René Provost (New York: Springer, 2011), 2.
11. Peter Ronayne, *Never Again? The United States and the Prevention and Punishment of Genocide since the Holocaust* (Lanham, MD: Rowman and Littlefield, 2001), 1.
12. Gareth Evans, *The Responsibility to Protect: Ending Mass Atrocities Once and for All* (Washington: Brookings Institution Press, 2008), 20.
13. Samuel Totten, email to author, September 17, 2011.
14. Mary Robinson, *Realizing Human Rights* (Oxford: Clarendon Press, 1998), 6.
15. Ramesh Thakur, *The United Nations, Peace and Security: From Collective Security to the Responsibility to Protect* (Cambridge: Cambridge University Press, 2006), 117.
16. Leo Kuper, *Genocide: Its Political Use in the Twentieth Century* (New Haven, CT: Yale University Press, 1981), 9.
17. Samantha Power, *"A Problem from Hell": America and the Age of Genocide* (New York: Basic Books, 2002), 59. Power quotes Hebert Evatt of Australia, who was president of the General Assembly at the time the Genocide Convention was adopted, as referring to this adoption as "an epoch-making event in the development of international law" (ibid.).
18. Beth Van Schaack, "The Crime of Political Genocide: Repairing the Genocide Convention's Blind Spot," *Yale Law Journal*, 106, no. 7 (1997): 2268.
19. The Secretariat Draft can be accessed at https://digitallibrary.un.org/record/611058?ln=en.
20. Douglas Irvin-Erickson, email to author, May 11, 2019.
21. Benjamin Meiches, email to author, May 10, 2019. Anton Weiss-Wendt similarly wrote, "His (compromise) proposal is rendered in the Secretariat draft of June 1947 (UN doc. E/447)" (email to author, May 13, 2019).
22. Raphael Lemkin, "Acts Constituting a General (Transnational) Danger Considered as Offences against the Law of Nations," trans. James T. Fussell, Prevent Genocide International, December 9, 2000, http://www.preventgenocide.org/lemkin/madrid1933-english.htm.
23. Donna-Lee Frieze, "Introduction: The 'Insistent Prophet,'" in Raphael Lemkin, *Totally Unofficial: The Autobiography of Raphael Lemkin*, ed. Donna-Lee Frieze (New Haven, CT: Yale University Press, 2013), xii.
24. Lemkin, "Acts Constituting a General (Transnational) Danger Considered as Offences against the Law of Nations."
25. Raphael Lemkin, *Totally Unofficial: The Autobiography of Raphael Lemkin*, ed. Donna Lee-Frieze (New Haven, CT: Yale University Press, 2013), 22.
26. Raphael Lemkin, *Axis Rule in Occupied Europe: Laws of Occupation, Analysis of Government, Proposals for Redress* (Clark, NJ: Lawbook Exchange, 2005), 79.
27. Ibid.
28. Ibid.
29. Ibid., 82–89.
30. For a full discussion of the connections among Lemkin's eight techniques of genocide, see Jeffrey Bachman, "Genocide and Imperialism," in *The Palgrave Encyclopedia of Imperialism and Anti-Imperialism*, ed. Immanuel Ness and Zak Cope (London: Palgrave Macmillan, 2019), https://link.springer.com/referencework entry/10.1007/978-3-030-29901-9_84.
31. Lemkin, *Axis Rule in Occupied Europe*, 85.
32. Weiss-Wendt, email to author.
33. United Nations, Draft Convention on the Crime of Genocide, 1947, https://digitallibrary.un.org/record/611058?ln=en.
34. United Nations, Draft Convention prepared by the Ad Hoc Committee on Genocide, 1948, http://www.preventgenocide.org/law/convention/drafts/.

35. International Court of Justice, "Reports of Judgments, Advisory Opinions and Orders: Reservations to the Convention on the Prevention and Punishment of the Crime of Genocide: Advisory Opinion of May 28th, 1951 " https://www.icj-cij.org/public/files/case-related/12/012-19510528-ADV-01-00-EN.pdf.
36. During International Court of Justice proceedings concerning reservations to the Genocide Convention, the United Kingdom questioned the utility of the Genocide Convention if it was to be "emasculated" by state reservations (International Court of Justice, "Pleadings, Oral Arguments, Documents, Reservations to the Convention on the Prevention and Punishment of the Crime of Genocide, Advisory Opinion of May 28th, 1951, Part II," 372, https://www.icj-cij.org/public/files/case-related/12/012-19510410-ORA-01-00-BI.pdf).
37. Convention on the Prevention and Punishment of the Crime of Genocide, United Nations Human Rights: Office of the High Commissioner, http://www.ohchr.org/EN/ProfessionalInterest/Pages/CrimeOfGenocide.aspx.
38. Gerry Simpson, *Great Powers and Outlaw States: Unequal Sovereigns in the International Legal Order* (Cambridge: Cambridge University Press, 2004), 49.
39. Malcolm N. Shaw, *International Law*, 7th ed. (Cambridge: Cambridge University Press, 2014), 156.
40. Ngaire Woods, "Order, Globalization, and Inequality in World Politics," in *Inequality, Globalization, and World Politics*, ed. Andrew Hurrell and Ngaire Woods (Oxford: Oxford University Press, 2002), 21.
41. Colin Warbrick, "The Principle of Sovereign Equality," in *The United Nations and the Principles of International Law: Essays in Memory of Michael Akehurst*, ed. Colin Warbrick and Vaughan Lowe (London: Routledge, 1994), 205.
42. Simpson, *Great Powers and Outlaw States*, 51.
43. Out of the 193 members of the United Nations, 152 states are parties to the Genocide Convention.
44. Michael Byers, *Custom, Power and the Power of Rules* (Cambridge: Cambridge University Press, 1999), 5.
45. Charles de Visscher, *Theory and Reality in Public International Law* (Princeton, NJ: Princeton University Press, 1957), 149.
46. Hans J. Morgenthau, *Politics among Nations: The Struggle for Power and Peace* (New York: Alfred A. Knopf, 1954), 270–271.
47. Georg Schwarzenberger, *Power Politics: A Study of World Society* (Westport, CT: Praeger, 1964), 199.
48. Simpson, Great Powers and Outlaw States, 63.
49. Ibid., 68.
50. Ibid., 67.
51. Ibid., 67–68.
52. Ibid., 68.
53. As chapter 4 discusses, the orthodox view requires unanimous acceptance of reservations for the reserving state to retain its status as a party to the treaty.
54. Simpson, *Great Powers and Outlaw States*, 68.
55. Ibid., 51.
56. Samuel Moyn (@samuelmoyn), "One other thing I learned studying law is that it is not its abuse but its use, mainly, that leads to domination and hierarchy," Twitter, December 28, 2020, https://twitter.com/samuelmoyn/status/1343530602902003713.
57. Adil Haque (@AdHaque110), "Discretionary non-application of laws is an exercise of domination and hierarchy tbh," Twitter, December 28, 2020, https://twitter.com/AdHaque110/status/1343532558894686214.
58. Robert Entman, *Projections of Power: Framing News, Public Opinion, and U.S. Foreign Policy* (Chicago: University of Chicago Press, 2004), 5. As the title of his

book makes clear, Entman is using the conception of framing in the context of media coverage of events related to U.S. foreign policy.

59. Michel-Rolph Trouillot, *Silencing the Past: Power and the Production of History* (Boston: Beacon Press, 1995), 114.
60. Ibid.
61. David Carr, "Narrative and the Real World: An Argument for Continuity," *History and Theory* 25, no. 2 (1986): 117.
62. Simpson, *Great Powers and Outlaw States*, 78.
63. Jennifer Welsh, "Taking Consequences Seriously: Objections to Humanitarian Intervention," in *Humanitarian Intervention and International Relations*, edited by Jennifer Welsh (Oxford: Oxford University Press, 2003), 63.
64. Thomas G. Weiss, "RtoP Alive and Well after Libya," *Ethics and International Affairs* 25, no. 3 (2011): 290.
65. Aidan Hehir, "The Illusion of Progress: Libya and the Future of R2P," *E-International Relations*, September 11, 2011, https://www.e-ir.info/2011/09/11/the-illusion-of-progress-libya-and-the-future-of-r2p/.

Chapter 1 Territorializing Prevention of Genocide

1. United States Office of the Secretary of Defense, "Discussion Paper: Rwanda," May 1, 1994, http://nsarchive2.gwu.edu//NSAEBB/NSAEBB356/rw050194.pdf.
2. China's draft resolution that harshly condemned the invasion was not voted on. A milder resolution sponsored by seven nonaligned states received widespread support but was opposed by the Soviet Union.
3. See, among others, Sean Murphy, *Humanitarian Intervention: The United Nations in an Evolving World Order* (Philadelphia: University of Pennsylvania Press, 1996), 99 and 104; Simon Chesterman, *Just War or Just Peace? Humanitarian Intervention and International Law* (Oxford: Oxford University Press, 2000), 73 and 80; Adam Roberts, "The United Nations and Humanitarian Intervention," in *Humanitarian Intervention and International Relations*, ed. Jennifer Welsh (Oxford: Oxford University Press, 2003), 78–79; James Mayall, "Humanitarian Intervention and International Society: Lessons from Africa," in *Humanitarian Intervention and International Relations*, ed. Jennifer Welsh, 125.
4. Mayall, "Humanitarian Intervention and International Society," 125.
5. Luke Glanville, "The Responsibility to Protect beyond Borders," *Human Rights Law Review* 12, no. 1 (2012): 8.
6. Samantha Power, *"A Problem from Hell": America and the Age of Genocide* (New York: Basic Books, 2002), 58.
7. Convention on the Prevention and Punishment of the Crime of Genocide, United Nations Human Rights: Office of the High Commissioner, http://www.ohchr.org/EN/ProfessionalInterest/Pages/CrimeOfGenocide.aspx.
8. Eyal Mayroz, "The Legal Duty to 'Prevent': After the Onset of 'Genocide,'" *Journal of Genocide Research* 14, no. 1 (2012): 81.
9. William Schabas, *Genocide in International Law: The Crime of Crimes* (Cambridge: Cambridge University Press, 2000), 72.
10. Hirad Abtahi and Philippa Webb, "Secrets and Surprises in the *Travaux Préparatoires* of the Genocide Convention," in *Arcs of Global Justice: Essays in Honor of William A. Schabas*, ed. Margaret M. deGuzman and Diane Marie Amann (Oxford: Oxford University Press, 2018), 299.
11. Ian Brownlie, *The Rule of Law in International Affairs: International Law at the Fiftieth Anniversary of the United Nations* (The Hague: Martinus Nijhoff, 1998), 287. Though he challenges this definition, Martti Koskenniemi similarly defines

Westphalian sovereignty as independence in relations between states: "independence in regard to a portion of the globe is the right to exercise therein, to the exclusion of any other States, the functions of a State" (*Sources of International Law* [Burlington, VT: Ashgate/Dartmouth, 2000], 242).

12. United Nations, United Nations Charter, 1945, https://www.un.org/en/about-us/un-charter/full-text.
13. Ibid.
14. Convention on the Prevention and Punishment of the Crime of Genocide.
15. The ICJ clarified this point in its ruling on Bosnia and Herzegovina v. Serbia and Montenegro. While defining what obligations are imposed on the Genocide Convention's contracting parties, the court observed "that what obligations the Convention imposes upon the parties to it depends on the ordinary meaning of the terms of the Convention read in their context and in the light of its object and purpose." It reviews the wording of Article I, which provides inter alia that "the Contracting Parties confirm that genocide, whether committed in time of peace or in time of war, is a crime under international law which they undertake to prevent and to punish." The court found that "Article I, in particular its undertaking to prevent, creates obligations distinct from those which appear in the subsequent Articles." See International Court of Justice. ' Reports of Judgments, Advisory Opinions and Orders: Case Concerning Application of the Convention on the Prevention and Punishment of the Crime of Genocide (Bosnia and Herzegovina v. Serbia and Montenegro), Judgment of 26 February 2007," 2007, https://www.icj-cij.org/public/files/case-related/91/091-20070226-JUD-01-00-EN.pdf.
16. Quoted in Peter Calvocoressi, *Nuremberg: The Facts, the Law and the Consequences* (New York: MacMillan, 1948), 57. For general information on the definition of crimes prosecuted at Nuremberg, see United States Holocaust Memorial Museum, "How Were the Crimes Defined?," in *Holocaust Encyclopedia*, November 5, 2020, http://www.ushmm.org/wlc/en/article.php?ModuleId=10007102.
17. Alexander Mitscherlich and Fred Mielke, "Judgment and Aftermath," in *The Nazi Doctors and the Nuremberg Code*, ed. George Annas and Michael Grodin (Oxford: Oxford University Press, 1995), 101. See also United States Holocaust Memorial Museum, "From the Indictment: Count Three—Crimes Against Humanity," https://www.ushmm.org/information/exhibitions/online-exhibitions/special-focus/doctors-trial/indictment/count-three.
18. Calvocoressi, *Nuremberg*, 57.
19. Ibid.
20. Convention on the Prevention and Punishment of the Crime of Genocide.
21. United Nations, United Nations Charter.
22. United Nations, Draft Convention on the Crime of Genocide, 1947, https://digitallibrary.un.org/record/611058?ln=en.
23. United Nations, Draft Convention prepared by the Ad Hoc Committee on Genocide, 1948, http://www.preventgenocide.org/law/convention/drafts/.
24. The use of "Law of Nations" in the Secretariat Draft is analogous to "international law." The use of the "law of nations" to refer to international law originated with Emerich de Vattel's classic work, *The Law of Nations* (Indianapolis, IN: Liberty Fund, 2009).
25. This appears to be the first time this point has been noticed or at least discussed.
26. United Nations, Draft Convention on the Crime of Genocide.
27. See Hirad Abtahi and Philippa Webb, *The Genocide Convention: The Travaux Préparatoires* (Leiden, the Netherlands: Martinus Nijhoff, 2008), 115, 124, 303, 333, and 534.

28. United Nations, Draft Convention on the Crime of Genocide.
29. Article XII states, "Irrespective of any provision in the foregoing articles, should the crimes as defined in this Convention be committed in any part of the world, or should there be serious reasons for suspecting that such crimes have been committed, *the High Contracting Parties may call upon the competent organs of the United Nation* to take measures for the suppression or prevention of such crimes" (emphasis added). Abtahi and Webb, *The Genocide Convention*, 1084.
30. Ibid.
31. Chapter VI, Article 36, Section 1, of the charter states, "The Security Council may, at any stage of a dispute of the nature referred to in Article 33 or of a situation of like nature [situations likely to endanger international peace and security], recommend appropriate procedures or methods of adjustment" (United Nations Charter).
32. Chapter VII, Article 41, of the charter states: "The Security Council may decide what measures not involving the use of armed force are to be employed to give effect to its decisions, and it may call upon the Members of the United Nations to apply such measures. These may include complete or partial interruption of economic relations and of rail, sea, air, postal, telegraphic, radio, and other means of communication, and the severance of diplomatic relations" (United Nations Charter). Chapter VII, Article 42, adds: "Should the Security Council consider that measures provided for in Article 41 would be inadequate or have proved to be inadequate, it may take such action by air, sea, or land forces as may be necessary to maintain or restore international peace and security. Such action may include demonstrations, blockade, and other operations by air, sea, or land forces of Members of the United Nations" (United Nations Charter).
33. Quoted in Abtahi and Webb, *The Genocide Convention*, 248.
34. Ibid.
35. Ibid.
36. This was not a roll-call vote. It is likely that Poland joined the Soviet Union, voting in favor of making the Security Council the United Nations organ to which all genocide referrals should be made. If my assumption is accurate, it would mean China, France, Lebanon, the United States, and Venezuela voted against the Soviet proposal.
37. Quoted in Abtahi and Webb, *The Genocide Convention*, 1007.
38. This was not a roll-call vote. It is likely that the Soviet Union was the lone no vote and that Poland abstained. Therefore, China would have been joined in support of its resolution by France, Lebanon, the United States, and Venezuela.
39. "Any signatory" was replaced with "any party" in Article VIII of the Revised Ad Hoc Committee Draft (United Nations, Draft Convention prepared by the Ad Hoc Committee on Genocide).
40. The General Assembly's Sixth Committee deals primarily with international legal matters. All United Nations members are permitted to participate in Sixth Committee proceedings.
41. Quoted in Abtahi and Webb, *The Genocide Convention*, 1734.
42. Quoted in ibid., 1735.
43. Quoted in ibid.
44. Quoted in ibid., 1743.
45. Anton Weiss-Wendt asserts that the Soviet Union strongly advocated its position because "the Security Council would be an ideal sounding board since any action adverse to the USSR could be vetoed" (*The Soviet Union and the Gutting of the UN Genocide Convention* [Madison: University of Wisconsin Press, 2017], 83).
46. Quoted in Abtahi and Webb, *The Genocide Convention*, 1750.

47. Hans Morgenthau's criticism of territorial sovereignty in relation to the Armenian genocide is relevant here. According to Morgenthau, "Technically, of course, I had no right to interfere. According to the cold-blooded legalities of the situation, the treatment of Turkish subjects by the Turkish government was purely a domestic affair" (quoted in Leo Kuper, *Genocide: Its Political Use in the Twentieth Century* [New Haven, CT: Yale University Press, 1981], 161).
48. As noted above, Article 42 of the charter states: "Should the Security Council consider that measures provided for in Article 41 would be inadequate or have proved to be inadequate, it may take such action by air, sea, or land forces as may be necessary to maintain or restore international peace and security. Such action may include demonstrations, blockade, and other operations by air, sea, or land forces of Members of the United Nations." Article 51 states, "Nothing in the present Charter shall impair the inherent right of individual or collective self-defense if an armed attack occurs against a Member of the United Nations, until the Security Council has taken measures necessary to maintain international peace and security. Measures taken by Members in the exercise of this right of self-defense shall be immediately reported to the Security Council and shall not in any way affect the authority and responsibility of the Security Council under the present Charter to take at any time such action as it deems necessary in order to maintain or restore international peace and security" (United Nations Charter). Article 2(4) states, "All Members shall refrain in their international relations from the threat or use of force against the territorial integrity or political independence of any state, or in any other manner inconsistent with the Purposes of the United Nations" (United Nations Charter).
49. Convention on the Prevention and Punishment of the Crime of Genocide.
50. This interpretation is limited to the combination of the language in the United Nations Charter and the Genocide Convention. As will be discussed in chapter 5 of this book, endorsement of R2P principles by world leaders revises the Security Council's authority as it pertains to intrastate violence, including genocide.
51. Convention on the Prevention and Punishment of the Crime of Genocide.
52. The Soviet Union referred to Article XII of the adopted text of the Genocide Convention as the "colonial clause" (quoted in Abtahi and Webb, *The Genocide Convention*, 1816).
53. Convention on the Prevention and Punishment of the Crime of Genocide.
54. For a further discussion of the extraterritorial application of human rights law, see, among others, Orna Ben-Naftali, "The Extraterritorial Application of Human Rights to Occupied Territories," *American Society of International Law Proceedings* 100 (March 29–April 1 2006): 90–95; Michael Dennis, "Application of Human Rights Treaties Extraterritorially during Times of Armed Conflict and Military Occupation," *American Society of International Law Proceedings* 100 (March29–April 1 2006): 86–90; Cordula Droege, "The Interplay between International Humanitarian Law and International Human Rights Law in Situations of Armed Conflict," *Israeli Law Review* 40, no. 2 (2007): 310–355; Noam Lubell, *Extraterritorial Use of Force against Non-State Actors* (Oxford: Oxford University Press, 2012).
55. Below I go into greater detail about the role of historical context in the development of the Genocide Convention, but it is important to note here that Article XII, written when the world was still in the colonial era, seems to exemplify the influence that considerations of national interest had on the convention's development.
56. As Abtahi and Webb point out, the Secretariat Draft contained a stronger emphasis on prevention than its successors did ("Secrets and Surprises in the *Travaux Préparatoires* of the Genocide Convention," 312).

57. For the common domestic legislature requirement, see United Nations, Draft Convention on the Crime of Genocide [Secretariat Draft], Article VI, and United Nations, Draft Convention prepared by the Ad Hoc Committee on Genocide [Ad Hoc Committee Draft], Article V.
58. United Nations, Draft Convention on the Crime of Genocide.
59. United Nations, Draft Convention prepared by the Ad Hoc Committee on Genocide.
60. Abtahi and Webb, *The Genocide Convention*, 535.
61. Quoted in ibid., 1815.
62. Quoted in ibid., 1816.
63. Quoted in ibid.
64. Quoted in ibid.
65. Quoted in ibid., 1817.
66. Quoted in ibid.
67. Quoted in ibid.
68. Quoted in ibid., 1818.
69. Ibid., 2028.
70. For the entire debate on Article XII, see Abtahi and Webb, *The Genocide Convention*, 1814–1823.
71. For a discussion of the connections between colonization, decolonization, and genocide, see Kuper, *Genocide*. Relatedly, Muhammad el-Farra argues that Algerian resistance to continued colonization was met with genocidal violence: "Entire villages are shelled, bombed, or burned; acts of genocide are committed against the inhabitants of towns and villages; an indiscriminate campaign of extermination is now taking place. . . . These are acts of genocide committed against people whose only crime is their love for liberty and their desire to preserve their own culture" ("The Algerian Tragedy," *Africa Today* 3, no. 4 [1956]: 7).
72. Quoted in Abtahi and Webb, *The Genocide Convention*, 1715.
73. Ibid., 1716.
74. Ibid.
75. Quoted in ibid., 1721.
76. Ibid.
77. Quoted in ibid., 1717.
78. Convention on the Prevention and Punishment of the Crime of Genocide.
79. International Court of Justice, Statute of the International Court of Justice, 1945, https://www.icj-cij.org/en/statute.
80. United Nations Charter.
81. Abtahi and Webb, *The Genocide Convention*, 525.
82. Ibid.
83. In fact, human rights treaties created after the Genocide Convention regularly include a treaty body that can consider individual complaints—of course, only with the state's prior consent.
84. According to William Schabas, in the case of *Bosnia v. Serbia*, the ICJ "made a major pronouncement on the duty to prevent genocide, declaring that this obligation, set out in exceedingly laconic terms both in the title and in art. 1 of the 1948 UNCG [United Nations Convention on the Prevention and Punishment of the Crime of Genocide], requires states to take action when genocide is threatened outside their own territory, to the extent that they may be able to exercise some influence. . . . The court's approach to the duty to prevent genocide dovetails neatly with recent developments in the political bodies of the United Nations recognizing a 'responsibility to protect,' and it provides further support for the entrenchment of this doctrine within customary international law" ("Genocide and the International Court of Justice: Finally, a Duty to Prevent the Crime of Crimes," *Genocide Studies and*

Prevention 2, no. 2 [2007]: 102). This is true to the extent that (1) action is limited to that which does not violate the sovereign territory of another state, and (2) the responsibility to protect is actionable only through the existing channels regarding the use of force—that is, through the Security Council..

85. In a review of a previous iteration of the ideas in this chapter, an anonymous referee incorrectly claimed that the ICJ "found that all states had a duty to prevent the genocide in Srebrenica." However, the same referee correctly noted that the duty to prevent genocide "was bounded by the remainder of international law—the implication being that Article 1 provides no authority for unilateral humanitarian intervention."
86. International Court of Justice, "Application of the Convention on the Prevention and Punishment of the Crime of Genocide (Bosnia and Herzegovina v. Serbia and Montenegro): Summary of the Judgment of 26 February 2007," https://www.icj-cij.org/public/files/case-related/91/13687.pdf.
87. Ibid. The ICJ also confirmed that the Genocide Convention's entry into force did not impose upon the "international community" (ibid.) an obligation to prevent genocide. Rather, the ICJ determined that such an obligation is limited to the authority that maintains control over the territory upon which genocide is being planned and/or committed.
88. Ibid.
89. Ibid.
90. Ibid.
91. Ibid.
92. For in-depth analysis of the concept of state responsibility for international crimes, see Nina H. B. Jørgensen, *The Responsibility of States for International Crimes* (Oxford: Oxford University Press, 2001); Antonio Cassese, *International Criminal Law* (Oxford: Oxford University Press, 2008).
93. International Law Commission, "Responsibility of States for Internationally Wrongful Acts," 2001, https://legal.un.org/ilc/texts/instruments/english/draft_articles/9_6_2001.pdf.
94. Ibid.
95. International Court of Justice, "Application of the Convention on the Prevention and Punishment of the Crime of Genocide (Bosnia and Herzegovina v. Serbia and Montenegro)."
96. Ibid.
97. Anja Seibert-Fohr, "State Responsibility for Genocide under the Genocide Convention," in *The UN Genocide Convention: A Commentary*, ed. Paola Gaeta (Oxford: Oxford University Press, 2009), 371.
98. Ibid., 363.
99. Quoted in Errol Harris, "The Problem of Sovereignty in International Relations," in *Philosophical Challenges and Opportunities of Globalization*, ed. Obliva Blanchette, Tomonobu Imamichi, and George F. Mclean (Washington: Council for Research in Values and Philosophy, 2002), 376.
100. Matthew Lippman, "The Convention on the Prevention and Punishment of the Crime of Genocide: Fifty Years Later," *Arizona Journal of International and Comparative Law* 15, no. 2 (1998): 505.
101. Ibid.

Chapter 2 Redefining the Crime of Genocide for Reasons of State

1. Beth Van Schaack, "The Crime of Political Genocide: Repairing the Genocide Convention's Blind Spot," *Yale Law Journal* 106, no. 7 (1997): 2268.

2. On the omission of political groups, see, among others, Van Schaack, "The Crime of Political Genocide"; Matthew Lippman, "The 1948 Convention on the Prevention and Punishment of the Crime of Genocide: Forty-Five Years Later," *Temple International and Comparative Law Journal* 8, no. 1 (1994): 1–84; David Nersessian, *Genocide and Political Groups* (Oxford: Oxford University Press, 2010); John Quigley, *The Genocide Convention: An International Law Analysis* (Burlington, VT: Ashgate, 2006); William Schabas, *Genocide in International Law: The Crime of Crimes* (Cambridge: Cambridge University Press, 2000). For significant details about the role of the Soviet Union, see Anton Weiss-Wendt, *The Soviet Union and the Gutting of the UN Genocide Convention* (Madison: University of Wisconsin Press, 2017). On the exclusion of cultural genocide from the Genocide Convention's prohibitions, see, among others, Lawrence Davidson, *Cultural Genocide* (New Brunswick, NJ: Rutgers University Press, 2012); Elisa Novic, *The Concept of Cultural Genocide: An International Law Perspective* (Oxford: Oxford University Press, 2016); A. Dirk Moses, "Raphael Lemkin, Culture, and the Concept of Genocide," in *The Oxford Handbook of Genocide Studies*, ed. Donald Bloxham and A. Dirk Moses, 19–41 (Oxford: Oxford University Press, 2010); Jeffrey Bachman, *Cultural Genocide: Law, Politics, and Global Manifestations* (London: Routledge, 2019).
3. Regarding Lemkin's flexibility on protection for political groups, see, among others, Weiss-Wendt, *The Soviet Union and the Gutting of the UN Genocide Convention*.
4. Hirad Abtahi and Philippa Webb, "Secrets and Surprises in the *Travaux Préparatoires* of the Genocide Convention," in *Arcs of Global Justice: Essays in Honor of William A. Schabas*, ed. Margaret M. deGuzman and Diane Marie Amann (Oxford: Oxford University Press, 2018), 305.
5. Ward Churchill writes that, in excluding cultural genocide from the Genocide Convention, the United States succeeded in "a maneuver serving to exempt a range of its own dirty linen from scrutiny" (*A Little Matter of Genocide: Holocaust and Denial in the Americas, 1492 to the Present* [San Francisco: City Lights Books, 1997], 365). However, this certainly also applies to the Soviet Union's efforts to omit protection for political groups.
6. Van Schaack, "The Crime of Political Genocide," 2261.
7. Ibid., 2268.
8. Lippman supports a broad expansion of the groups protected under the Genocide Convention, but he also supports a more modest and widely acceptable proposal that would add only political groups to those already protected ("The 1948 Convention on the Prevention and Punishment of the Crime of Genocide," 75).
9. Ibid.
10. Lawrence LeBlanc, *The United States and the Genocide Convention* (Durham, NC: Duke University Press, 1991), 85.
11. Quoted in Raphael Lemkin, *Totally Unofficial: The Autobiography of Raphael Lemkin*, ed. Donna Lee-Frieze (New Haven, CT: Yale University Press, 2013), 161. A slightly different account is provided by Douglas Irvin-Erickson, who wrote that the Brazilian ambassador told Lemkin that "some of the revolutions which happen in our countries could be classified as destruction of political groups and we would not like to have our internal difficulties aired all the time by international bodies" (*Raphael Lemkin and the Concept of Genocide* [Philadelphia: University of Pennsylvania Press, 2016], 180). This last point is also relevant to the issues discussed in chapter 1 of this book.
12. This, too, is a position consistent with that offered by some Latin American countries. For example, the Venezuelan ambassador told Lemkin, "Political

groups are nowhere defined. They are indefinable. They lack permanency and consistency" (quoted in Lemkin, *Totally Unofficial*, 161).

13. LeBlanc, *The United States and the Genocide Convention*, 87.
14. Ibid., 85.
15. Ibid., 87.
16. Ibid.
17. Jeffrey Bachman, *The United States and Genocide: (Re)Defining the Relationship* (London: Routledge, 2017), 25–26.
18. For detailed accounts of genocide in East Pakistan, see, among others, Suhail Islam and Syed Hassan, "The Wretched of the Nations: The West's Role in Human Rights Violations in the Bangladesh War of Independence," in *Genocide, War Crimes and the West: History and Complicity*, ed. Adam Jones, 201–213 (London: Zed Books, 2004); Gary J. Bass, *The Blood Telegram: Nixon, Kissinger, and a Forgotten Genocide* (New York: Vintage Books, 2013); Srinath Raghavan, *1971: A Global History of the Creation of Bangladesh* (Cambridge, MA: Harvard University Press, 2013). Similar dynamics were present during deliberations over genocide in Cambodia, Iraq, Bosnia, and Rwanda. Especially in the latter three cases, the "fog" produced by the armed conflicts made it possible for some states to deny clear knowledge about what was happening and to promote cease-fires and political settlements.
19. Simon Chesterman cites at least one million people killed and up to ten million refugees (*Just War or Just Peace? Humanitarian Intervention and International Law* [Oxford: Oxford University Press, 2000], 72). Ben Kiernan cites a range of 300,000–1,000,000 people killed (*Blood and Soil: A World History of Genocide and Extermination from Sparta to Darfur* [New Haven, CT: Yale University Press, 2007], 572). Islam and Hassan cite an even greater range, from hundreds of thousands to as many as 3,000,000 dead ("The Wretched of the Nations," 205). Samantha Power cites 1,000,000–2,000,000 people killed and the rape of 200,000 girls and women (*"A Problem from Hell": American and the Age of Genocide* [New York: Basic Books, 2002], 82).
20. Quoted in Bass, *The Blood Telegram*, 58.
21. Bachman, *The United States and Genocide*, 97–98.
22. See, among others, Van Schaack, "The Crime of Political Genocide"; Lippman, "The 1948 Convention on the Prevention and Punishment of the Crime of Genocide"; LeBlanc, *The United States and the Genocide Convention*; Nersessian, *Genocide and Political Groups*; Quigley, *The Genocide Convention*; Schabas, *Genocide in International Law*. For significant details about the role of the Soviet Union, see Weiss-Wendt, *The Soviet Union and the Gutting of the UN Genocide Convention*. See also Lawrence LeBlanc, "The United Nations Genocide Convention and Political Groups: Should the United States Propose an Amendment?" *Yale Journal of International Law* 2, no. 3 (1988): 268–295.
23. United Nations General Assembly, "The Crime of Genocide," 1946, https://digitallibrary.un.org/record/209873?ln=en.
24. United Nations, Draft Convention on the Crime of Genocide, 1947, https://digitallibrary.un.org/record/611058?ln=en.
25. United Nations, Draft Convention prepared by the Ad Hoc Committee on Genocide, 1948, http://www.preventgenocide.org/law/convention/drafts/.
26. Raphael Lemkin, "Genocide," *American Scholar* 15, no. 2 (1946): 229.
27. Raphael Lemkin, "Acts Constituting a General (Transnational) Danger Considered as Offences against the Law of Nations," trans. James T. Fussell, Prevent Genocide International, December 9, 2000, www.preventgenocide.org/emkin /madrid1933-english.htmemkin.

28. Raphael Lemkin, *Axis Rule in Occupied Europe: Laws of Occupation, Analysis of Government, Proposals for Redress* (Clark, NJ: Lawbook Exchange, 2005), 79.
29. Ibid.
30. Raphael Lemkin, "Genocide: A Modern Crime," *Free World* 4 (April 1945): 39.
31. Raphael Lemkin, "The Nature of Genocide," n.d., 14, folder 2, box 2, Raphaël Lemkin Collection, P-154, American Jewish Historical Society, New York.
32. Lemkin, *Totally Unofficial*, 152.
33. Quoted in ibid., 157.
34. Ibid.
35. Irvin-Erickson, *Raphael Lemkin and the Concept of Genocide*, 180.
36. Quoted in Weiss-Wendt, *The Soviet Union and the Gutting of the UN Genocide Convention*, 101.
37. Ibid.
38. Anton Weiss-Wendt, "Hostage of Politics: Raphael Lemkin on 'Soviet Genocide,'" *Journal of Genocide Research* 7, no. 4 (2005): 551.
39. Hirad Abtahi and Philippa Webb, *The Genocide Convention: The Travaux Préparatoires* (Leiden, the Netherlands: Martinus Nijhoff, 2008), 229.
40. Quoted in ibid., 230.
41. Quoted in ibid.
42. Quoted in ibid., 161.
43. Quoted in ibid.
44. Quoted in ibid., 1041.
45. Examples are China and Brazil (ibid., 702 and 1238, respectively).
46. An example is Venezuela (ibid., 1312).
47. Ibid., 1314.
48. Ibid., 1393–1394.
49. Ibid., 718–719.
50. Ibid., 1392.
51. Schabas, *Genocide in International Law*, 138.
52. Quoted in ibid., 139.
53. Though Lemkin was more frustrated by the exclusion of cultural genocide, which he referred to as "the most important part of the Convention" (quoted in Moses, "Raphael Lemkin, Culture, and the Concept of Genocide," 37), the genocide studies literature, broadly speaking, has been more critical of the omission of political groups.
54. Van Schaack, "The Crime of Political Genocide," 2268.
55. Nersessian, *Genocide and Political Groups*, 62.
56. Ibid.
57. Ibid., 63.
58. The Soviet Union was joined in opposition by its satellites, which supported Soviet positions at a near-perfect rate, and numerous Latin American states. One Latin American delegate explained the general opposition to the inclusion of political groups: "On our continent, we are always having a revolution. Then we dance a rumba and forget it. But if this treaty includes political groups, the loser of the revolution can claim before the world that the winner violated the genocide pact and must be punished" (quoted in Weiss-Wendt, *The Soviet Union and the Gutting of the UN Genocide Convention*, 99).
59. Power, *"A Problem from Hell,"* 69.
60. Stephen Feinstein, "Understanding the 'G' Word," in *Will Genocide Ever End?*, ed. Carol Rittner, John Roth, and James Smith (St. Paul, MN: Paragon House, 2002), 41.
61. Leo Kuper, *Genocide: Its Political Use in the Twentieth Century* (New Haven, CT: Yale University Press, 1981), 97.
62. Nersessian, *Genocide and Political Groups*, 106.

63. Relatedly, Weiss-Wendt writes, "In accordance with the basic principle of American diplomacy, the US opposed anything that the USSR favoured" ("Hostage of Politics," 554).
64. Matthew Lippman, "The Convention on the Prevention and Punishment of the Crime of Genocide: Fifty Years Later," *Arizona Journal of International and Comparative Law* 15, no. 2 (1998): 452.
65. See, among others, Power, *A Problem from Hell*; Irvin-Erickson, *Raphael Lemkin and the Concept of Genocide*; Weiss-Wendt, *The Soviet Union and the Gutting of the UN Genocide Convention*; LeBlanc, *The United States and the Genocide Convention*.
66. LeBlanc, *The United States and the Genocide Convention*, 41–42.
67. For a detailed analysis of the U.S. role in what is referred to as genocide, see Bachman, *The United States and Genocide*, 78–96. See also Douglas Kammen and Katharine McGregor, "Introduction: The Contours of Mass Violence in Indonesia, 1965–68," in *The Contours of Mass Violence in Indonesia, 1965–1968*, ed. Douglas Kammen and Katharine McGregor (Honolulu: University of Hawaii Press, 2012), 1–24; Benedict Anderson, *Violence and the State in Suharto's Indonesia* (Ithaca, NY: Cornell University Press, 2009); Helen Fein, "Revolutionary and Antirevolutionary Genocides: A Comparison of State Murders in Democratic Kampuchea, 1975 to 1979, and in Indonesia, 1965 to 1966," *Comparative Studies in Society and History* 35, no. 4 (1993): 796–823; Robert Cribb, "Genocide in Indonesia, 1965–1966," *Journal of Genocide Research* 3, no. 2 (2001): 219–239; Kai Thaler, "Foreshadowing Future Slaughter: From the Indonesian Killings of 1965–1966 to the 1974–1999 Genocide in East Timor," *Genocide Studies and Prevention* 7, no. 2 (2012): 204–222.
68. Elsewhere I have argued that the United States is responsible for genocide in Vietnam (Bachman, *The United States and Genocide*, 156–174). See also Jean-Paul Sartre, *On Genocide* (Boston: Beacon Press, 1968). For an opposing argument, see Hugo Adam Bedau, "Genocide in Vietnam?" in *Philosophy, Morality, and International Affairs*, ed. Virginia Held, Sidney Morgenbesser, and Thomas Nagel (Oxford: Oxford University Press, 1974), 5–46.
69. Convention on the Prevention and Punishment of the Crime of Genocide, United Nations Human Rights: Office of the High Commissioner, accessed September 1, 2017, http://www.ohchr.org/EN/ProfessionalInterest/Pages/CrimeOfGenocide.aspx.
70. Moses, "Raphael Lemkin, Culture, and the Concept of Genocide," 38.
71. Makau Mutua, "Savages, Victims, and Saviors: The Metaphor of Human Rights," *Harvard International Law Journal* 42, no. 1 (2001): 220.
72. Adam Jones, *Genocide: A Comprehensive Introduction*, 3rd ed. (London: Routledge, 2017), 43.
73. Lippman, "The 1948 Convention on the Prevention and Punishment of the Crime of Genocide," 74.
74. Ibid., 76.
75. See, among others, Davidson, *Cultural Genocide*; Novic, *The Concept of Cultural Genocide*; Moses, "Raphael Lemkin, Culture, and the Concept of Genocide"; Lindsey Kingston, "The Destruction of Identity: Cultural Genocide and Indigenous Peoples." *Journal of Human Rights* 14, no. 1 (2015): 63–83; Patrick Wolfe, "Settler Colonialism and the Elimination of the Native," *Journal of Genocide Research* 8, no. 4 (2006): 387–409; David Nersessian, "Cultural Genocide," in *Genocide: A Reader*, ed. Jens Meierhenrich, 80–81 (Oxford: Oxford University Press, 2014); Damien Short, "Cultural Genocide and Indigenous Peoples: A Sociological Approach," *International Journal of Human Rights* 14, no. 6 (2010): 833–848; Andrew Woolford, Jeff Benvenuto, and Alexander Hinton, *Colonial Genocide in Indigenous North America* (Durham, NC: Duke University Press,

2014); Bachman, *Cultural Genocide*; Ruth Amir, "Cultural Genocide in Canada: It Did Happen Here," *Aboriginal Policy Studies* 7, no. 1 (2018): 103–126; Andrew Woolford, *This Benevolent Experiment: Indigenous Boarding Schools, Genocide, and Redress in Canada and the United States* (Lincoln: University of Nebraska Press, 2015); Robert van Krieken, "The Barbarism of Civilization: Cultural Genocide and the 'Stolen Generations,'" *British Journal of Sociology* 50, no. 2 (1999): 297–315.

76. Julian Burger, *Report from the Frontier: The State of the World's Indigenous Peoples* (London: Zed Books, 1987), 31.
77. Nersessian, "Cultural Genocide," 81.
78. In his separate opinion in the case of *Bosnia v. Serbia*, Judge Elihu Lauterpacht argued that crimes committed in Bosnia that were labeled "ethnic cleansing" were actually acts of genocide. He argued that "the forced migration of civilians, more commonly known as 'ethnic cleansing,' is, in truth, part of a deliberate campaign by the Serbs to eliminate Muslim control of, and presence in, substantial parts of Bosnia-Herzegovina. . . . It is difficult to regard the Serbian acts as other than acts of genocide. . . . They are clearly directed against an ethnical or religious group as such, and they are intended to destroy that group, if not in whole certainly in part, to the extent necessary to ensure that the group no longer occupied the parts of Bosnia-Herzegovina coveted by the Serbs" (International Court of Justice, "Application of the Convention on the Prevention and Punishment of the Crime of Genocide [Bosnia and Herzegovina v. Serbia and Montenegro]: Provisional measures: Separate Opinion of Judge Lauterpacht," September 13, 1993, https://www.icj-cij.org/public/files/case-related/91/091-19930913-ORD-01-05-EN.pdf).
79. Martin Shaw, *What Is Genocide?* (Malden, MA: Polity Press, 2007), 48.
80. Ward Churchill, *Kill the Indian, Save the Man: The Genocidal Impact of American Indian Residential Schools* (San Francisco: City Light Books, 2004), 7. See also Lemkin, *Axis Rule in Occupied Europe*, 79, note 1.
81. United Nations, Draft Convention on the Crime of Genocide.
82. United Nations, Draft Convention prepared by the Ad Hoc Committee on Genocide.
83. Quoted in Abtahi and Webb, *The Genocide Convention*, 234.
84. Lemkin, "Genocide," 228.
85. Quoted in Abtahi and Webb, *The Genocide Convention*, 234.
86. Quoted in ibid., 837.
87. Ibid., 890.
88. Ibid., 727.
89. Quoted in ibid., 1502.
90. Ibid., 2049.
91. Ibid.
92. Ibid., 1503.
93. Quoted in ibid., 727.
94. Quoted in Schabas, *Genocide in International Law*, 183. The international declaration on human rights referred to by France became the Universal Declaration of Human Rights (UDHR), which was adopted by the General Assembly on December 10, 1948, one day after the adoption of the Genocide Convention. The UDHR contains two references to culture, one of which specifically regards cultural rights: "Everyone has the right freely to participate in the cultural life of the community, to enjoy the arts and to share in scientific advancement and its benefits" (United Nations, Universal Declaration of Human Rights, 1948, Article 27, https://www.ohchr.org/en/udhr/documents/udhr_translations/eng.pdf.) Also, on December 16, 1966, the General Assembly adopted the International Covenant on Economic, Social and Cultural Rights.
95. Quoted in Abtahi and Webb, *The Genocide Convention*,, 1506.

96. Quoted in ibid., 1514.
97. Kuper, *Genocide*, 15.
98. Ibid. Lemkin would agree. He distinguished between what might be considered cultural adaptation and forced assimilation. In this regard, Lemkin believed in both the idea of a benevolent colonizer, from which the colonized could benefit, and the idea that some cultures will die off through organic processes. See Novic, *The Concept of Cultural Genocide*, 21–22.
99. Churchill, *A Little Matter of Genocide*, 364.
100. Ibid, 365.
101. Ibid.
102. Power, *A Problem from Hell*, 65–70.
103. Shamiran Mako, "Cultural Genocide and Key International Instruments: Framing the Indigenous Experience," *International Journal on Minority and Group Rights* 19, no. 2 (2012): 177.
104. Churchill, *A Little Matter of Genocide*, 406.
105. Quoted in ibid., 245.
106. Quoted in ibid.
107. United States Department of the Interior, Office of Indian Affairs, "Rules Governing the Court of Indian Offenses," March 30, 1883, https://rclinton.files.wordpress.com/2007/11/code-of-indian-offenses.pdf.
108. Ibid.
109. Eduardo Hernandez-Chavez, "Language Policy in the United States: A History of Cultural Genocide," in *Linguistic Human Rights: Overcoming Linguistic Discrimination*, ed. Tove Skutnabb-Kangas and Robert Phillipson (The Hague: Mouton de Gruyter, 1995), 145.
110. Ibid.
111. United States Department of the Interior, Bureau of Indian Affairs, *Annual Report of the Commissioner of Indian Affairs to the Secretary of Interior* (Washington: Government Printing Office, 1886), xxiii.
112. Sharon O'Brien, "Federal Indian Policies and the International Protection of Human Rights," in *American Indian Policy in the Twentieth Century*, ed. Vine Deloria Jr. (Norman: University of Oklahoma Press, 1985), 35–61.
113. Churchill, *A Little Matter of Genocide*, 248.
114. Ibid.
115. United States Congress. "An Act Relative to Employment for Certain Adult Indians on or Near Indian Reservations." Public Laws of the Eighty-Fourth Congress, Second Session, Public Law 959, August 3, 1956, https://www.govinfo.gov/content/pkg/STATUTE-70/pdf/STATUTE-70-Pg986.pdf..
116. Churchill, *A Little Matter of Genocide*, see note that begins on page 366 and ends on page 367.
117. Ibid.
118. United Nations, "List of former Trust and Non-Self-Governing Territories," https://www.un.org/dppa/decolonization/en/history/former-trust-and-nsgts.
119. Remi P. Clignet and Philip J. Foster, "French and British Colonial Education in Africa," *Comparative Education Review,* 8, no. 2 (1964): 191.
120. Ibid.
121. Ibid.
122. Alf Andrew Heggoy, "Education in French Algeria: An Essay on Cultural Conflict," *Comparative Education Review* 17, no. 2 (1973): 180.
123. Ibid.
124. Ibid., 182..
125. Derwent Whittlesey, "British and French Colonial Technique in West Africa," *Foreign Affairs*, 15, no. 2 (January 1937): 369.

126. Ibid.
127. Clignet and Foster provide specific statistics regarding the enrollment of Africans in French schools in numerous French colonies ("French and British Colonial Education in Africa," 194).
128. Ibid. See also Bob W. White, "Talk about School: Education and the Colonial Project in French and British Africa (1860–1960)," *Comparative Education*, 32, no. 1 (1996), 9–25; Heggoy, "Education in French Algeria"; Whittlesey, "British and French Colonial Technique in West Africa."
129. White, "Talk about School."14.
130. Albert Charton, "Technical Education in French West Africa," in *Africans Learn to be French*, ed. William Bryant Mumford (New York: Negro University Press, 1970), 120.
131. Nuffield Foundation and Colonial Office, *African Education: A Study of Educational Policy and Practice in British Tropical Africa* (Oxford: Oxford University Press, 1953), 80.
132. Quoted in White, "Talk about School," 14.
133. Raphael Antonetti, "Reorganization of Education in French Equatorial Africa [1926]," reproduced in *Education and Nation-Building in Africa*, ed. L. Gray Cowan, James O'Connell, and David G. Scanlon (New York: Frederick A. Praeger, 1965), 54.
134. Charton, "Technical Education in French West Africa," 131.
135. Clignet and Foster, "French and British Colonial Education in Africa," 195.
136. Ibid.
137. Whittlesey, "British and French Colonial Technique in West Africa," 369.
138. White, "Talk about School."
139. Nuffield Foundation and Colonial Office, *African Education*, 3.
140. Ibid.
141. Clignet and Foster, "French and British Colonial Education in Africa." 194.
142. White, "Talk about School," 18.
143. Nuffield Foundation and Colonial Office, *African Education*, 69.
144. Ibid.
145. Mutua, "Savages, Victims, and Saviors," 233.
146. Hans Morgenthau, "What Is the National Interest of the United States?," *Annals of the American Academy of Political and Social Science* 282, no. 1 (1952): 4.

Chapter 3 The ICJ as Enabler of State Impunity for Genocide

1. Anja Seibert-Fohr, "State Responsibility for Genocide under the Genocide Convention," in *The UN Genocide Convention: A Commentary*, ed. Paola Gaeta (Oxford: Oxford University Press, 2009), 349. For more on the concept of state responsibility for genocide, see Jens David Ohlin, "State Responsibility for Conspiracy, Incitement, and Attempt to Commit Genocide," in *The UN Genocide Convention*, ed. Gaeta, 374–380; Paolo Palchetti, "State Responsibility for Complicity in Genocide," in *The UN Genocide Convention*, ed. Gaeta, 381–393; Marko Milanović, "State Responsibility for Genocide," *European Journal of International Law* 17, no. 3 (2006): 553–604, and "State Responsibility for Genocide: A Follow-Up," *European Journal of International Law* 18, no. 4 (2007): 669–694.
2. See Nina H. B. Jørgensen, *The Responsibility of States for International Crimes* (Oxford: Oxford University Press, 2001); Antonio Cassese, *International Criminal Law* (Oxford: Oxford University Press, 2008).
3. International Law Commission, "Responsibility of States for Internationally Wrongful Acts," 2001, http://legal.un.org/ilc/texts/instruments/english/draft_articles/9_6_2001.pdf.

4. For a summary of the ruling and the criteria established, see International Court of Justice, "Application of the Convention on the Prevention and Punishment of the Crime of Genocide (Bosnia and Herzegovina v. Serbia and Montenegro): Summary of the Judgement of 26 February 2007," https://www.icj-cij.org/public/files/case-related/91/13687.pdf.
5. The ICJ has been criticized for failing to seek complete and unredacted evidence from Serbia, including minutes from meetings of the Supreme Defense Council of Serbia; enforcing a high standard of proof, in particular for complicity in genocide; and relying heavily on International Criminal Tribunal for the Former Yugoslavia jurisprudence, especially when determining that genocide was limited to the murders in Srebrenica. See Susana SáCouto, "Reflections on the Judgment of the International Court of Justice in Bosnia's Genocide Case against Serbia and Montenegro," *Human Rights Brief* 15, no. 1 (2007): 2–4; Antonio Cassese, "On the Use of Criminal Law Notions in Determining State Responsibility," *Journal of International Criminal Justice* 5, no. 4 (2007): 875; Paola Gaeta, "On What Conditions Can a State Be Held Responsible for Genocide?," *European Journal of International Law* 18, no. 4 (2007): 631.
6. International Court of Justice, "Application of the Convention on the Prevention and Punishment of the Crime of Genocide (The Gambia v. Myanmar): Request for the Indication of Provisional Measures: Order of January 23, 2020," https://www.icj-cij.org/public/files/case-related/178/178-20200123-ORD-01-00-EN.pdf. For a brief discussion of The Gambia's complaint, assertion of standing, and request for provisional measures against Myanmar, see Anna Meijknecht, "Hague Case Law: Latest Developments," *Netherlands International Law Review* 67, no. 3 (2020): 581–583.
7. In the case of *The Gambia v. Myanmar*, see the ICJ's decision on provisional measures that concluded that there is sufficient grounding to "establish prima facie the existence of a dispute between the Parties relating to the interpretation, application or fulfilment of the Genocide Convention" and that, "prima facie, it [the ICJ] has jurisdiction pursuant to Article IX of the Genocide Convention to deal with the case" (International Court of Justice, "Application of the Convention on the Prevention and Punishment of the Crime of Genocide (The Gambia v. Myanmar): Request for the Indication of Provisional Measures: Order of January 23, 2020").
8. International Court of Justice, "Reports of Judgments, Advisory Opinions and Orders: Reservations to the Convention on the Prevention and Punishment of the Crime of Genocide: Advisory Opinion of May 28th, 1951," https://www.icj-cij.org/public/files/case-related/12/012-19510528-ADV-01-00-EN.pdf.
9. Articles 19–22 of the VCLT codify the ICJ's advisory opinion on reservations to the Genocide Convention. Article 19 allows states to make treaty reservations when signing, ratifying, accepting, approving, or acceding to a treaty, unless the treaty expressly prohibits reservations. The VCLT also incorporates the ICJ's standard for the permissibility of reservations: they must be compatible with the object and purpose of the treaty. Additionally, according to the VCLT and as the ICJ previously advised, an objection to a reservation does not affect the party status of the reserving state, meaning that the reserving state maintains its party status. Furthermore, an objection does not affect the status of the treaty between the reserving and objecting states, unless so indicated by the objecting state. See United Nations, Vienna Convention on the Law of Treaties, 1969, https://legal.un.org/ilc/texts/instruments/english/conventions/1_1_1969.pdf.
10. The first twenty-two state parties, by their dates of ratification, are Ethiopia (July 1); Australia (July 8); Norway (July 22); Iceland (August 29); and Ecuador (December 21), all in 1949; and Panama (January 11); Guatemala (January 13);

Israel (March 9); Monaco (March 30); Jordan (April 3); Liberia (June 20); the Philippines (July 7); Saudi Arabia (July 13); Bulgaria (July 21); Turkey (July 31); El Salvador (September 28); Sri Lanka (October 12); and Cambodia, Costa Rica, France, Haiti, and South Korea (October 14), all in 1950.

11. Prior to the Genocide Convention's entry into force, three states made reservations to Articles IX and XII: Belarus on December 16, 1949, and August 11, 1954, respectively; the Soviet Union on December 16, 1949, and May 3, 1954, respectively; and Ukraine on December 16, 1949 and November 15, 1954, respectively. However, they did not become state parties until more than three years after the convention entered into force.
12. Ecuador also objected to reservations made by Belarus, the Soviet Union, and Ukraine when those states signed the Genocide Convention.
13. During the first half of November 1950, the Genocide Convention received two additional state parties: Romania ratified the treaty on November 2, 1950, and Poland did the same on November 14. However, both made reservations to Articles IX and XII, which had already been objected to by Ecuador when Czechoslovakia and Bulgaria made reservations (as well as objecting to the reservation of the Philippines in the case of Article IX). Also, on November 15, Australia objected to reservations made by Czechoslovakia, Bulgaria, and the Philippines. Thus, the addition of two state parties did not change the situation. The Genocide Convention still did not have the requisite number of parties for entry into force if states maintaining reservations that had been objected to were not included.
14. United Nations General Assembly, Resolution 478(V), 16 November 1950, https://digitallibrary.un.org/record/862766?ln=en.
15. International Court of Justice, "Reports of Judgments, Advisory Opinions and Orders, Reservations to the Convention on the Prevention and Punishment of the Crime of Genocide: Advisory Opinion of May 28th, 1951, https://www.icj-cij.org/public/files/case-related/12/012-19510528-ADV-01-00-EN.pdf.
16. Ibid.
17. Ibid.
18. Ibid.
19. Ibid.
20. Ibid.
21. Ibid.
22. Ibid.
23. Anton Weiss-Wendt, *The Soviet Union and the Gutting of the UN Genocide Convention* (Madison: University of Wisconsin Press, 2017), 369.
24. International Court of Justice, "Pleadings, Oral Arguments, Documents, Reservations to the Convention on the Prevention and Punishment of the Crime of Genocide, Advisory Opinion of May 28, 1951," https://www.icj-cij.org/public/files/case-related/12/11767.pdf.
25. Ibid.
26. Weiss-Wendt, *The Soviet Union and the Gutting of the UN Genocide Convention*, 158.
27. International Court of Justice, "Pleadings, Oral Arguments, Documents." This was a convenient position for the United States to take, seeing that it had threatened to undermine the adoption of the Genocide Convention if substantive obligations under the convention had included the prohibition of acts constituting cultural genocide. With the ultimate exclusion of cultural genocide, it was easier for the United States to argue that reservations were likely to be of a contractual or procedural sort rather than substantial in nature.

28. Ibid.
29. International Court of Justice, "Pleadings, Oral Arguments, Documents, Reservations to the Convention on the Prevention and Punishment of the Crime of Genocide, Advisory Opinion of May 28th, 1951, Part II," https://www.icj-cij.org/public/files/case-related/12/012-19510410-ORA-01-00-BI.pdf.
30. Ibid.
31. It is also important to note that the United States would have made a reservation to the article containing acts constituting cultural genocide had such an article been retained in the adopted text of the Genocide Convention. This completely contradicts the U.S. position that the convention's essential elements include "the definition of the crime of genocide" and that "reservations may frequently be technical qualifications of a treaty rather than substantial limitations of its obligations."
32. International Court of Justice, "Pleadings, Oral Arguments, Documents, . . . Part II."
33. Ibid.
34. Ibid.
35. Ibid.
36. Ibid.
37. Ibid.
38. Ibid.
39. International Court of Justice, "Pleadings, Oral Arguments, Documents."
40. International Court of Justice, Advisory Opinions and Orders, Reservations to the Convention on the Prevention and Punishment of the Crime of Genocide Advisory Opinion of May 28, 1951, Dissenting Opinion of Judges Guerrero, Sir Arnold McNair, Read, Hsu Mo, https://www.icj-cij.org/public/files/case-related/12/012-19510528-ADV-01-01-EN.pdf.
41. Ibid.
42. Ibid.
43. Ibid.
44. International Court of Justice, Advisory Opinions and Orders, Reservations to the Convention on the Prevention and Punishment of the Crime of Genocide Advisory Opinion of May 28, 1951, Dissenting Opinion of Judges Alvarez, https://www.icj-cij.org/public/files/case-related/12/012-19510528-ADV-01-02-EN.pdf.
45. Heather Elko McKibben and Shaina D. Western, "'Reserved Ratification': An Analysis of States' Entry of Reservations upon Ratification of Human Rights Treaties," *British Journal of Political Science* 50, no. 2 (2020): 688.
46. International Court of Justice, Advisory Opinions and Orders, Reservations to the Convention on the Prevention and Punishment of the Crime of Genocide Advisory Opinion of May 28, 1951, Dissenting Opinion of Judges Guerrero, Sir Arnold McNair, Read, Hsu Mo.
47. Spain's reservation, which was withdrawn in 2009, was an outright one, meaning that Spain preemptively rejected the ICJ's jurisdiction in all Genocide Convention cases. In its reservation, the United States does not explicitly reject ICJ jurisdiction, but it does require that it give prior consent to ICJ jurisdiction on a case-by-case basis. In the case that Serbia attempted to bring against it, the United States delivered the following response: "The United States reservation is clear and unambiguous. The United States has not given the specific consent it requires. It will not do so. Thus, there is no jurisdiction, prima facie or otherwise" (International Court of Justice, "Public Sitting Held on Tuesday 11 May 1999, at 4.30 pm, in the Peace Palace, Vice-President Weeramantry, Acting President,

Presiding in the Case Concerning .Legality of the Use of Force (Yugoslavia v. United States of America): Request for the Indication of Provisional Measures: Verbatim Record," 1999, 14, https://www.icj-cij.org/public/files/case-related/114/114-19990511-ORA-01-00-BI.pdf).

48. Ibid.
49. International Court of Justice, "Reports of Judgments, Advisory Opinions and Orders: Case Concerning Armed Activities on the Territory of the Congo (New Application, 2002): (Democratic Republic of the Congo v. Rwanda): Jurisdiction of the Court and Admissibility of the Application Judgment of 3 February 2006," https://www.icj-cij.org/public/files/case-related/126/126-20060203-JUD-01-00-EN.pdf.
50. International Court of Justice, "Reports of Judgments, Advisory Opinions and Orders: Case Concerning Application of the Convention on the Prevention and Punishment of the Crime of Genocide (Bosnia and Herzegovina v. Serbia and Montenegro), Judgment of 26 February 2007." https://www.icj-cij.org/public/files/case-related/91/091-20070226-JUD-01-00-EN.pdf..
51. Ibid.
52. International Court of Justice, "Reports of Judgments, Advisory Opinions and Orders: Case Concerning Application of the Convention on the Prevention and Punishment of the Crime of Genocide (Bosnia and Herzegovina v. Serbia and Montenegro): Preliminary Objections: Judgment of July 11, 1996," https://www.icj-cij.org/public/files/case-related/91/091-19960711-JUD-01-00-EN.pdf.
53. International Court of Justice, "Pleadings, Oral Arguments, Documents, . . . Part II."
54. John Quigley, *The Genocide Convention: An International Law Analysis* (Burlington, VT: Ashgate, 2006), 221.
55. International Law Commission, *Yearbook of the International Law Commission, 2001* (New York: United Nations, 2007), vol. 2, part 2, 67, https://legal.un.org/ilc/publications/yearbooks/english/ilc_2001_v2_p2.pdf.
56. Quigley, *The Genocide Convention*, 220.
57. The states that maintain or formerly made Article IX reservations are Albania (withdrawn), Algeria, Argentina, Bahrain, Bangladesh, Belarus (withdrawn), Bulgaria (withdrawn), China, Czechoslovakia (withdrawn), Hungary (withdrawn), India, Malaysia, Mongolia (withdrawn), Montenegro, Morocco, the Philippines, Poland (withdrawn), Romania (withdrawn), Rwanda (withdrawn), Russia (withdrawn), Serbia, Singapore, Spain (withdrawn), Ukraine (withdrawn), the United Arab Emirates, United States, Venezuela, Viet Nam, and Yemen.
58. See Jeffrey S. Bachman, *The United States and Genocide: (Re)Defining the Relationship* (London: Routledge, 2017), chapters 4–6.
59. Ibid., 176.
60. Jeffrey S. Bachman, "A 'Synchronized Attack' on Life: The Saudi-Led Coalition's 'Hidden and Holistic' Genocide in Yemen and the Shared Responsibility of the US and UK," *Third World Quarterly* 40, no. 2 (2019): 298–316. See, in particular, pages 306–309.
61. Newlines Institute for Strategy and Policy, "The Uyghur Genocide: An Examination of China's Breaches of the 1948 Genocide Convention," March 2021, 4, https://newlinesinstitute.org/wp-content/uploads/Chinas-Breaches-of-the-GC3-2.pdf.
62. Ibid. For an important work on China's persecution of Uyghurs, see Sean R. Roberts, *The War on the Uyghurs: China's Internal Campaign against a Muslim Minority* (Princeton, NJ: Princeton University Press, 2020).
63. International Court of Justice, Advisory Opinions and Orders, Reservations to the Convention on the Prevention and Punishment of the Crime of Genocide

Advisory Opinion of May 28, 1951, Dissenting Opinion of Judges Guerrero, Sir Arnold McNair, Read, Hsu Mo.

64. Madeline Morris, "Few Reservations about Reservations," *Chicago Journal of International Law* 1, no. 2 (2000): 343.
65. Ibid. See also Pok Yin S. Chow, "Reservations as Unilateral Acts? Examining the International Law Commission's Approach to Reservations," *International and Comparative Law Quarterly* 66, no. 2 (2017): 339.
66. Dan Hammer, "Allowing Genocide? An Analysis of Armed Activities on the Territory of the Congo, Jurisdictional Reservations, and the Legitimacy of the International Court of Justice," *Minnesota Journal of International Law* 16, no. 2 (2007): 513.
67. Mark Gibney, "State Responsibility and the 'Object and Purpose' of the Genocide Convention," *International Studies Journal* 4, nos. 2–3 (2007–2008): 147.
68. Kasey L. McCall-Smith, "Mind the Gaps: The ILC Guide to Practice on Reservations to Human Rights Treaties," *International Community Law Review* 16, no. 2 (2014): 304.
69. As mentioned in n. 57, the Soviet Union withdrew its Article IX reservation (in 1989).

Chapter 4 The P-5 and Discretionary Nonapplication of the Genocide Convention

1. Robert Entman, *Projections of Power: Framing News, Public Opinion, and U.S. Foreign Policy* (Chicago: University of Chicago Press, 2004), 5. As the title of his book makes clear, Entman is using this conception of framing in the context of media coverage of events related to U.S. foreign policy.
2. A. Dirk Moses, *The Problems of Genocide: Permanent Security and the Language of Transgression* (Cambridge: Cambridge University Press, 2021), 7.
3. Ibid.
4. Michel-Rolph Trouillot, *Silencing the Past: Power and the Production of History* (Boston: Beacon Press, 1995), 114.
5. Ibid.
6. David Carr, "Narrative and the Real World: An Argument for Continuity," *History and Theory* 25, no. 2 (1986): 117.
7. Hirad Abtahi and Philippa Webb, "Secrets and Surprises in the *Travaux Préparatoires* of the Genocide Convention," in *Arcs of Global Justice: Essays in Honor of William A. Schabas*, ed. Margaret M. deGuzman and Diane Marie Amann (Oxford: Oxford University Press, 2018), 305.
8. The scholars I corresponded with are William Schabas (email to author, September 17, 2011), Leila Nadya Sadat (email to author, September 26, 2011), Beth Van Schaack (email to author, September 19, 2011), and Samuel Totten (email to author, September 17, 2011). I reviewed Helen Fein's (*Human Rights and Wrongs: Slavery, Terror, Genocide* [Boulder, CO: Paradigm Publishers, 2007]) and Ben Kiernan's (*Blood and Soil: A World History of Genocide and Extermination from Sparta to Darfur* [New Haven, CT: Yale University Press, 2007]) publications. Four of these six scholars agreed that genocide was committed in Bangladesh (Van Schaack leaned toward recognizing the violence as genocide, and only Schabas did not consider it as genocide). Everyone except Schabas recognized genocide in Bosnia, though Totten limited genocide to Srebrenica. And there was unanimous agreement that genocide was committed in Rwanda. In Alexander Laban Hinton's genocide studies canon, Bangladesh is located in the "Second Circle," Rwanda is part of the "Triad," and Bosnia is in the "Twentieth-Century Core" ("Critical Genocide Studies," *Genocide Studies and Prevention* 7, no. 1 [2012]: 13).

9. For detailed accounts of genocide in East Pakistan, see, among others, Suhail Islam and Syed Hassan, "The Wretched of the Nations: The West's Role in Human Rights Violations in the Bangladesh War of Independence," in *Genocide, War Crimes and the West: History and Complicity*, ed. Adam Jones, 201–213 (London: Zed Books, 2004); Gary J. Bass, *The Blood Telegram: Nixon, Kissinger, and a Forgotten Genocide* (New York: Vintage Books, 2013); Srinath Raghavan, *1971: A Global History of the Creation of Bangladesh* (Cambridge, MA: Harvard University Press, 2013). As noted in chapter 2, similar dynamics were present during deliberations over genocide in Cambodia, Iraq, Bosnia, and Rwanda.
10. Simon Chesterman, *Just War or Just Peace? Humanitarian Intervention and International Law* (Oxford: Oxford University Press, 2000), 72; Carol Rittner, "Are Women Human?," in *Rape: Weapon of War and Genocide*, ed. Carol Rittner and John K. Roth (St. Paul, MN: Paragon House, 2012), 5.
11. Kaylan Chaudhuri, *Genocide in Bangladesh* (New Delhi: Orient Longman, 1972), 199.
12. Leo Kuper, *Genocide: Its Political Use in the Twentieth Century* (New Haven, CT: Yale University Press, 1981), 79.
13. Quoted in Bass, *The Blood Telegram*, 58.
14. Quoted in ibid., 77.
15. Quoted in ibid., 78.
16. United Nations Security Council, "Official Records: Twenty-Sixth Year, 1606th Meeting: 4 December 1971," https://undocs.org/en/S/PV.1606(OR).
17. Quoted in Hirad Abtahi and Philippa Webb, *The Genocide Convention: The Travaux Préparatoires* (Leiden, the Netherlands: Martinus Nijhoff, 2008), 1045.
18. United Nations Security Council, "Official Records: Twenty-Sixth Year, 1606th Meeting." For a discussion of international law and the use of force against armed bands that cross territorial borders, see Ian Brownlie, "International Law and the Activities of Armed Bands," *International and Comparative Law Quarterly* 7, no. 4 (1958): 712–735. The same discussion can be applied to cases of armed bands within a state's territory.
19. United Nations Security Council, "Official Records: Twenty-Sixth Year, 1606th Meeting."
20. Ibid.
21. Ibid.
22. Ibid.
23. United Nations Security Council, "Official Records: Twenty-Sixth Year, 1607th Meeting: 5 December 1971," 20, https://undocs.org/en/S/PV.1607(OR).
24. United Nations Security Council, "Official Records: Twenty-Sixth Year, 1606th Meeting."
25. Ibid.
26. Ibid.
27. Ibid.
28. Interestingly, while arguing for the omission of political groups from the Genocide Convention, the Soviet Union had raised its concern that its own response to internal subversion would be used politically against it through accusations of genocide.
29. United Nations Security Council, "Official Records: Twenty-Sixth Year, 1607th Meeting."
30. United Nations Security Council, "Argentina, Belgium, Burundi, Italy, Japan, Nicaragua, Sierra Leone and Somalia: draft resolution," December 5, 1971, https://undocs.org/en/S/10423.
31. United Nations Security Council, "Official Records: Twenty-Sixth Year, 1606th Meeting."

32. Ibid.
33. Ibid.
34. Ibid.
35. Ibid.
36. Ibid.
37. For a further discussion of how groups targeted in East Pakistan fit within those protected by the Genocide Convention, see Jeffrey S. Bachman, *The United States and Genocide: (Re)Defining the Relationship* (London: Routledge, 2017), 97–98.
38. PBS, *Frontline*, "Ghosts of Rwanda: Timeline," April 1, 2004, http://www.pbs.org/wgbh/pages/frontline/shows/ghosts/etc/crontext.html.
39. During the June 8, 1994, Security Council meeting, the United States referred to "acts of genocide" in Rwanda (United Nations Security Council, "Forty-Ninth Year, 3388th Meeting, Wednesday, 8 June 1994," https://digitallibrary.un.org/record/162815?ln=en). The Security Council also adopted Resolution 925, which refers to "acts of genocide" [United Nations Security Council, "Resolution 925 (1994)," June 8, 1994, https://undocs.org/en/S/RES/925(1994)].
40. United Nations Security Council, "Forty-Ninth Year, 3326th Meeting, Thursday, 6 January 1994," https://undocs.org/en/S/PV.3326.
41. United Nations Security Council, "Forty-Ninth Year, 3368th Meeting, Thursday, 21 April 1994," https://digitallibrary.un.org/record/186509?ln=en.
42. There is evidence of atrocities committed by the RPF, but that is not the focus here. For more on suspected RPF crimes, see Susan Thomson, *Rwanda: From Genocide to Precarious Peace* (New Haven, CT: Yale University Press, 2018).
43. United Nations Security Council, "Forty-Ninth Year, 3377th Meeting, Monday, 16 May 1994" https://undocs.org/en/S/PV.3377.
44. Ibid.
45. United Nations Security Council, "Forty-Ninth Year, 3368th Meeting."
46. United Nations Security Council, "Resolution 912 (1994)," April 21, 1994, https://undocs.org/en/S/RES/912(1994).
47. United Nations Security Council, "Forty-Ninth Year, 3371st Meeting, Saturday, 30 April 1994," https://undocs.org/en/S/PV.3371.
48. United Nations Security Council, "Statement by the President of the Security Council, 30 April 1994," https://undocs.org/S/PRST/1994/21.
49. Ibid.
50. PBS, *Frontline*, "Ghosts of Rwanda."
51. United Nations Security Council, "Resolution 918 (1994)," May 17, 1994, https://digitallibrary.un.org/record/197563?ln=en.
52. Ibid. The resolution reiterated that in the context of the violence in Rwanda, "the killing of members of an ethnic group with the intention of destroying such a group, in whole or in part, constitutes a crime punishable under international law."
53. Ibid.
54. United Nations Security Council, "Forty-Ninth Year, 3377th Meeting."
55. Ibid.
56. PBS, *Frontline*, "Ghosts of Rwanda."
57. It is worth noting the passive manner in which "acts of genocide" were first officially recognized by the Security Council. The resolution noted "with the gravest concern *the reports* indicating that acts of genocide have occurred in Rwanda" (United Nations Security Council, "Resolution 925 (1994)," June 8, 1994, https://undocs.org/en/S/RES/925(1994) (emphasis added).
58. United Nations Security Council, "Forty-Ninth Year, 3388th Meeting, Wednesday, 8 June 1994," https://undocs.org/en/S/PV.3388.
59. Ibid.

60. United Nations Security Council, "Forty-Ninth Year, 3392nd Meeting, Wednesday, 22 June 1994," https://undocs.org/en/S/PV.3392.
61. United Nations Security Council, "Forty-Ninth Year, 3377th Meeting."
62. Ibid.
63. United Nations Security Council, "Forty-Ninth Year, 3388th Meeting."
64. Ibid.
65. United Nations Security Council, "Forty-Ninth Year, 3392nd Meeting."
66. United Nations Security Council, "Forty-Ninth Year, 3377th Meeting."
67. United Nations Security Council, "Forty-Ninth Year, 3388th Meeting."
68. Ibid.
69. United Nations Security Council, "Forty-Ninth Year, 3392nd Meeting." Nonetheless, Resolution 929, adopted on the same day, did not describe the violence in Rwanda as genocide. See United Nations Security Council, "Resolution 929 (1994)." June 22, 1994." "Resolution 929 (1994)," June 22, 1994, https://undocs.org/en/S/RES/929(1994).
70. United Nations Security Council, "Forty-Ninth Year, 3377th Meeting."
71. United Nations Security Council, "Forty-Ninth Year, 3388th Meeting."
72. Ibid.
73. United Nations Security Council, "Forty-Ninth Year, 3392nd Meeting."
74. United Nations Security Council, "Forty-Ninth Year, 3388th Meeting."
75. Ibid.
76. Ibid.
77. Quoted from André Guichaoua, *From War to Genocide: Criminal Politics in Rwanda, 1990–1994* (Madison: University of Wisconsin Press, 2017), 202, in Thomson, *Rwanda*, 21.
78. Thomson, *Rwanda*, 21.
79. Rabia Ali and Lawrence Lifschultz describe this nationalistic fervor: "Insular, parochial, ethnocentric, this was a vision of a purified nation-state in which there was no room for the 'Other'. The ingathering of a people into the bosom of the 'mother country' meant in this instance the acquisition of the territory on which they lived. Serbia's nationalist ideology was unequivocal on this issue: the destiny of all Serbs was to live in one state, and since all land on which Serbs lived was by definition Serb land, it rightfully belonged to 'Greater Serbia'. They, alone, would unilaterally define its boundaries and remove any community which by their account did not 'belong'" ("Why Bosnia?," *Third World Quarterly* 15, no. 3 [1994]: 368).
80. For detailed accounts of the violence in Bosnia, see, among others, Beverly Allen, *Rape Warfare: The Hidden Genocide in Bosnia-Herzegovina and Croatia* (Duluth: University of Minnesota Press, 1996); Norman Cigar, *Genocide in Bosnia: The Policy of "Ethnic Cleansing"* (College Station: Texas A&M University Press, 2000); Thomas Cushman and Stjepan Mestrovic, *This Time We Knew: Western Responses to Genocide in Bosnia* (New York: New York University Press, 1996); Kiernan, *Blood and Soil*; Samantha Power, *"A Problem from Hell": America and the Age of Genocide* (New York: Basic Books, 2002).
81. Resolution 713 was the first passed by the Security Council concerning the breakup of the former Yugoslavia. The resolution called for the immediate implementation of "a general and complete embargo on all deliveries of weapons and military equipment to Yugoslavia until the Council decides otherwise following consultation between the Secretary-General and the Government of Yugoslavia" (United Nations Security Council, "Resolution 713 [1991])," September 25, 1991, https://undocs.org/S/RES/713(1991).
82. Power, *"A Problem from Hell,"* 249.

83. United Nations Security Council, "Letter Dated 24 May 1994 from the Secretary-General to the President of the Security Council," https://digitallibrary.un.org/record/232969?ln=en.
84. United Nations Security Council, "Letter Dated 9 February 1993 from the Secretary-General Addressed to the President of the Security Council," https://undocs.org/S/25274.
85. Ibid.
86. Raphael Lemkin, *Axis Rule in Occupied Europe: Laws of Occupation, Analysis of Government, Proposals for Redress* (Clark, NJ: Lawbook Exchange, 2005), 79.
87. United Nations Security Council, "Provisional Verbatim Record of the 3106th Meeting," August 13, 1992, https://undocs.org/en/S/PV.3106.
88. United Nations Security Council, "Provisional Verbatim Record of the 3135th Meeting," November 13, 1992, https://undocs.org/en/S/PV.3135.
89. United Nations Security Council, "Provisional Verbatim Record of the 3106th Meeting."
90. United Nations Security Council, "Resolution 757 (1992)," May 30,1992, https://undocs.org/S/RES/757(1992).
91. United Nations Security Council, "Resolution 771 (1992)," August 13, 1992, 1, https://undocs.org/S/RES/771(1992).
92. United Nations Security Council, "Provisional Verbatim Record of the 3082nd Meeting," May 30, 1992, https://undocs.org/en/S/PV.3082.
93. United Nations Security Council, "Provisional Verbatim Record of the 3208th Meeting," May 6, 1993, https://undocs.org/en/S/PV.3208.
94. United Nations Security Council, "Provisional Verbatim Record of the 3228th Meeting," June 4, 1993, https://undocs.org/en/S/PV.3228.
95. Ibid.
96. United Nations Security Council, "Provisional Verbatim Record of the 3247th Meeting," June 29, 1993, https://undocs.org/en/S/PV.3247. This as close as one can come to describing Lemkin's two phases of genocide without using his exact words.
97. United Nations Security Council, "Provisional Verbatim Record of the 3333rd Meeting," February 3, 1994, https://undocs.org/en/S/PV.3333.
98. United Nations Security Council, "Provisional Verbatim Record of the 3192nd Meeting," April 3, 1993, https://undocs.org/en/S/PV.3192.
99. United Nations Security Council, "Provisional Verbatim Record of the 3257th Meeting," July 22, 1993, https://undocs.org/en/S/PV.3257https://undocs.org/en/S/PV.3192.
100. United Nations Security Council, "Forty-Ninth Year, 3367th Meeting, Thursday, 21 April 1994," 49, https://undocs.org/en/S/PV.3367.
101. United Nations Security Council, "Provisional Verbatim Record of the 3082nd Meeting"; United Nations Security Council, "Provisional Verbatim Record of the 3135th Meeting."
102. United Nations Security Council, "Resolution 827 (1993)," May 25, 1993, https://undocs.org/S/RES/827(1993).
103. International Court of Justice, "Application of the Convention on the Prevention and Punishment of the Crime of Genocide (Bosnia and Herzegovina v. Serbia and Montenegro): Provisional measures: Separate Opinion of Judge Lauterpacht," September 13, 1993, https://www.icj-cij.org/public/files/case-related/91/091-19930913-ORD-01-05-EN.pdf.
104. See Donna-Lee Frieze, "The Destruction of Sarajevo's *Vijećnica*: A Case of Genocidal Cultural Destruction?," in *New Directions in Genocide Research*, ed. Adam Jones (London: Routledge, 2012), 57–75.

105. United Nations Security Council, "Letter Dated 20 May 1992 from the Permanent Representative of Egypt to the United Nations Addressed to the Secretary-General," https://digitallibrary.un.org/record/144080?ln=en.
106. United Nations Security Council, "Letter Dated 27 May 1992 from the Minister for Foreign Affairs of Bosnia and Herzegovina Addressed to the President of the Security Council," https://digitallibrary.un.org/record/143668?ln=en.
107. United Nations Security Council, "Provisional Verbatim Record of the 3119th Meeting," October 6, 1992," https://undocs.org/en/S/PV.3119.
108. United Nations Security Council, "Provisional Verbatim Record of the 3135th Meeting."
109. United Nations Security Council, "Provisional Verbatim Record of the 3137th Meeting," November 16, 1992, https://undocs.org/en/S/PV.3137.
110. United Nations Security Council, "Provisional Verbatim Record of the 3136th Meeting," November 16, 1992, https://undocs.org/en/S/PV.3136.
111. Ibid.
112. Ibid.
113. Ibid.
114. United Nations Security Council, "Provisional Verbatim Record of the 3137th Meeting."
115. United Nations Security Council, "Provisional Verbatim Record of the 3217th Meeting," May 25, 1993, https://undocs.org/en/S/PV.3217.
116. Ibid.
117. United Nations Security Council, "Letter Dated 30 May 1993 from the Permanent Representative of Bosnia and Herzegovina to the United Nations Addressed to the President of the Security Council," https://digitallibrary.un.org/record/167096?ln=en.
118. United Nations Security Council, "Letter Dated 30 March 1994 from the Deputy Permanent Representative of Bosnia and Herzegovina to the United Nations Addressed to the President of the Security Council," https://digitallibrary.un.org/record/185282?ln=en.
119. United Nations Security Council, "Forty-Ninth Year, 3367th Meeting."
120. Ibid.
121. Ibid.
122. Ibid.
123. United Nations Security Council, "Forty-Ninth Year, 3370th Meeting, Wednesday, 27 April 1994," https://undocs.org/en/S/PV.3370.
124. Ibid.
125. Ibid.
126. United Nations Security Council, "Letter Dated 1 July 1994 from the Permanent Representative of Croatia to the United Nations Addressed to the President of the Security Council," https://digitallibrary.un.org/record/190062?ln=en.
127. United Nations Security Council, "Provisional Verbatim Record of the 3428th Meeting," September 23, 1994," https://undocs.org/en/S/PV.3428.
128. Ibid.
129. Ibid.
130. Ibid.
131. Ibid.
132. Ibid.
133. United Nations Security Council, "Forty-Ninth Year, 3370th Meeting."
134. Ibid.
135. United Nations Security Council, "Fiftieth Year, 3512th Meeting, Friday, 31 March 1995," https://undocs.org/en/S/PV.3512.

136. United Nations Security Council, "Fiftieth Year, 3575th Meeting, Friday, 8 September 1995," https://undocs.org/en/S/PV.3575.
137. Ibid.
138. United Nations Security Council, "Letter Dated 24 February 1995 from the Permanent Representative of Morocco to the United Nations Addressed to the President of the Security Council," https://digitallibrary.un.org/record/173479?ln=en.
139. United Nations Security Council, "Fiftieth Year, 3512th Meeting."
140. United Nations Security Council, "Fiftieth Year, 3543rd Meeting, Friday, 16 June 1995," https://undocs.org/en/S/PV.3543.
141. Moses, *The Problems of Genocide*, 7.

Chapter 5 The Responsibility to Protect and P-5 Impunity

1. International Commission on Intervention and State Sovereignty, *The Responsibility to Protect* (Ottawa: International Development Research Centre, 2001), https://idl-bnc-idrc.dspacedirect.org/bitstream/handle/10625/18432/IDL-18432.pdf?sequence=6&isAllowed=y.
2. A. Dirk Moses, *The Problems of Genocide: Permanent Security and the Language of Transgression* (Cambridge: Cambridge University Press, 2021), 19.
3. Ibid., 9.
4. Kofi Annan, "Two Concepts of Sovereignty," *Economist*, September 18, 1999, http://www.economist.com/node/324795.
5. International Commission on Intervention and State Sovereignty, *The Responsibility to Protect.*
6. United Nations General Assembly, "Resolution Adopted by the General Assembly on 16 September 2005." https://www.un.org/en/development/desa/population/migration/generalassembly/docs/globalcompact/A_RES_60_1.pdf.
7. Ibid.
8. United Nations, Draft Convention on the Crime of Genocide, 1947, https://digitallibrary.un.org/record/611058?ln=en.
9. As Moses writes, the hierarchy of international crimes creates the space in which such arguments can be made: "Alternatively, state violence can be excused as legitimately political—that is, motivated by security concerns—rather than illegitimately ethnic in motivation. That is, by defining genocide in such narrow terms, governments can undertake drastic measures against population groups in the name of security, self-preservation, 'military necessity,' and opposing 'terrorists'" (*The Problems of Genocide*, 9).
10. Hirad Abtahi and Philippa Webb, *The Genocide Convention: The Travaux Préparatoires* (Leiden, the Netherlands: Martinus Nijhoff, 2008), 1737. See "Genocide: Just Another Crime under International Law?" in chapter 1 of this book.
11. International Commission on Intervention and State Sovereignty, *The Responsibility to Protect.*
12. Adam Jones, *Genocide: A Comprehensive Introduction* (London: Routledge, 2010), 21.
13. John Quigley, *The Genocide Convention: An International Law Analysis* (Burlington, VT: Ashgate, 2006), 10.
14. Josef Kunz, "The United Nations Convention on Genocide," *American Journal of International Law* 43, no. 4 (1949): 743.
15. Matthew Lippman, "The 1948 Convention on the Prevention and Punishment of the Crime of Genocide: Forty-Five Years Later," *Temple International and Comparative Law Journal* 8, no. 1 (1994): 77.

16. Matthew Lippman, "The Convention on the Prevention and Punishment of the Crime of Genocide: Fifty Years Later," *Arizona Journal of International and Comparative Law* 15, no. 2 (1998): 507.
17. Lawrence LeBlanc, "The Intent to Destroy Groups in the Genocide Convention: The Proposed U.S. Understanding," *American Journal of International Law* 78, no. 2 (1984): 382.
18. Ibid.
19. Kurt Jonassohn, "What Is Genocide?" in *Genocide Watch*, edited by Helen Fein (New Haven, CT: Yale University Press, 1992), 19.
20. Ibid.
21. Ibid., 21.
22. Helen Fein, "Genocide, Terror, Life Integrity, and War Crimes: The Case for Discrimination," in *Genocide: Conceptual and Historical Dimensions*, ed. George Andreopoulos (Philadelphia: University of Pennsylvania Press, 1994), 97.
23. International Criminal Tribunal for Rwanda, "In the Appeals Chamber, Case No. ICTR-2001-66-A," https://unictr.irmct.org/sites/unictr.org/files/case-documents/ictr-01-66/appeals-chamber-judgements/en/080312.pdf.
24. Ibid.
25. International Commission on Intervention and State Sovereignty, *The Responsibility to Protect.*
26. International Criminal Court, Rome Statute of the International Criminal Court, 1998, https://www.icc-cpi.int/resource-library/documents/rs-eng.pdf.
27. Ibid.
28. Ibid.
29. Ibid.
30. International Commission on Intervention and State Sovereignty, *The Responsibility to Protect.*
31. United Nations, Draft Convention on the Crime of Genocide, 1947, https://digitallibrary.un.org/record/611058?ln=en.
32. International Criminal Court, Rome Statute of the International Criminal Court.
33. International Commission on Intervention and State Sovereignty, *The Responsibility to Protect.*
34. United Nations, United Nations Charter, 1945, https://www.un.org/en/about-us/un-charter/full-text.
35. International Commission on Intervention and State Sovereignty, *The Responsibility to Protect.*
36. Alex Stark, Introduction to *The Responsibility to Protect: Challenges and Opportunities in Light of the Libyan Intervention*, edited by Alex Stark, 4, *e-International Relations*, November 2011, https://www.e-ir.info/publication/the-r2p-challenges-and-opportunities-in-light-of-the-libyan-intervention.
37. Aidan Hehir, "The Illusion of Progress: Libya and the Future of R2P," *e-International Relations*, September 11, 2011, https://www.e-ir.info/2011/09/11/the-illusion-of-progress-libya-and-the-future-of-r2p/.
38. Ibid.
39. Since October 2011, China has applied its veto to eleven resolutions on Syria and the Middle East. Russia has done the same seventeen times. What might be less well known is that the United States has vetoed five resolutions on Palestine since the 2005 World Summit, at which R2P was endorsed. For records of veto use, see United Nations, "Security Council—Veto List," January 20, 2022, https://research.un.org/en/docs/sc/quick.
40. An example of a direct reference can be found in Resolution 1970. This resolution, which preceded the one that authorized the use of force in Libya

(Resolution 1973), recalled "the Libyan authorities' *responsibility to protect* its population" (United Nations Security Council, "Resolution 1970 (2011)," February 26, 2011, [emphasis added], https://undocs.org/S/RES/1970(2011)). An example of a fragmented R2P reference can be found in Resolution 2098, which stressed that "the Government of the DRC bears primary *responsibility for* security, *protection of civilians*, national reconciliation, peacebuilding and development in the country" (United Nations Security Council, "Resolution 2098 (2013)," March 28, 2013, [emphasis added], https://undocs.org/S/RES/2098(2013)).

41. A complete list of the applicable United Nations Security Council resolutions is located in the bibliography (see resolutions 1739–2559)
42. France and the United Kingdom also abstained from voting on one resolution each.
43. For a detailed exposition of the violence in Yemen through a genocide studies lens, and an analysis of the shared responsibility for that violence of the United States and United Kingdom, see Jeffrey S. Bachman, "A 'Synchronized Attack' on Life: The Saudi-Led Coalition's 'Hidden and Holistic' Genocide in Yemen and the Shared Responsibility of the US and UK," *Third World Quarterly* 40, no. 2 (2019): 298–316.
44. Moses, *The Problems of Genocide*, 492.
45. For a summary of what is meant by illiberal and liberal permanent security, see ibid., 37–42.
46. Ibid., 492.
47. Jeffrey Bachman, "Cases Studied in *Genocide Studies and Prevention* and *Journal of Genocide Research* and Implications for the Field of Genocide Studies," *Genocide Studies and Prevention* 14, no. 1 (2020): 8–10.
48. Julia Hoffmann, and André Nollkaemper, "Concluding Observations," in *Responsibility to Protect: From Principle to Practice*, ed. Julia Hoffmann, and André Nollkaemper (Amsterdam: Amsterdam University Press, 2012), 356.
49. Ademola Abass, "The African Union and the Responsibility to Protect: Principles and Limitations," in *Responsibility to Protect: From Principle to Practice*, ed. Julia Hoffmann and André Nollkaemper (Amsterdam: Amsterdam University Press, 2012), 222.
50. Hoffmann, and Nollkaemper, "Concluding Observations," 360.
51. Ibid.
52. Ibid., 369.
53. I refer to this as the "Samantha Power Effect" (Jeffrey S. Bachman, *The United States and Genocide: (Re)Defining the Relationship* [London: Routledge, 2017], 8–11) because Power's *"A Problem from Hell": American and the Age of Genocide* (New York: Basic Books, 2002) helped make ubiquitous the narrative of the United States as an essentially benign bystander that needs to muster the necessary leadership and political will to do more to prevent genocide without looking at the ways in which the United States has contributed to the commission of genocide.
54. An example of this reciprocal behavior can be found in how China responds to U.S. State Department reports on human rights in China with its own reports on human rights in the United States. See Chen Qingqing and Bai Yunyi, "China Issues Annual US Human Rights Report amid Escalating Washington-Led West's Attack on Beijing," *Global Times*, March 24, 2001, https://www.globaltimes.cn/page/202103/1219297.shtml.
55. Heather M. Roff, *Global Justice, Kant and the Responsibility to Protect: A Provisional Duty* (London: Routledge, 2013), 9.

CONCLUSION

1. Louis Henkin, *How Nations Behave: Law and Foreign Policy*, 2nd ed. (New York: Columbia University Press, 1979), 62.
2. Ibid.
3. Ibid., 62–63.
4. Ibid., 63.
5. José E. Alvarez, "Do Liberal States Behave Better? A Critique of Slaughter's Liberal Theory," *European Journal of International Law* 12, no. 2 (2001): 192.
6. Anne-Marie Slaughter, "International Law in a World of Liberal States," *European Journal of International Law* 6, no. 3 (1995): 532.
7. Ibid., 533.
8. Ibid., 532–533.
9. Susan Marks, "The End of History? Reflections on Some International Legal Theses," *European Journal of International Law* 8, no. 3 (1997): 473.
10. David Luban, "Just War and Human Rights," *Philosophy and Public Affairs* 9, no. 2 (1980): 160–181.
11. Benjamin Meiches, *The Politics of Annihilation: A Genealogy of Genocide* (Minneapolis: University of Minnesota Press, 2019), 12.
12. Gerry Simpson, *Great Powers and Outlaw States: Unequal Sovereigns in the International Legal Order* (Cambridge: Cambridge University Press, 2004), 76–83.
13. Ibid., 78.
14. Ibid., 76.
15. Slaughter, "International Law in a World of Liberal States," 509.
16. Wolfgang Wagner, Wouter Werner, and Michal Onderco, "Rogues, Pariahs, Outlaws: Theorizing Deviance in International Relations," in *Deviance in International Relations*, ed. Wolfgang Wagner, Wouter Werner, and Michal Onderco (London: Palgrave Macmillan, 2014), 8.
17. James Christensen, "Arming the Outlaws: On the Moral Limits of the Arms Trade," *Political Studies* 67, no. 1 (2019): 117.
18. Miroslav Nincic, *Renegade Regimes: Confronting Deviant Behavior in World Politics* (New York: Columbia University Press, 2005), 2 and 5.
19. John Rawls, *The Law of Peoples* (Cambridge, MA: Harvard University Press, 2002), 5.
20. Ibid., 3.
21. Jack Donnelly, "Sovereign Inequalities and Hierarchy in Anarchy: American Power and International Society," *European Journal of International Relations* 12, no. 2 (2006): 146.
22. Anthony Lake, "Confronting Backlash States," *Foreign Affairs* (March/April 1994), https://www.foreignaffairs.com/articles/iran/1994-03-01/confronting-backlash-states.
23. Ibid.
24. Ibid.
25. Ibid.
26. Sally-Ann Totman, *How Hollywood Projects Foreign Policy* (New York: Palgrave Macmillan, 2009), 34; Lake, "Confronting Backlash States"; Elizabeth N. Saunders, "Setting Boundaries: Can International Society Exclude 'Rogue States'?," *International Studies Review* 8, no. 1 (2006): 23; Mary Caprioli and Peter F. Trumbore, "Rhetoric versus Reality: Rogue States in International Conflict," *Journal of Conflict Resolution* 49, no. 5 (2005): 771.
27. Totman, *How Hollywood Projects Foreign Policy*, 34; Lake, "Confronting Backlash States"; Saunders, "Setting Boundaries," 23; Caprioli and Trumbore, "Rhetoric

versus Reality," 771; K. P. O'Reilly, "Perceiving Rogue States: The Use of the 'Rogue State' Concept by U.S. Foreign Policy Elites," *Foreign Policy Analysis* 3, no. 4 (2007): 305.

28. Totman, *How Hollywood Projects Foreign Policy*, 34; Lake, "Confronting Backlash States"; Saunders, "Setting Boundaries," 23; Caprioli and Trumbore, "Rhetoric versus Reality," 771; Mary Caprioli and Peter F. Trumbore, "Identifying 'Rogue' States and Testing Their Interstate Conflict Behavior," *European Journal of International Relations* 9, no. 3 (2003): 395; O'Reilly, "Perceiving Rogue States," 305.
29. Totman, *How Hollywood Projects Foreign Policy*, 34; Lake, "Confronting Backlash States"; Saunders, "Setting Boundaries," 23; Caprioli and Trumbore, "Rhetoric versus Reality," 771; Caprioli and Trumbore, "Identifying 'Rogue' States and Testing Their Interstate Conflict Behavior," 395; O'Reilly, "Perceiving Rogue States," 305.
30. Totman, *How Hollywood Projects Foreign Policy*, 34; Lake, "Confronting Backlash States"; Saunders, "Setting Boundaries," 23; Jonathan B. Schwartz, "Dealing with a 'Rogue State': The Libya Precedent," *American Journal of International Law* 101, no. 3 (2007): 553; Caprioli and Trumbore, "Rhetoric versus Reality," 771; O'Reilly, "Perceiving Rogue States," 305.
31. Totman, *How Hollywood Projects Foreign Policy*, 34; Maria Garbielsen Jumbert, "How Sudan's 'Rogue' State Label Shaped US Responses to the Darfur Conflict: What's the Problem and Who's in Charge?" *Third World Quarterly* 35, no. 2 (2014): 285; Caprioli and Trumbore, "Rhetoric versus Reality," 781, and "Identifying 'Rogue' States and Testing Their Interstate Conflict Behavior," 395.
32. Totman, *How Hollywood Projects Foreign Policy*, 34; Caprioli and Trumbore, "Rhetoric versus Reality," 781; O'Reilly, "Perceiving Rogue States," 305.
33. Robert Rotberg, "The Threat from Rogue States," *Boston Globe*, November 6, 2004, https://www.belfercenter.org/publication/threat-rogue-states.
34. Ibid.
35. Saunders, "Setting Boundaries," 28; Wagner, Werner, and Onderco, "Rogues, Pariahs, Outlaws," 8; Rotberg, "The Threat from Rogue States."
36. Donnelly, "Sovereign Inequalities and Hierarchy in Anarchy," 146.
37. Elizabeth Anderson, "Outlaws," *Good Society* 23, no. 1 (2014): 114.
38. A. Dirk Moses, *The Problems of Genocide: Permanent Security and the Language of Transgression* (Cambridge: Cambridge University Press, 2021), 39–40.
39. Convention on the Prevention and Punishment of the Crime of Genocide, United Nations Human Rights: Office of the High Commissioner, accessed September 1, 2017, http://www.ohchr.org/EN/ProfessionalInterest/Pages/CrimeOfGenocide.aspx.
40. Alexander Laban Hinton, "Critical Genocide Studies," *Genocide Studies and Prevention* 7, no. 1 (2012): 11–12.
41. Moses, *The Problems of Genocide*, 492.
42. Hinton, "Critical Genocide Studies," 12–13.
43. Jeffrey Bachman, "Cases Studied in *Genocide Studies and Prevention* and *Journal of Genocide Research* and Implications for the Field of Genocide Studies," *Genocide Studies and Prevention* 14, no. 1 (2020): 6.
44. Ibid., 14.
45. Ibid., 8–10.
46. Jeffrey S. Bachman, *The United States and Genocide: (Re)Defining the Relationship* (London: Routledge, 2017), 8–11.
47. Samantha Power, *"A Problem from Hell": America and the Age of Genocide* (New York: Basic Books, 2002), xvi.
48. Ibid., xvii–xviii.

49. Madeleine K. Albright and William S. Cohen, *Preventing Genocide: A Blueprint for U.S. Policymakers* (Washington: United States Holocaust Memorial Museum, 2008), ix.
50. Ibid., xx.
51. Ibid.
52. Hinton, "Critical Genocide Studies," 13. Rwanda is also located in the triad, which includes the Holocaust and the Armenian genocide and is one level above the twentieth-century core and only one level below the prototype case, the Holocaust.
53. Ibid., 12.
54. Power, *"A Problem from Hell,"* 173.
55. Bachman, *The United States and Genocide*, 11.
56. See ibid., 78–155..
57. Others who have not overlooked U.S. violence, and that of other Western states, deserve recognition. In addition to the writing of Moses and Hinton, the work of Noam Chomsky is perhaps the best known. See almost any of his works on U.S. foreign policy, but specifically *Rogue States: The Rule of Force in World Affairs* (Boston: South End Press, 2000). See also Adam Jones's edited volume, *Genocide, War Crimes and the West: History and Complicity* (London: Zed Books, 2004). In his introduction to the volume, Jones coins the term "democrisy" to refer to "the strain of hypocrisy that attaches to regimes that are avowedly democratic in character, that allow comparative freedom and immunity from naked state violence domestically, but that initiate or participate in atrocious actions beyond their borders" (Adam Jones, "Introduction: History and Complicity," in *Genocide, War Crimes and the West* [London: Zed Books, 2004], 9).

Bibliography

Abass, Ademola. "The African Union and the Responsibility to Protect: Principles and Limitations." In *Responsibility to Protect: From Principle to Practice*, edited by Julia Hoffmann and André Nollkaemper, 213–236. Amsterdam: Amsterdam University Press, 2012.

Abtahi, Hirad, and Philippa Webb. *The Genocide Convention: The Travaux Préparatoires*. Leiden, the Netherlands: Martinus Nijhoff, 2008.

Abtahi, Hirad, and Philippa Webb. "Secrets and Surprises in the *Travaux Préparatoires* of the Genocide Convention." In *Arcs of Global Justice: Essays in Honor of William A. Schabas*, edited by Margaret M. deGuzman and Diane Marie Amann, 299–319. Oxford: Oxford University Press, 2018.

Afoaku, Osita G., and Okechukwu Ukaga. "United Nations Security Council Reform: A Critical Analysis of Enlargement Options." *Journal of Third World Studies* 18, no. 2 (2001): 149–169.

Akhavan, Payam, and René Provost. "Moving from Repression to Prevention of Genocide." In *Confronting Genocide*, edited by Payam Akhavan and René Provost, 1–10. New York: Springer, 2011.

Albright, Madeleine K., and William S. Cohen. *Preventing Genocide: A Blueprint for U.S. Policymakers*. Washington: United States Holocaust Memorial Museum, 2008.

Ali, Rabia, and Lawrence Lifschultz. "Why Bosnia?" *Third World Quarterly* 15, no. 3 (1994): 367–401.

Allen, Beverly. *Rape Warfare: The Hidden Genocide in Bosnia-Herzegovina and Croatia*. Duluth: University of Minnesota Press, 1996.

Alvarez, José E. "Do Liberal States Behave Better? A Critique of Slaughter's Liberal Theory." *European Journal of International Law* 12, no. 2 (2001): 183–246.

Amir, Ruth. "Cultural Genocide in Canada: It Did Happen Here." *Aboriginal Policy Studies* 7, no. 1 (2018): 103–126.

Anderson, Benedict. *Violence and the State in Suharto's Indonesia*. Ithaca, NY: Cornell University Press, 2009.

Anderson, Elizabeth. "Outlaws." *Good Society* 23, no. 1 (2014): 103–114.

Annan, Kofi. "Two Concepts of Sovereignty." *Economist*, September 18, 1999. http://www.economist.com/node/324795.

Antonetti, Raphael. "Reorganization of Education in French Equatorial Africa [1926]." Reproduced in *Education and Nation-Building in Africa*, edited by L. Gray Cowan, James O'Connell, and David G. Scanlon, 53–58. New York: Frederick A. Praeger, 1965.

Bachman, Jeffrey. "Cases Studied in *Genocide Studies and Prevention* and *Journal of Genocide Research* and Implications for the Field of Genocide Studies." *Genocide Studies and Prevention* 14, no. 1 (2020): 2–20.

Bachman, Jeffrey, ed. *Cultural Genocide: Law, Politics, and Global Manifestations*. London: Routledge, 2019.

Bachman, Jeffrey. "Genocide and Imperialism." In *The Palgrave Encyclopedia of Imperialism and Anti-Imperialism*, edited by Immanuel Ness and Zak Cope. London: Palgrave Macmillan, 2019. https://link.springer.com/referenceworkentry/10.1007/978-3-030-29901-9_84.

Bachman, Jeffrey S. "A 'Synchronized Attack' on Life: The Saudi-Led Coalition's 'Hidden and Holistic' Genocide in Yemen and the Shared Responsibility of the US and UK." *Third World Quarterly* 40, no. 2 (2019): 298–316.

Bachman, Jeffrey S. *The United States and Genocide: (Re)Defining the Relationship*. London: Routledge, 2017.

Bass, Gary J. *The Blood Telegram: Nixon, Kissinger, and a Forgotten Genocide*. New York: Vintage Books, 2013.

Bedau, Hugo Adam. "Genocide in Vietnam?" In *Philosophy, Morality, and International Affairs*, edited by Virginia Held, Sidney Morgenbesser, and Thomas Nagel, 5–46. Oxford: Oxford University Press, 1974.

Ben-Naftali, Orna. "The Extraterritorial Application of Human Rights to Occupied Territories." *American Society of International Law Proceedings* 100 (March 29–April 1 2006): 90–95.

Bosco, David. *Five to Rule Them All: The UN Security Council and the Making of the Modern World*. Oxford: Oxford University Press, 2009.

Brownlie, Ian. "International Law and the Activities of Armed Bands." *International and Comparative Law Quarterly* 7, no. 4 (1958): 712–735.

Brownlie, Ian. *The Rule of Law in International Affairs: International Law at the Fiftieth Anniversary of the United Nations*. The Hague: Martinus Nijhoff, 1998.

Burger, Julian. *Report from the Frontier: The State of the World's Indigenous Peoples*. London: Zed Books, 1987.

Byers, Michael. *Custom, Power and the Power of Rules*. Cambridge: Cambridge University Press, 1999.

Calvocoressi, Peter. *Nuremberg: The Facts, the Law and the Consequences*. New York: MacMillan, 1948.

Caprioli, Mary, and Peter F. Trumbore. "Identifying 'Rogue' States and Testing Their Interstate Conflict Behavior." *European Journal of International Relations* 9, no. 3 (2003): 377–406.

Caprioli, Mary, and Peter F. Trumbore. "Rhetoric versus Reality: Rogue States in International Conflict." *Journal of Conflict Resolution* 49, no. 5 (2005): 770–791.

Carr, David. "Narrative and the Real World: An Argument for Continuity." *History and Theory* 25, no. 2 (1986): 117–131.

Cassese, Antonio. *International Criminal Law*. Oxford: Oxford University Press, 2008.

Cassese, Antonio. "On the Use of Criminal Law Notions in Determining State Responsibility." *Journal of International Criminal Justice* 5, no. 4 (2007): 875–887.

Charton, Albert. "Technical Education in French West Africa." In *Africans Learn to be French*, edited by William B. Mumford, 113–136. New York: Negro University Press, 1970.

Chaudhuri, Kaylan. *Genocide in Bangladesh*. New Delhi: Orient Longman, 1972.

Chen Qingqing and Bai Yunyi. "China Issues Annual US Human Rights Report amid Escalating Washington-Led West's Attack on Beijing." *Global Times*, March 24, 2001. https://www.globaltimes.cn/page/202103/1219297.shtml.

Chesterman, Simon. *Just War or Just Peace? Humanitarian Intervention and International Law*. Oxford: Oxford University Press, 2000.

Chomsky, Noam. *Rogue States: The Rule of Force in World Affairs*. Boston: South End Press, 2000.

Chow, Pok Yin S. "Reservations as Unilateral Acts? Examining the International Law Commission's Approach to Reservations." *International and Comparative Law Quarterly* 66, no. 2 (2017): 335–365.

Christensen, James. "Arming the Outlaws: On the Moral Limits of the Arms Trade." *Political Studies* 67, no. 1 (2019): 116–131.

Churchill, Ward. *Kill the Indian, Save the Man: The Genocidal Impact of American Indian Residential Schools*. San Francisco: City Light Books, 2004.

Churchill, Ward. *A Little Matter of Genocide: Holocaust and Denial in the Americas, 1492 to the Present*. San Francisco: City Lights Books, 1997.

Cigar, Norman. *Genocide in Bosnia: The Policy of "Ethnic Cleansing."* College Station: Texas A&M University Press, 2000.

Clignet, Remi P., and Philip J. Foster. "French and British Colonial Education in Africa." *Comparative Education Review* 8, no. 2 (1964): 191–198.

Convention on the Prevention and Punishment of the Crime of Genocide. United Nations Human Rights: Office of the High Commissioner. http://www.ohchr.org/EN/ProfessionalInterest/Pages/CrimeOfGenocide.aspx.

Cribb, Robert. "Genocide in Indonesia, 1965–1966." *Journal of Genocide Research* 3, no. 2 (2001): 219–239.

Cushman, Thomas, and Stjepan Mestrovic. *This Time We Knew: Western Responses to Genocide in Bosnia*. New York: New York University Press, 1996.

Davidson, Lawrence. *Cultural Genocide*. New Brunswick, NJ: Rutgers University Press, 2012.

De Vattel, Emerich. *The Law of Nations*. Indianapolis, IN: Liberty Fund, 2009.

De Visscher, Charles. *Theory and Reality in Public International Law*. Princeton, NJ: Princeton University Press, 1957.

Dennis, Michael. "Application of Human Rights Treaties Extraterritorially during Times of Armed Conflict and Military Occupation." *American Society of International Law Proceedings*, 100 (March 29–April 1 2006): 86–90.

Donnelly, Jack. "Sovereign Inequalities and Hierarchy in Anarchy: American Power and International Society." *European Journal of International Relations* 12, no. 2 (2006): 139–170.

Droege, Cordula. "The Interplay between International Humanitarian Law and International Human Rights Law in Situations of Armed Conflict." *Israeli Law Review* 40, no. 2 (2007): 310–355.

El-Farra, Muhammad. "The Algerian Tragedy." *Africa Today* 3, no. 4 (1956): 7–9.

Entman, Robert. *Projections of Power: Framing News, Public Opinion, and U.S. Foreign Policy*. Chicago: University of Chicago Press, 2004.

Evans, Gareth. *The Responsibility to Protect: Ending Mass Atrocities Once and for All*. Washington: Brookings Institution Press, 2008.

Fein, Helen, "Genocide, Terror, Life Integrity, and War Crimes: The Case for Discrimination." In *Genocide: Conceptual and Historical Dimensions*, edited by George Andreopoulos, 95–108. Philadelphia: University of Pennsylvania Press, 1994.

Fein, Helen. *Human Rights and Wrongs: Slavery, Terror, Genocide*. Boulder, CO: Paradigm Publishers, 2007.

Fein, Helen. "Revolutionary and Antirevolutionary Genocides: A Comparison of State Murders in Democratic Kampuchea, 1975 to 1979, and in Indonesia, 1965 to 1966." *Comparative Studies in Society and History* 35, no. 4 (1993): 796–823.

Feinstein, Stephen. "Understanding the 'G' Word." In *Will Genocide Ever End?*, edited by Carol Rittner, John Roth, and James Smith, 39–44. St. Paul, MN: Paragon House, 2002.

Frieze, Donna-Lee. "The Destruction of Sarajevo's *Vijećnica*: A Case of Genocidal Cultural Destruction?" In *New Directions in Genocide Research*, edited by Adam Jones, 57–75. London: Routledge, 2012.

Frieze, Donna-Lee. "Introduction: The 'Insistent Prophet.'" In Raphael Lemkin, *Totally Unofficial: The Autobiography of Raphael Lemkin*, edited by Donna-Lee Frieze, ix–xxvii. New Haven, CT: Yale University Press, 2013.

Gaeta, Paola. "On What Conditions Can a State Be Held Responsible for Genocide?" *European Journal of International Law* 18, no. 4 (2007): 631–648.

Gibney, Mark. "State Responsibility and the 'Object and Purpose' of the Genocide Convention." *International Studies Journal* 4, nos. 2–3 (2007–2008): 141–150.

Glanville, Luke. "The Responsibility to Protect beyond Borders." *Human Rights Law Review* 12, no. 1 (2012): 1–32.

Guichaoua, André. *From War to Genocide: Criminal Politics in Rwanda, 1990–1994.* Madison: University of Wisconsin Press, 2017.

Hammer, Dan. "Allowing Genocide? An Analysis of Armed Activities on the Territory of the Congo, Jurisdictional Reservations, and the Legitimacy of the International Court of Justice." *Minnesota Journal of International Law* 16, no. 2 (2007): 495–523.

Haque, Adil (@AdHaque110). "Discretionary non-application of laws is an exercise of domination and hierarchy tbh." Twitter, December 28, 2020. https://twitter.com/AdHaque110/status/1343532558894686214.

Harris, Errol. "The Problem of Sovereignty in International Relations." In *Philosophical Challenges and Opportunities of Globalization*, edited by Obliva Blanchette, Tomonobu Imamichi, and George F. Mclean, 371–386. Washington: Council for Research in Values and Philosophy, 2002.

Heggoy, Alf Andrew. "Education in French Algeria: An Essay on Cultural Conflict." *Comparative Education Review* 17, no. 2 (1973): 180–197.

Hehir, Aidan. "The Illusion of Progress: Libya and the Future of R2P." *E-International Relations*, September 11, 2011. https://www.e-ir.info/2011/09/11/the-illusion-of-progress-libya-and-the-future-of-r2p/.

Henkin, Louis. *How Nations Behave: Law and Foreign Policy*. 2nd ed. New York: Columbia University Press, 1979.

Hernandez-Chavez, Eduardo. "Language Policy in the United States: A History of Cultural Genocide." In *Linguistic Human Rights: Overcoming Linguistic Discrimination*, edited by Tove Skutnabb-Kangas and Robert Phillipson, 141–158. The Hague: Mouton de Gruyter, 1995.

Hinton, Alexander Laban. "Critical Genocide Studies." *Genocide Studies and Prevention* 7, no. 1 (2012): 4–15.

Hoffmann, Julia, and André Nollkaemper. "Concluding Observations." In *Responsibility to Protect: From Principle to Practice*, edited by Julia Hoffmann and André Nollkaemper, 355–372. Amsterdam: Amsterdam University Press, 2012.

International Commission on Intervention and State Sovereignty. *The Responsibility to Protect*. Ottawa: International Development Research Centre, 2001. https://idl-bnc-idrc.dspacedirect.org/bitstream/handle/10625/18432/IDL-18432.pdf?sequence=6&isAllowed=y.

International Court of Justice. "Advisory Opinions and Orders, Reservations to the Convention on the Prevention and Punishment of the Crime of Genocide Advisory Opinion of May 28, 1951: Dissenting Opinion of Judge Alvarez." https://www.icj-cij.org/en/case/12/advisory-opinions.

International Court of Justice. "Advisory Opinions and Orders, Reservations to the Convention on the Prevention and Punishment of the Crime of Genocide

Advisory Opinion of May 28, 1951: Dissenting Opinion of Judges Guerrero, Sir Arnold McNair, Read, Hsu Mo." https://www.icj-cij.org/en/case/12/advisory-opinions.

International Court of Justice. "Application of the Convention on the Prevention and Punishment of the Crime of Genocide (Bosnia and Herzegovina v. Serbia and Montenegro): Provisional measures: Separate Opinion of Judge Lauterpacht." September 13, 1993. https://www.icj-cij.org/public/files/case-related/91/091-19930913-ORD-01-05-EN.pdf.

International Court of Justice. "Application of the Convention on the Prevention and Punishment of the Crime of Genocide (Bosnia and Herzegovina v. Serbia and Montenegro): Summary of the Judgment of 26 February 2007." https://www.icj-cij.org/public/files/case-related/91/13687.pdf.

International Court of Justice. "Pleadings, Oral Arguments, Documents: Reservations to the Convention on the Prevention and Punishment of the Crime of Genocide: Advisory Opinion of May 28th, 1951." https://www.icj-cij.org/public/files/case-related/12/11767.pdf.

International Court of Justice. "Pleadings, Oral Arguments, Documents: Reservations to the Convention on the Prevention and Punishment of the Crime of Genocide, Advisory Opinion of May 28th, 1951, Part II." https://www.icj-cij.org/public/files/case-related/12/012-19510410-ORA-01-00-BI.pdf.

International Court of Justice. "Public Sitting Held on Tuesday 11 May 1999, at 4.30 pm, in the Peace Palace, Vice-President Weeramantry, Acting President, Presiding in the Case Concerning .Legality of the Use of Force (Yugoslavia v. United States of America): Request for the Indication of Provisional Measures: Verbatim Record." 1999. https://www.icj-cij.org/public/files/case-related/114/114-19990511-ORA-01-00-BI.pdf.

International Court of Justice. "Reports of Judgments, Advisory Opinions and Orders: Application of the Convention on the Prevention and Punishment of the Crime of Genocide (The Gambia v. Myanmar): Request for the Indication of Provisional Measures: Order of January 23, 2020." https://www.icj-cij.org/public/files/case-related/178/178-20200123-ORD-01-00-EN.pdf.

International Court of Justice. "Reports of Judgments, Advisory Opinions and Orders: Case Concerning Application of the Convention on the Prevention and Punishment of the Crime of Genocide (Bosnia and Herzegovina v. Serbia and Montenegro): Preliminary Objections: Judgment of July 11, 1996." https://www.icj-cij.org/public/files/case-related/91/091-19960711-JUD-01-00-EN.pdf.

International Court of Justice. "Reports of Judgments, Advisory Opinions and Orders: Case Concerning Application of the Convention on the Prevention and Punishment of the Crime of Genocide (Bosnia and Herzegovina v. Serbia and Montenegro), Judgment of 26 February 2007." 2007. https://www.icj-cij.org/public/files/case-related/91/091-20070226-JUD-01-00-EN.pdf.

International Court of Justice. "Reports of Judgments, Advisory Opinions and Orders: Case Concerning Armed Activities on the Territory of the Congo (New Application, 2002): (Democratic Republic of the Congo v. Rwanda): Jurisdiction of the Court and Admissibility of the Application Judgment of 3 February 2006." https://www.icj-cij.org/public/files/case-related/126/126-20060203-JUD-01-00-EN.pdf.

International Court of Justice. "Reports of Judgments, Advisory Opinions and Orders: Reservations to the Convention on the Prevention and Punishment of the Crime of Genocide: Advisory Opinion of May 28th, 1951." https://www.icj-cij.org/public/files/case-related/12/012-19510528-ADV-01-00-EN.pdf.

International Court of Justice. Statute of the International Court of Justice. 1945. https://www.icj-cij.org/en/statute.

International Criminal Court. Rome Statute of the International Criminal Court. 1998. https://www.icc-cpi.int/resource-library/documents/rs-eng.pdf.

International Criminal Tribunal for Rwanda. "In the Appeals Chamber, Case No. ICTR-2001-66-A." https://unictr.irmct.org/sites/unictr.org/files/case-documents/ictr-01-66/appeals-chamber-judgements/en/080312.pdf.

International Law Commission. "Responsibility of States for Internationally Wrongful Acts." 2001. http://legal.un.org/ilc/texts/instruments/nglish/draft_articles/9_6_2001.pdf.

International Law Commission. *Yearbook of the International Law Commission, 2001.* Vol. 2, Part 2. New York: United Nations, 2007. https://legal.un.org/ilc/publications/yearbooks/nglish/ilc_2001_v2_p2.pdf.

Irvin-Erickson, Douglas. Email to author. May 11, 2019.

Irvin-Erickson, Douglas. *Raphael Lemkin and the Concept of Genocide.* Philadelphia: University of Pennsylvania Press, 2016.

Islam, Suhail, and Syed Hassan. "The Wretched of the Nations: The West's Role in Human Rights Violations in the Bangladesh War of Independence." In *Genocide, War Crimes and the West: History and Complicity,* edited by Adam Jones, 201–213. London: Zed Books, 2004.

Jonassohn, Kurt. "What Is Genocide?" In *Genocide Watch,* edited by Helen Fein, 17–26. New Haven, CT: Yale University Press, 1992.

Jones, Adam. *Genocide: A Comprehensive Introduction.* London: Routledge, 2010.

Jones, Adam. *Genocide: A Comprehensive Introduction.* 3rd ed. London: Routledge, 2017.

Jones, Adam, ed. *Genocide, War Crimes and the West: History and Complicity.* London: Zed Books, 2004.

Jones, Adam. "Introduction: History and Complicity." In *Genocide, War Crimes and the West,* edited by Adam Jones, 3–30. London: Zed Books, 2004.

Jørgensen, Nina H. B. *The Responsibility of States for International Crimes.* Oxford: Oxford University Press, 2001.

Jumbert, Maria Garbielsen. "How Sudan's 'Rogue' State Label Shaped US Responses to the Darfur Conflict: What's the Problem and Who's in Charge?" *Third World Quarterly* 35, no. 2 (2014): 284–299.

Kammen, Douglas, and Katharine McGregor. "Introduction: The Contours of Mass Violence in Indonesia, 1965–68." In *The Contours of Mass Violence in Indonesia, 1965–1968,* edited by Douglas Kammen and Katharine McGregor, 1–24. Honolulu: University of Hawaii Press, 2012.

Kiernan, Ben. *Blood and Soil: A World History of Genocide and Extermination from Sparta to Darfur.* New Haven, CT: Yale University Press, 2007.

Kingston, Lindsey. "The Destruction of Identity: Cultural Genocide and Indigenous Peoples." *Journal of Human Rights* 14, no. 1 (2015): 63–83.

Koskenniemi, Martti. *Sources of International Law.* Burlington, VT: Ashgate/Dartmouth, 2000.Kunz, Josef. "The United Nations Convention on Genocide." *American Journal of International Law* 43, no. 4 (1949): 738–746.

Kuper, Leo. *Genocide: Its Political Use in the Twentieth Century.* New Haven, CT: Yale University Press, 1981.

Lake, Anthony. "Confronting Backlash States." *Foreign Affairs* (March–April 1994). https://www.foreignaffairs.com/articles/iran/1994-03-01/confronting-backlash-states.

Lazreg, Marnia. *Torture and the Twilight of Empire: From Algiers to Baghdad*. Princeton, NJ: Princeton University Press, 2016.

LeBlanc, Lawrence. "The Intent to Destroy Groups in the Genocide Convention: The Proposed U.S. Understanding." *American Journal of International Law* 78, no. 2 (1984): 369–385.

LeBlanc, Lawrence. "The United Nations Genocide Convention and Political Groups: Should the United States Propose an Amendment?" *Yale Journal of International Law* 2, no. 3 (1988): 268–295.

LeBlanc, Lawrence. *The United States and the Genocide Convention*. Durham, NC: Duke University Press, 1991.

Lemkin, Raphael. "Acts Constituting a General (Transnational) Danger Considered as Offences against the Law of Nations." Translated by James T. Fussell. Prevent Genocide International, December 9, 2000. http://www.preventgenocide.org/lemkin/madrid1933-english.htm.

Lemkin, Raphael. *Axis Rule in Occupied Europe: Laws of Occupation, Analysis of Government, Proposals for Redress*. Clark, NJ: Lawbook Exchange, 2005.

Lemkin, Raphael. "Genocide." *American Scholar* 15, no. 2 (1946): 227–230.

Lemkin, Raphael. "Genocide: A Modern Crime." *Free World* 4 (April 1945): 39–43.

Lemkin, Raphael. "The Nature of Genocide." N.d. Folder 2, box 2, N. D. Raphaël Lemkin Collection, P-154, American Jewish Historical Society, New York.

Lemkin, Raphael. *Totally Unofficial: The Autobiography of Raphael Lemkin*. Edited by Donna Lee-Frieze. New Haven, CT: Yale University Press, 2013.

Lippman, Matthew. "The 1948 Convention on the Prevention and Punishment of the Crime of Genocide: Forty-Five Years Later." *Temple International and Comparative Law Journal* 8, no. 1 (1994): 1–84.

Lippman, Matthew. "The Convention on the Prevention and Punishment of the Crime of Genocide: Fifty Years Later." *Arizona Journal of International and Comparative Law* 15, no. 2 (1998): 415–514.

Luban, David. "Just War and Human Rights." *Philosophy and Public Affairs* 9, no. 2 (1980): 160–181.

Lubell, Noam. *Extraterritorial Use of Force against Non-State Actors*. Oxford: Oxford University Press, 2012.

Mako, Shamiran. "Cultural Genocide and Key International Instruments: Framing the Indigenous Experience." *International Journal on Minority and Group Rights* 19, no. 2 (2012): 175–194.

Marks, Susan. "The End of History? Reflections on Some International Legal Theses." *European Journal of International Law* 8, no. 3 (1997): 449–477.

Mayall, James. "Humanitarian Intervention and International Society: Lessons from Africa." In *Humanitarian Intervention and International Relations*, edited by Jennifer Welsh, 120–141. Oxford: Oxford University Press, 2003.

Mayroz, Eyal. "The Legal Duty to 'Prevent': After the Onset of 'Genocide.' " *Journal of Genocide Research* 14, no. 1 (2012): 79–98.

McCall-Smith, Kasey L. "Mind the Gaps: The ILC Guide to Practice on Reservations to Human Rights Treaties." *International Community Law Review* 16, no. 2 (2014): 263–305.

McKibben, Heather Elko, and Shaina D. Western. " 'Reserved Ratification': An Analysis of States' Entry of Reservations upon Ratification of Human Rights Treaties." *British Journal of Political Science* 50, no. 2 (2020): 687–712.

Meiches, Benjamin. Email to author. May 10, 2019.

Meiches, Benjamin. *The Politics of Annihilation: A Genealogy of Genocide*. Minneapolis: University of Minnesota Press, 2019.

Meijknecht, Anna. "Hague Case Law: Latest Developments." *Netherlands International Law Review* 67, no. 3 (2020): 581–583.

Milanović, Marko. "State Responsibility for Genocide." *European Journal of International Law* 17, no. 3 (2006): 553–604.

Milanović, Marko. "State Responsibility for Genocide: A Follow-Up." *European Journal of International Law* 18, no. 4 (2007): 669–694.

Mitscherlich, Alexander, and Fred Mielke. "Judgment and Aftermath." In *The Nazi Doctors and the Nuremberg Code*, edited by George Annas and Michael Grodin, 94–120. Oxford: Oxford University Press, 1995.

Morgenthau, Hans J. *Politics among Nations: The Struggle for Power and Peace*. New York: Alfred A. Knopf, 1954.

Morgenthau, Hans. "What Is the National Interest of the United States?" *Annals of the American Academy of Political and Social Science* 282, no. 1 (1952): 1–7.

Morris, Madeline. "Few Reservations about Reservations." *Chicago Journal of International Law* 1, no. 2 (2000): 341–346.

Moses, A. Dirk. *The Problems of Genocide: Permanent Security and the Language of Transgression*. Cambridge: Cambridge University Press, 2021.

Moses, A. Dirk. "Raphael Lemkin, Culture, and the Concept of Genocide." In *The Oxford Handbook of Genocide Studies*, edited by Donald Bloxham and A. Dirk Moses, 19–41. Oxford: Oxford University Press, 2010.

Moyn, Samuel (@samuelmoyn). "One other thing I learned studying law is that it is not its abuse but its use, mainly, that leads to domination and hierarchy." Twitter, December 28, 2020. https://twitter.com/samuelmoyn/status/1343530602902003713.

Murphy, Sean D. *Humanitarian Intervention: The United Nations in an Evolving World Order*. Philadelphia: University of Pennsylvania Press, 1996.

Mutua, Makau. "Savages, Victims, and Saviors: The Metaphor of Human Rights." *Harvard International Law Journal* 42, no. 1 (2001): 201–245.

Naimark, Norman. *Stalin's Genocides*. Princeton, NJ: Princeton University Press, 2010.

Nersessian, David. "Cultural Genocide." In *Genocide: A Reader*, edited by Jens Meierhenrich, 80–81. Oxford: Oxford University Press, 2014.

Nersessian, David. *Genocide and Political Groups*. Oxford: Oxford University Press, 2010.

Newlines Institute for Strategy and Policy. "The Uyghur Genocide: An Examination of China's Breaches of the 1948 Genocide Convention." March 2021. https://newlinesinstitute.org/wp-content/uploads/Chinas-Breaches-of-the-GC3-2.pdf.

Nincic, Miroslav. *Renegade Regimes: Confronting Deviant Behavior in World Politics*. New York: Columbia University Press, 2005.

Novic, Elisa. *The Concept of Cultural Genocide: An International Law Perspective*. Oxford: Oxford University Press, 2016.

Nuffield Foundation and Colonial Office. *African Education: A Study of Educational Policy and Practice in British Tropical Africa*. Oxford: Oxford University Press, 1953.

O'Brien, Sharon. "Federal Indian Policies and the International Protection of Human Rights." In *American Indian Policy in the Twentieth Century*, edited by Vine Deloria Jr., 35–61. Norman: University of Oklahoma Press, 1985.

Ohlin, Jens David. "State Responsibility for Conspiracy, Incitement, and Attempt to Commit Genocide." In *The UN Genocide Convention: A Commentary*, edited by Paola Gaeta, 374–380. Oxford: Oxford University Press, 2009.

Oppenheim, Lassa. *International Law*, Vol. 1—Peace. 8th ed. by Hersch Lauterpacht. London: Longmans, Green & Co. 1955.

Oppenheim, Lassa. *International Law: A Treatise*. Vol. 1. 2nd ed. London: Longmans, Green & Co. 1912.

O'Reilly, K. P. "Perceiving Rogue States: The Use of the 'Rogue State' Concept by U.S. Foreign Policy Elites." *Foreign Policy Analysis* 3, no. 4 (2007): 295–315.

Palchetti, Paolo. "State Responsibility for Complicity in Genocide." In *The UN Genocide Convention: A Commentary*, edited by Paola Gaeta, 381–393. Oxford: Oxford University Press, 2009.

PBS. *Frontline*, "Ghosts of Rwanda: Timeline." April 1, 2004. http://www.pbs.org/wgbh/pages/frontline/shows/ghosts/etc/crontext.html.

Power, Samantha. *"A Problem from Hell": America and the Age of Genocide*. New York: Basic Books, 2002.

Quigley, John. *The Genocide Convention: An International Law Analysis*. Burlington, VT: Ashgate, 2006.

Raghavan, Srinath. *1971: A Global History of the Creation of Bangladesh*. Cambridge, MA: Harvard University Press, 2013.

Rawls, John. *The Law of Peoples*. Cambridge, MA: Harvard University Press, 2002.

Rittner, Carol. "Are Women Human?" In *Rape: Weapon of War and Genocide*, edited by Carol Rittner and John K. Roth, 1–14. St. Paul, MN: Paragon House, 2012.

Roberts, Adam. "The United Nations and Humanitarian Intervention." In *Humanitarian Intervention and International Relations*, edited by Jennifer Welsh, 71–97. Oxford: Oxford University Press, 2003.

Roberts, Sean R. *The War on the Uyghurs: China's Internal Campaign against a Muslim Minority*. Princeton, NJ: Princeton University Press, 2020.

Robinson, Mary. *Realizing Human Rights*. Oxford: Clarendon Press, 1998.

Roff, Heather M. *Global Justice, Kant and the Responsibility to Protect: A Provisional Duty*. London: Routledge, 2013.

Ronayne, Peter. *Never Again? The United States and the Prevention and Punishment of Genocide since the Holocaust*. Lanham, MD: Rowman and Littlefield, 2001.

Rotberg, Robert. "The Threat from Rogue States." *Boston Globe*, November 6, 2004. https://www.belfercenter.org/publication/threat-rogue-states.

SáCouto, Susana. "Reflections on the Judgment of the International Court of Justice in Bosnia's Genocide Case against Serbia and Montenegro." *Human Rights Brief* 15, no. 1 (2007): 2–4.

Sadat, Leila Nadya. Email to author. September 26, 2011.

Sartre, Jean-Paul Sartre. *On Genocide*. Boston: Beacon Press, 1968.

Saunders, Elizabeth N. "Setting Boundaries: Can International Society Exclude 'Rogue States'?" *International Studies Review* 8, no. 1 (2006): 23–53.

Schabas, William. Email to author. September 17, 2011.

Schabas, William. "Genocide and the International Court of Justice: Finally, a Duty to Prevent the Crime of Crimes." *Genocide Studies and Prevention* 2, no. 2 (2007): 101–122.

Schabas, William. *Genocide in International Law: The Crime of Crimes*. Cambridge: Cambridge University Press, 2000.

Schiller, Barry. "Life in a Symbolic Universe: Comments on the Genocide Convention and International Law." *Southwestern University Law Review* 9, no. 1(1977): 47–83.

Schwartz, Jonathan B. "Dealing with a 'Rogue State': The Libya Precedent." *American Journal of International Law* 101, no. 3 (2007): 553–580.

Schwarzenberger, Georg. *Power Politics: A Study of World Society.* Westport, CT: Praeger, 1964.

Seibert-Fohr, Anja. "State Responsibility for Genocide under the Genocide Convention." In *The UN Genocide Convention: A Commentary*, edited by Paola Gaeta, 349–373. Oxford: Oxford University Press, 2009.

Shaw, Malcolm N. *International Law.* 7th ed. Cambridge: Cambridge University Press, 2014.

Shaw, Martin. *What Is Genocide?* Malden, MA: Polity Press, 2007.

Short, Damien. "Cultural Genocide and Indigenous Peoples: A Sociological Approach." *International Journal of Human Rights* 14, no. 6 (2010): 833–848.

Simpson, Gerry. *Great Powers and Outlaw States: Unequal Sovereigns in the International Legal Order.* Cambridge: Cambridge University Press, 2004.

Slaughter, Anne-Marie. "International Law in a World of Liberal States." *European Journal of International Law* 6, no. 3 (1995): 503–538.

Soyinka, Wole. *The Burden of Memory, the Muse of Forgiveness.* Oxford: Oxford University Press, 1999.

Stark, Alex. Introduction to *The Responsibility to Protect: Challenges and Opportunities in Light of the Libyan Intervention*, edited by Alex Stark, 4–6. *e-International Relations*, November 2011. https://www.e-ir.info/publication/the-r2p-challenges-and-opportunities-in-light-of-the-libyan-intervention/.

Thakur, Ramesh. *The United Nations, Peace and Security: From Collective Security to the Responsibility to Protect.* Cambridge: Cambridge University Press, 2006.

Thaler, Kai. "Foreshadowing Future Slaughter: From the Indonesian Killings of 1965–1966 to the 1974–1999 Genocide in East Timor." *Genocide Studies and Prevention* 7, no. 2 (2012): 204–222.

Thomson, Susan. *Rwanda: From Genocide to Precarious Peace.* New Haven, CT: Yale University Press, 2018.

Totman, Sally-Ann. *How Hollywood Projects Foreign Policy.* New York: Palgrave Macmillan, 2009.

Totten, Samuel. Email to author. September 17, 2011.

Trouillot, Michel-Rolph. *Silencing the Past: Power and the Production of History.* Boston: Beacon Press, 1995.

United Nations. Draft Convention on the Crime of Genocide. 1947. https://digitallibrary.un.org/record/611058?ln=en.

United Nations. Draft Convention prepared by the Ad Hoc Committee on Genocide. 1948. http://www.preventgenocide.org/law/convention/drafts/.

United Nations. "List of former Trust and Non-Self-Governing Territories." https://www.un.org/dppa/decolonization/en/history/former-trust-and-nsgts.

United Nations. "Security Council—Veto List." January 20, 2022. https://research.un.org/en/docs/sc/quick.

United Nations. United Nations Charter. 1945. https://www.un.org/en/about-us/un-charter/full-text.

United Nations. Universal Declaration of Human Rights. 1948. https://www.ohchr.org/en/udhr/documents/udhr_translations/eng.pdf

United Nations. Vienna Convention on the Law of Treaties. 1969. https://legal.un.org/ilc/texts/instruments/english/conventions/1_1_1969.pdf.

United Nations General Assembly. "The Crime of Genocide." 1946. https://digitallibrary.un.org/record/209873?ln=en.

United Nations General Assembly. Resolution 478(V), 16 November 1950. Available https://digitallibrary.un.org/record/862766?ln=en.

United Nations General Assembly. "Resolution Adopted by the General Assembly on 16 September 2005." https://www.un.org/en/development/desa/population/migration/generalassembly/docs/globalcompact/A_RES_60_1.pdf.

United Nations Security Council. "Argentina, Belgium, Burundi, Italy, Japan, Nicaragua, Sierra Leone and Somalia: draft resolution." December 5, 1971. https://undocs.org/en/S/10423.

United Nations Security Council. "Fiftieth Year, 3512th Meeting, Friday, 31 March 1995." https://undocs.org/en/S/PV.3512.

United Nations Security Council. "Fiftieth Year, 3543rd Meeting, Friday, 16 June 1995." https://undocs.org/en/S/PV.3543.

United Nations Security Council. "Fiftieth Year, 3575th Meeting, Friday, 8 September 1995." https://undocs.org/en/S/PV.3575.

United Nations Security Council. "Forty-Ninth Year, 3367th Meeting, Thursday, 21 April 1994." https://undocs.org/en/S/PV.3367.

United Nations Security Council. "Forty-Ninth Year, 3368th Meeting, Thursday, 21 April 1994." https://digitallibrary.un.org/record/186509?ln=en.

United Nations Security Council. "Forty-Ninth Year, 3370th Meeting, Wednesday, 27 April 1994." https://undocs.org/en/S/PV.3370.

United Nations Security Council. "Forty-Ninth Year, 3371st Meeting, Saturday, 30 April 1994." https://undocs.org/en/S/PV.3371.

United Nations Security Council. "Forty-Ninth Year, 3377th Meeting, Monday, 16 May 1994." https://undocs.org/en/S/PV.3377.

United Nations Security Council. "Forty-Ninth Year, 3388th Meeting, Wednesday, 8 June 1994." https://digitallibrary.un.org/record/162815?ln=en.

United Nations Security Council. "Forty-Ninth Year, 3392nd Meeting, Wednesday, 22 June 1994." https://undocs.org/en/S/PV.3392.

United Nations Security Council. "Letter Dated 1 July 1994 from the Permanent Representative of Croatia to the United Nations Addressed to the President of the Security Council." https://digitallibrary.un.org/record/190062?ln=en.

United Nations Security Council. "Letter Dated 20 May 1992 from the Permanent Representative of Egypt to the United Nations Addressed to the Secretary-General." https://digitallibrary.un.org/record/144080?ln=en.

United Nations Security Council. "Letter Dated 24 February 1995 from the Permanent Representative of Morocco to the United Nations Addressed to the President of the Security Council." https://digitallibrary.un.org/record/173479?ln=en.

United Nations Security Council. "Letter Dated 24 May 1994 from the Secretary-General to the President of the Security Council." https://digitallibrary.un.org/record/232969?ln=en.

United Nations Security Council. "Letter Dated 27 May 1992 from the Minister for Foreign Affairs of Bosnia and Herzegovina Addressed to the President of the Security Council." https://digitallibrary.un.org/record/143668?ln=en.

United Nations Security Council. "Letter Dated 30 March 1994 from the Deputy Permanent Representative of Bosnia and Herzegovina to the United Nations Addressed to the President of the Security Council." https://digitallibrary.un.org/record/185282?ln=en.

United Nations Security Council. "Letter Dated 30 May 1993 from the Permanent Representative of Bosnia and Herzegovina to the United Nations Addressed to the President of the Security Council." https://digitallibrary.un.org/record/167096?ln=en.

United Nations Security Council. "Official Records: Twenty-Sixth Year, 1606th Meeting: 4 December 1971." https://undocs.org/en/S/PV.1606(OR).

United Nations Security Council. "Official Records: Twenty-Sixth Year, 1607th Meeting: 5 December 1971." https://undocs.org/en/S/PV.1607(OR).

United Nations Security Council. "Provisional Verbatim Record of the 3082nd Meeting." May 30, 1992. https://undocs.org/en/S/PV.3082.

United Nations Security Council. "Provisional Verbatim Record of the 3106th Meeting." August 13, 1992. https://undocs.org/en/S/PV.3106.

United Nations Security Council. "Provisional Verbatim Record of the 3119th Meeting," October 6, 1992. https://undocs.org/en/S/PV.3119.

United Nations Security Council. "Provisional Verbatim Record of the 3135th Meeting. November 13, 1992. https://undocs.org/en/S/PV.3135.

United Nations Security Council. "Provisional Verbatim Record of the 3136th Meeting." November 16, 1992. https://undocs.org/en/S/PV.3136.

United Nations Security Council. "Provisional Verbatim Record of the 3137th Meeting." November 16, 1992. https://undocs.org/en/S/PV.3137.

United Nations Security Council. "Provisional Verbatim Record of the 3192nd Meeting," April 3, 1993. https://undocs.org/en/S/PV.3192.

United Nations Security Council, "Provisional Verbatim Record of the 3208th Meeting," May 6, 1993. https://undocs.org/en/S/PV.3208.

United Nations Security Council. "Provisional Verbatim Record of the 3217th Meeting," May 25, 1993. https://undocs.org/en/S/PV.3217.

United Nations Security Council. "Provisional Verbatim Record of the 3228th Meeting." June 4, 1993. https://undocs.org/en/S/PV.3228.

United Nations Security Council. "Provisional Verbatim Record of the 3247th Meeting," June 29, 1993. https://undocs.org/en/S/PV.3247.

United Nations Security Council. "Provisional Verbatim Record of the 3257th Meeting." July 22, 1993. https://undocs.org/en/S/PV.3257.

United Nations Security Council. "Provisional Verbatim Record of the 3326th Meeting." January 6, 1994. https://undocs.org/en/S/PV.3326

United Nations Security Council. "Provisional Verbatim Record of the 3333rd Meeting." February 3, 1994. https://undocs.org/en/S/PV.3333.

United Nations Security Council. "Provisional Verbatim Record of the 3428th Meeting." September 23, 1994. https://undocs.org/en/S/PV.3428.

United Nations Security Council. "Resolution 713 (1991)," September 25, 1991. https://undocs.org/S/RES/713(1991).

United Nations Security Council. "Resolution 757 (1992)." May 30, 1992. https://undocs.org/S/RES/757(1992).

United Nations Security Council. "Resolution 771 (1992)." August 13, 1992. https://undocs.org/S/RES/771(1992).

United Nations Security Council. "Resolution 827 (1993)." May 25, 1993. https://undocs.org/S/RES/827(1993).

United Nations Security Council. "Resolution 912 (1994)," April 21, 1994. https://undocs.org/en/S/RES/912(1994).

United Nations Security Council. "Resolution 918 (1994)." May 17, 1994. https://digitallibrary.un.org/record/197563?ln=en.

United Nations Security Council. "Resolution 925 (1994)," June 8, 1994. https://undocs.org/en/S/RES/925(1994).

United Nations Security Council. "Resolution 929 (1994)." June 22, 1994. https://undocs.org/en/S/RES/929(1994).

United Nations Security Council. "Resolution 1739 (2007)." January 10, 2007. https://undocs.org/S/RES/1793(2007).

United Nations Security Council. "Resolution 1756 (2007)." May 15, 2007. https://undocs.org/S/RES/1756(2007).

United Nations Security Council. "Resolution 1801 (2008)." February 20, 2008. https://undocs.org/S/RES/1801(2008).

United Nations Security Council. "Resolution 1807 (2008)." March 31, 2008. https://undocs.org/S/RES/1807(2008).

United Nations Security Council. "Resolution 1814 (2008)." May 15, 2008. https://undocs.org/S/RES/1814(2008).

United Nations Security Council. "Resolution 1856 (2008)." December 22, 2008. https://undocs.org/S/RES/1856(2008).

United Nations Security Council. "Resolution 1857 (2008). December 22, 2008. https://undocs.org/S/RES/1857(2008).

United Nations Security Council. "Resolution 1863 (2009)." February 26, 2011. https://undocs.org/S/RES/1863(2009).

United Nations Security Council. "Resolution 1896 (2009)." January 16, 2009. https://undocs.org/S/RES/1896(2009).

United Nations Security Council. "Resolution 1906 (2009)." December 7, 2009. https://undocs.org/S/RES/1906(2009).

United Nations Security Council. "Resolution 1910 (2010)." January 28, 2010. https://undocs.org/S/RES/1910(2010).

United Nations Security Council. "Resolution 1923 (2010)." May 25, 2010. https://undocs.org/S/RES/1923(2010).

United Nations Security Council. "Resolution 1925 (2010)." May 28, 2010. https://undocs.org/S/RES/1925(2010).

United Nations Security Council. "Resolution 1949 (2010)." November 23, 2010. https://undocs.org/S/RES/1949(2010).

United Nations Security Council. "Resolution 1952 (2010)." November 29, 2010. https://undocs.org/S/RES/1952(2010).

United Nations Security Council. "Resolution 1962 (2010)." December 20, 2010. https://undocs.org/S/RES/1962(2010).

United Nations Security Council. "Resolution 1964 (2010)." December 22, 2010. https://undocs.org/S/RES/1964(2010).

United Nations Security Council. "Resolution 1970 (2011)." February 26, 2011. https://undocs.org/S/RES/1970(2011).

United Nations Security Council. "Resolution 1973 (2011)." March 17, 2011. https://undocs.org/S/RES/1973(2011).

United Nations Security Council. "Resolution 1975 (2011)." March 30, 2011. https://undocs.org/S/RES/1975(2011).

United Nations Security Council. "Resolution 1991 (2011)." June 28, 2011. https://undocs.org/S/RES/1991(2011).

United Nations Security Council. "Resolution 1996 (2011)." July 8, 2011. https://undocs.org/S/RES/1996(2011).

United Nations Security Council. "Resolution 2000 (2011)." July 27, 2011. https://undocs.org/S/RES/2000(2011).

United Nations Security Council. "Resolution 2010 (2011)." September 30, 2011. https://undocs.org/S/RES/2010(2011).

United Nations Security Council. "Resolution 2014 (2011)." October 21, 2011. https://undocs.org/S/RES/2014(2011).

United Nations Security Council. "Resolution 2021 (2011)." November 29, 2011. https://undocs.org/S/RES/2021(2011).

United Nations Security Council. "Resolution 2031 (2011)." December 22, 2011. https://undocs.org/S/RES/2031(2011).

United Nations Security Council. "Resolution 2040 (2012)." March 12, 2012. https://undocs.org/S/RES/2040(2012).

United Nations Security Council. "Resolution 2053 (2012)." June 27, 2012. https://undocs.org/S/RES/2053(2012).

United Nations Security Council. "Resolution 2057 (2012)." July 5, 2012. https://undocs.org/S/RES/2057(2012).

United Nations Security Council. "Resolution 2062 (2012)." July 26, 2012. https://undocs.org/S/RES/2062(2012).

United Nations Security Council. "Resolution 2071 (2012)." October 12, 2012. https://undocs.org/S/RES/2071(2012).

United Nations Security Council. "Resolution 2076 (2012)." November 20, 2012. https://undocs.org/S/RES/2076(2012).

United Nations Security Council. "Resolution 2078 (2012)." November 28, 2012. https://undocs.org/S/RES/2078(2012).

United Nations Security Council. "Resolution 2085 (2012)." December 20, 2012. https://undocs.org/S/RES/2085(2012).

United Nations Security Council. "Resolution 2088 (2013)." January 13, 2013. https://undocs.org/S/RES/2088(2013).

United Nations Security Council. "Resolution 2090 (2013)." February 13, 2013. https://undocs.org/S/RES/2090(2013).

United Nations Security Council. "Resolution 2093 (2013)." March 6, 2013. https://undocs.org/S/RES/2093(2013).

United Nations Security Council. "Resolution 2098 (2013)." March 28, 2013. https://undocs.org/S/RES/2098(2013).

United Nations Security Council. "Resolution 2109 (2013)." July 11, 2013. https://undocs.org/S/RES/2109(2013).

United Nations Security Council. "Resolution 2112 (2013)." July 30, 2013. https://undocs.org/S/RES/2112(2013).

United Nations Security Council. "Resolution 2116 (2013)." September 18, 2013. https://undocs.org/S/RES/2116(2013).

United Nations Security Council. "Resolution 2121 (2013)." October 10, 2013. https://undocs.org/S/RES/2121(2013).

United Nations Security Council. "Resolution 2127 (2013)." December 5, 2013. https://undocs.org/S/RES/2127(2013).

United Nations Security Council. "Resolution 2134 (2014)." January 28, 2014. https://undocs.org/S/RES/2134(2014).

United Nations Security Council. "Resolution 2136 (2014)." January 30, 2014. https://undocs.org/S/RES/2136(2014).

United Nations Security Council. "Resolution 2137 (2014)." February 13, 2014. https://undocs.org/S/RES/2137(2014).

United Nations Security Council. "Resolution 2139 (2014)." February 22, 2014. https://undocs.org/S/RES/2139(2014).

United Nations Security Council. "Resolution 2144 (2014)." March 14, 2014. https://undocs.org/S/RES/2144(2014).

United Nations Security Council. "Resolution 2147 (2014)." March 28, 2014. https://undocs.org/S/RES/2147(2014).

United Nations Security Council. "Resolution 2149 (2014)." April 10, 2014. https://undocs.org/S/RES/2149(2014).

United Nations Security Council. "Resolution 2155 (2014)." May 27, 2014. https://undocs.org/S/RES/2155(2014).

United Nations Security Council. "Resolution 2162 (2014)." June 25, 2014. https://undocs.org/S/RES/2162(2014).

United Nations Security Council. "Resolution 2164 (2014)." June 25, 2014. https://undocs.org/S/RES/2164(2014).

United Nations Security Council. "Resolution 2165 (2014)." July 14, 2014. https://undocs.org/S/RES/2165(2014).

United Nations Security Council. "Resolution 2176 (2014)." September 15, 2014. https://undocs.org/S/RES/2176%20(2014).

United Nations Security Council. "Resolution 2187 (2014)." November 25, 2014. https://undocs.org/S/RES/2187%20(2014).

United Nations Security Council. "Resolution 2188 (2014)." December 9, 2014. https://undocs.org/S/RES/2188%20(2014).

United Nations Security Council. "Resolution 2190 (2014)." December 15, 2014. https://undocs.org/S/RES/2190%20(2014).

United Nations Security Council. "Resolution 2196 (2015)." January 22, 2015. https://undocs.org/S/RES/2196%20(2015).

United Nations Security Council. "Resolution 2198 (2015)." January 29, 2015. https://undocs.org/S/RES/2198%20(2015).

United Nations Security Council. "Resolution 2200 (2015)." February 12, 2015. https://undocs.org/S/RES/2200%20(2015).

United Nations Security Council. "Resolution 2206 (2015)." March 3, 2015. https://undocs.org/S/RES/2206%20(2015).

United Nations Security Council. "Resolution 2211 (2015)." March 26, 2015. https://undocs.org/S/RES/2211%20(2015).

United Nations Security Council. "Resolution 2213 (2015)." March 27, 2015. https://undocs.org/S/RES/2213(2015).

United Nations Security Council. "Resolution 2217 (2015)." April 28, 2015. https://undocs.org/S/RES/2217(2015).

United Nations Security Council. "Resolution 2223 (2015)." May 28, 2015. https://undocs.org/S/RES/2223(2015).

United Nations Security Council. "Resolution 2226 (2015)." June 25, 2015. https://undocs.org/S/RES/2226(2015).

United Nations Security Council. "Resolution 2227 (2015)." June 29, 2015. https://undocs.org/S/RES/2227(2015).

United Nations Security Council. "Resolution 2228 (2015)." June 29, 2015. https://undocs.org/S/RES/2228(2015).

United Nations Security Council. "Resolution 2237 (2015)." September 2, 2015. https://undocs.org/S/RES/2237(2015).

United Nations Security Council. "Resolution 2239 (2015)." September 17, 2015. https://undocs.org/S/RES/2239(2015).

United Nations Security Council. "Resolution 2241 (2015)." October 9, 2015. https://undocs.org/S/RES/2241(2015).

United Nations Security Council. "Resolution 2244 (2015)." October 23, 2015. https://undocs.org/S/RES/2244(2015).

United Nations Security Council. "Resolution 2248 (2015)." November 12, 2015. https://undocs.org/S/RES/2248(2015).

United Nations Security Council. "Resolution 2252 (2015)." December 15, 2015. https://undocs.org/S/RES/2252(2015).

United Nations Security Council. "Resolution 2254 (2015)." December 18, 2015. https://undocs.org/S/RES/2254(2015).

United Nations Security Council. "Resolution 2258 (2015)." December 22, 2015. https://undocs.org/S/RES/2258(2015).

United Nations Security Council. "Resolution 2262 (2016)." January 27, 2016. https://undocs.org/S/RES/2262(2016).

United Nations Security Council. "Resolution 2265 (2016)." February 10, 2016. https://undocs.org/S/RES/2265(2016).

United Nations Security Council. "Resolution 2275 (2016)." March 24, 2016. https://undocs.org/S/RES/2275(2016).

United Nations Security Council. "Resolution 2277 (2016)." March 30, 2016. https://undocs.org/S/RES/2277(2016).

United Nations Security Council. "Resolution 2279 (2016)." April 1, 2016. https://undocs.org/S/RES/2279(2016).

United Nations Security Council. "Resolution 2284 (2016)." April 28, 2016. https://undocs.org/S/RES/2284(2016).

United Nations Security Council. "Resolution 2288 (2016)." May 25, 2016. https://undocs.org/S/RES/2288(2016).

United Nations Security Council. "Resolution 2290 (2016)." May 31, 2016. https://undocs.org/S/RES/2290(2016).

United Nations Security Council. "Resolution 2293 (2016)." June 23, 2016. https://undocs.org/S/RES/2293(2016).

United Nations Security Council. "Resolution 2295 (2016)." June 29, 2016. https://undocs.org/S/RES/2295(2016).

United Nations Security Council. "Resolution 2296 (2016)." June 29, 2016. https://undocs.org/S/RES/2296(2016).

United Nations Security Council. "Resolution 2297 (2016)." July 7, 2016. https://undocs.org/S/RES/2297(2016).

United Nations Security Council. "Resolution 2301 (2016)." July 26, 2016. https://undocs.org/S/RES/2301(2016).

United Nations Security Council. "Resolution 2303 (2016)." July 29, 2016. https://undocs.org/S/RES/2303(2016).

United Nations Security Council. "Resolution 2304 (2016)." August 12, 2016. https://undocs.org/S/RES/2304(2016).

United Nations Security Council. "Resolution 2317 (2016)." November 10, 2016. https://undocs.org/S/RES/2307(2016).

United Nations Security Council. "Resolution 2327 (2016)." December 16, 2016. https://undocs.org/S/RES/2327(2016).

United Nations Security Council. "Resolution 2332 (2016)." December 21, 2016. https://undocs.org/en/S/RES/2332(2016).

United Nations Security Council. "Resolution 2333 (2016)." December 23, 2016. https://undocs.org/S/RES/2333(2016).

United Nations Security Council. "Resolution 2337 (2017)." January 19, 2017. https://undocs.org/S/RES/2337(2017).

United Nations Security Council. "Resolution 2339 (2017)." January 27, 2017. https://undocs.org/S/RES/2339(2017).

United Nations Security Council. "Resolution 2340 (2017)." February 8, 2017. https://undocs.org/S/RES/2340(2017).

United Nations Security Council. "Resolution 2348 (2017)." March 31, 2017. https://undocs.org/S/RES/2348(2017).

United Nations Security Council. "Resolution 2360 (2017)." June 21, 2017. https://undocs.org/S/RES/2360(2017).

United Nations Security Council. "Resolution 2363 (2017)." June 29, 2017. https://undocs.org/S/RES/2363(2017).

United Nations Security Council. "Resolution 2364 (2017)." June 29, 2017. https://undocs.org/S/RES/2364(2017).

United Nations Security Council. "Resolution 2372 (2017)." August 30, 2017. https://undocs.org/S/RES/2372(2017).

United Nations Security Council. "Resolution 2373 (2017)." August 30, 2017. https://undocs.org/S/RES/2373(2017).

United Nations Security Council. "Resolution 2374 (2017)." September 5, 2017. https://undocs.org/S/RES/2374(2017).

United Nations Security Council. "Resolution 2385 (2017)." November 14, 2017. https://undocs.org/S/RES/2385(2017).

United Nations Security Council. "Resolution 2387 (2017)." November 15, 2017. https://undocs.org/S/RES/2387(2017).

United Nations Security Council. "Resolution 2389 (2017)." December 8, 2017. https://undocs.org/S/RES/2389(2017).

United Nations Security Council. "Resolution 2393 (2017)." December 19, 2017. https://undocs.org/S/RES/2393(2017).

United Nations Security Council. "Resolution 2399 (2018)." January 30, 2018. https://undocs.org/S/RES/2399(2018).

United Nations Security Council. "Resolution 2406 (2018)." March 15, 2018. https://undocs.org/S/RES/2406(2018).

United Nations Security Council. "Resolution 2409 (2018)." March 27, 2018. https://undocs.org/S/RES/2409(2018).

United Nations Security Council. "Resolution 2423 (2018)." June 28, 2018. https://undocs.org/S/RES/2423(2018).

United Nations Security Council. "Resolution 2428 (2018)." July 13, 2018. https://undocs.org/S/RES/2428(2018).

United Nations Security Council. "Resolution 2429 (2018)." July 13, 2018. https://undocs.org/S/RES/2429(2018).

United Nations Security Council. "Resolution 2431 (2018)." July 30, 2018. https://undocs.org/S/RES/2431(2018).

United Nations Security Council. "Resolution 2433 (2018)." August 30, 2018. https://undocs.org/S/RES/2433(2018).

United Nations Security Council. "Resolution 2439 (2018)." October 30, 2018. https://undocs.org/S/RES/2439(2018).

United Nations Security Council. "Resolution 2444 (2018)." November 14, 2018. https://undocs.org/S/RES/2444(2018).

United Nations Security Council. "Resolution 2448 (2018)." December 13, 2018. https://undocs.org/S/RES/2448(2018).

United Nations Security Council. "Resolution 2449 (2018)." December 13, 2018. https://undocs.org/S/RES/2449(2018).

United Nations Security Council. "Resolution 2459 (2019)." March 15, 2019. https://undocs.org/S/RES/2459(2019).

United Nations Security Council. "Resolution 2463 (2019)." March 29, 2019. https://undocs.org/S/RES/2463(2019).

United Nations Security Council. "Resolution 2480 (2019)." June 28, 2019. https://undocs.org/S/RES/2480(2019).

United Nations Security Council. "Resolution 2485 (2019)." August 29, 2019. https://undocs.org/S/RES/2485(2019).

United Nations Security Council. "Resolution 2499 (2019)." November 15, 2019. https://undocs.org/S/RES/2499(2019).

United Nations Security Council. "Resolution 2502 (2019)." December 19, 2019. https://undocs.org/S/RES/2502(2019).

United Nations Security Council. "Resolution 2514 (2020)." March 12, 2020. https://undocs.org/en/S/RES/2514(2020).

United Nations Security Council. "Resolution 2521 (2020)." May 29, 2020. https://undocs.org/en/S/RES/2521(2020).

United Nations Security Council. "Resolution 2524 (2020)." June 3, 2020. https://undocs.org/en/S/RES/2524(2020).

United Nations Security Council. "Resolution 2525 (2020)." June 3, 2020. https://undocs.org/en/S/RES/2525(2020).

United Nations Security Council. "Resolution 2531 (2020)." June 6, 2020. https://undocs.org/en/S/RES/2531(2020).

United Nations Security Council. "Resolution 2539 (2020)." August 28, 2020. https://undocs.org/en/S/RES/2539(2020).

United Nations Security Council. "Resolution 2552 (2020)." November 12, 2020. https://undocs.org/en/S/RES/2552(2020).

United Nations Security Council. "Resolution 2556 (2020)." December 18, 2020. https://undocs.org/en/S/RES/2556(2020).

United Nations Security Council. "Resolution 2559 (2020)." December 22, 2020. https://undocs.org/en/S/RES/2559(2020).

United Nations Security Council. "Statement by the President of the Security Council, 30 April 1994." https://undocs.org/S/PRST/1994/21.

United States Congress. "An Act Relative to Employment for Certain Adult Indians on or Near Indian Reservations." Public Laws of the Eighty-Fourth Congress, Second Session, Public Law 959, August 3, 1956. https://www.govinfo.gov/content/pkg/STATUTE-70/pdf/STATUTE-70-Pg986.pdf.

United States Department of the Interior, Bureau of Indian Affairs. *Annual Report of the Commissioner of Indian Affairs to the Secretary of Interior.* Washington: Government Printing Office, 1886.

United States Department of the Interior, Office of Indian Affairs. "Rules Governing the Court of Indian Offenses." March 30, 1883. https://rclinton.files.wordpress.com/2007/11/code-of-indian-offenses.pdf.

United States Holocaust Memorial Museum. "From the Indictment: Count Three—Crimes Against Humanity." https://www.ushmm.org/information/exhibitions/online-exhibitions/special-focus/doctors-trial/indictment/count-three.

United States Holocaust Memorial Museum. "How Were the Crimes Defined?" In *Holocaust Encyclopedia*, November 5, 2020. https://encyclopedia.ushmm.org/content/en/article/how-were-the-crimes-defined.

United States Office of the Secretary of Defense. "Discussion Paper: Rwanda." May 1, 1994. http://nsarchive2.gwu.edu//NSAEBB/NSAEBB356/rw050194.pdf.

Van Krieken, Robert. "The Barbarism of Civilization: Cultural Genocide and the 'Stolen Generations.'" *British Journal of Sociology* 50, no. 2 (1999): 297–315.

Van Schaack, Beth. "The Crime of Political Genocide: Repairing the Genocide Convention's Blind Spot." *Yale Law Journal* 106, no. 7 (1997): 2259–2291.

Van Schaack, Beth. Email to author, September 19, 2011.

Venter, Albert. "Reform of the United Nations Security Council: A Comment on the South African Position." *International Journal on World Peace* 20, no. 4 (2003): 29–47.

Wagner, Wolfgang, Wouter Werner, and Michal Onderco. "Rogues, Pariahs, Outlaws: Theorizing Deviance in International Relations." In *Deviance in International Relations*, edited by Wolfgang Wagner, Wouter Werner, and Michal Onderco, 1–14. London: Palgrave Macmillan, 2014.

Warbrick, Colin. "The Principle of Sovereign Equality." In *The United Nations and the Principles of International Law: Essays in Memory of Michael Akehurst*, edited by Colin Warbrick and Vaughan Lowe, 204–229. London: Routledge, 1994.

Weiss, Thomas G. "RtoP Alive and Well after Libya." *Ethics and International Affairs* 25, no. 3 (2011): 287–292.

Weiss-Wendt, Anton. Email to author. May 13, 2019.

Weiss-Wendt, Anton. "Hostage of Politics: Raphael Lemkin on 'Soviet Genocide.'" *Journal of Genocide Research* 7, no. 4 (2005): 551–559.

Weiss-Wendt, Anton. *The Soviet Union and the Gutting of the UN Genocide Convention*. Madison: University of Wisconsin Press, 2017.

Welsh, Jennifer. "Taking Consequences Seriously: Objections to Humanitarian Intervention." In *Humanitarian Intervention and International Relations*, edited by Jennifer Welsh, 52–70. Oxford: Oxford University Press, 2003.

White, Bob W. "Talk about School: Education and the Colonial Project in French and British Africa (1860–1960)." *Comparative Education* 32, no. 1 (1996): 9–25.

Whittlesey, Derwent. "British and French Colonial Technique in West Africa." *Foreign Affairs*, 15, no. 2 (January 1937): 362–373.

Wolfe, Patrick. "Settler Colonialism and the Elimination of the Native." *Journal of Genocide Research* 8, no. 4 (2006): 387–409.

Woods, Ngaire. "Order, Globalization, and Inequality in World Politics." In *Inequality, Globalization, and World Politics*, edited by Andrew Hurrell and Ngaire Woods, 8–35. Oxford: Oxford University Press, 2002.

Woolford, Andrew. *This Benevolent Experiment: Indigenous Boarding Schools, Genocide, and Redress in Canada and the United States*. Lincoln: University of Nebraska Press, 2015.

Woolford, Andrew, Jeff Benvenuto, and Alexander Hinton, eds. *Colonial Genocide in Indigenous North America*. Durham, NC: Duke University Press, 2014.

Index

About the Author

Jeffrey S. Bachman is a senior professorial lecturer in human rights at the American University School of International Service in Washington, DC. He is the author of *The United States and Genocide: (Re)Defining the Relationship* and editor of *Cultural Genocide: Law, Politics, and Global Manifestations*.

Available titles in the Genocide, Political Violence, Human Rights series:

Nanci Adler, ed., *Understanding the Age of Transitional Justice: Crimes, Courts, Commissions, and Chronicling*

Bree Akesson and Andrew R. Basso, *From Bureaucracy to Bullets: Extreme Domicide and the Right to Home*

Jeffrey S. Bachman, *The Politics of Genocide: From the Genocide Convention to the Responsibility to Protect*

Alan W. Clarke, *Rendition to Torture*

Alison Crosby and M. Brinton Lykes, *Beyond Repair? Mayan Women's Protagonism in the Aftermath of Genocidal Harm*

Lawrence Davidson, *Cultural Genocide*

Daniel Feierstein, *Genocide as Social Practice: Reorganizing Society under the Nazis and Argentina's Military Juntas*

Joseph P. Feldman, *Memories before the State: Postwar Peru and the Place of Memory, Tolerance, and Social Inclusion*

Alexander Laban Hinton, ed., *Transitional Justice: Global Mechanisms and Local Realities after Genocide and Mass Violence*

Alexander Laban Hinton, Thomas La Pointe, and Douglas Irvin-Erickson, eds., *Hidden Genocides: Power, Knowledge, Memory*

Douglas A. Kammen, *Three Centuries of Conflict in East Timor*

Eyal Mayroz, *Reluctant Interveners: America's Failed Responses to Genocide from Bosnia to Darfur*

Pyong Gap Min, *Korean "Comfort Women": Military Brothels, Brutality, and the Redress Movement*

Walter Richmond, *The Circassian Genocide*

S. Garnett Russell, *Becoming Rwandan: Education, Reconciliation, and the Making of a Post-Genocide Citizen*

Victoria Sanford, Katerina Stefatos, and Cecilia M. Salvi, eds., *Gender Violence in Peace and War: States of Complicity*

Irina Silber, *Everyday Revolutionaries: Gender, Violence, and Disillusionment in Postwar El Salvador*

Samuel Totten and Rafiki Ubaldo, eds., *We Cannot Forget: Interviews with Survivors of the 1994 Genocide in Rwanda*

Eva van Roekel, *Phenomenal Justice: Violence and Morality in Argentina*

Anton Weiss-Wendt, *A Rhetorical Crime: Genocide in the Geopolitical Discourse of the Cold War*

Kerry Whigham, *Resonant Violence: Affect, Memory, and Activism in Post-Genocide Societies*

Timothy Williams, *The Complexity of Evil: Perpetration and Genocide*

Ronnie Yimsut, *Facing the Khmer Rouge: A Cambodian Journey*

Natasha Zaretsky, *Acts of Repair: Justice, Truth, and the Politics of Memory in Argentina*

Kolibri 360 GmbH
Ferdinand-Jühlke-Straße 7
99095 Erfurt, Deutschland
produktsicherheit@kolibri360.de